# TWENTIETH CENTURY VIEWS

The aim of this series is to present the best in contemporary critical opinion on major authors, providing a twentieth century perspective on their changing status in an era of profound revaluation.

Maynard Mack, *Series Editor*
Yale University

# HESSE

## A COLLECTION OF CRITICAL ESSAYS

Edited by

*Theodore Ziolkowski*

Prentice-Hall, Inc.  *Englewood Cliffs, N.J.*

A SPECTRUM BOOK

Library of Congress Cataloging in Publication Data

ZIOLKOWSKI, THEODORE, comp.
    Hesse; a collection of critical essays.

    (A Spectrum Book: Twentieth century views)
    CONTENTS: Mann, T. Introduction to Demian.—Gide, A.
Preface to The Journey to the East.—Buber, M. Hermann
Hesse in the service of the spirit. [etc.]
    1. Hesse, Hermann, 1877–1962.
PT2617.E85Z9893        838'.9'1209        73–11431
ISBN 0–13–387183–5
ISBN 0–13–387175–4 (pbk.)

10  9  8  7  6  5  4  3  2  1

PRENTICE-HALL INTERNATIONAL, INC. (London)
PRENTICE-HALL OF AUSTRALIA PTY. LTD. (Sydney)
PRENTICE-HALL OF CANADA LTD. (Toronto)
PRENTICE-HALL OF INDIA PRIVATE LIMITED (New Delhi)
PRENTICE-HALL OF JAPAN, INC. (Tokyo)

# Acknowledgments

Acknowledgment is gratefully made to Suhrkamp Verlag, Frankfurt am Main, for permission to reprint excerpts from the following poems in German: "Entgegenkommen," "Der letzte Glasperlenspieler," "Stufen," and "Nach dem Lesen in der Summa contra Gentiles" from *Das Glasperlenspiel*, by Hermann Hesse (Copyright 1943 by Fretz & Wasmuth AG, Zürich) and to translate excerpts from unpublished letters of Hermann Hesse. Suhrkamp Verlag and Farrar, Straus & Giroux, Inc., have also given generous permission to reprint excerpts and to translate lines from the following poems: "Späte Prüfung" from *Späte Gedichte*, by Hermann Hesse (Copyright 1953, 1961, 1963 by Suhrkamp Verlag); "Sterbelied des Dichters," "Nach dem Abend im Hirschen," "Jede Nacht," "Abend mit Doktor Ling," and "Armer Teufel am Morgen nach dem Maskenball" from *Krisis*, by Hermann Hesse (Copyright 1928 by S. Fischer Verlag, Berlin).

In some instances the reprinted excerpts from the following translations of Hesse's works have been modified with the understanding of the publishers:

"Life Story Briefly Told," "A Guest at the Spa," and "Journey to Nuremberg" from *Autobiographical Writings*, translated by Denver Lindley (Copyright 1971, 1972 by Farrar, Straus & Giroux, Inc.). Reprinted by permission of Farrar, Straus & Giroux, Inc. and Jonathan Cape Ltd.

*Demian*, translated by Michael Roloff and Michael Lebeck. Copyright 1925 by Fischer Verlag. Copyright © 1965 by Harper & Row, Publishers, Inc. British edition published by Peter Owen, London. Reprinted by permission of Harper & Row, Publishers, Inc., and Peter Owen, London.

*The Glass Bead Game*, translated by Richard and Clara Winston (Copyright 1969 by Holt, Rinehart & Winston, Inc.). Reprinted by permission of Holt, Rinehart & Winston, Inc. and Jonathan Cape Ltd.

*The Journey to the East*, translated by Hilda Rosner (Copyright

1956 by Herman Hesse). Reprinted by permission of Farrar, Straus & Giroux, Inc. and Peter Owen, London.

*Klingsor's Last Summer,* translated by Richard and Clara Winston (Copyright 1970 by Farrar, Straus & Giroux, Inc.). Reprinted by permission of Farrar, Straus & Giroux, Inc. and Jonathan Cape Ltd.

*Narcissus and Goldmund,* translated by Ursule Molinaro (Copyright 1968 by Farrar, Straus & Giroux, Inc.). Reprinted by permission of Farrar, Straus & Giroux, Inc. and Peter Owen, London.

*Steppenwolf,* translated by Basil Creighton and revised by Joseph Mileck and Horst Frenz, Rinehart Editions (Copyright 1963 by Holt, Rinehart & Winston, Inc.). Reprinted by permission of Holt, Rinehart & Winston, Inc.

# Contents

# Introduction

## by Theodore Ziolkowski

## I

Rarely, since a generation of young Europeans decked themselves out in the blue frock coat and yellow vest of Goethe's Werther, has the youth culture of an age responded so rapturously to a writer as, today, to Hermann Hesse. Images from his novels have shaped the consciousness of young Americans in the sixties and early seventies and provided them with signposts of orientation in a reality that often seems to imitate his art. A Berkeley bar called "The Steppenwolf," a Philadelphia coffeehouse known as "The Magic Theater," and "Demian's Rathskeller" in Princeton—these were (and are) landmarks for the generation that shopped in such boutiques as "The Bead Game" and rocked to the sounds of "Steppenwolf," a group whose members performed in costumes suggesting figures from Hesse's novel. *Mademoiselle* printed Hesse's views on Peace, while *Seventeen* cited Hesse, along with Paul McCartney of the Beatles and Neil Armstrong of the Moon, in an article on graphology ("What A Boy's Handwriting Tells You"). The Hallmark Company brought out greeting cards bearing "Words of Love" from *Siddhartha*. The humor magazine *National Lampoon* featured a "classy comics illustrated" version of *Siddhartha,* and that same novel had the distinction of being parodied in *The New Yorker.*[1] The Hesse cult was duly noted and appraised by *Time, Life, Look, The Saturday Review,* and other witnesses of popular culture—not to mention Charles Schulz in his "Peanuts" comic strip.

At first glance these facts would seem to be of interest to no one but sociologists and psychologists of youth. Yet some people are deeply perturbed by this Hessomania—and I don't mean only the worried mothers who attend public lectures on Hesse to learn some-

[1] Roger Angell, "Sad Arthur," *The New Yorker* (March 14, 1970).

1

thing about the new Pied Piper who has enchanted their children. The Hesse phenomenon has also brought the literary critics out to the barricades. Stephen Koch, writing in *The New Republic* (July 13, 1968), points out that the young generation's "capacity for cultural co-option scares the hell out of a lot of people, myself sometimes included." While conceding that "the final third of *Steppenwolf* is one of the great moments of modern literature," Koch asserts that "Hesse's thought is irretrievably adolescent, so that in his chosen role of artist of ideas, he is inevitably second-rate. . . ." Koch is annoyed not so much at Hesse himself, who "despite his faults . . . is a graceful and generally unpretentious artist." He is dismayed, rather, by what he regards as Hesse's pernicious influence on the young, who have adopted him as their spiritual leader. George Steiner, reporting on the Hesse vogue in *The New Yorker* (January 18, 1969), concedes that there are certain "memorable passages" in *Steppenwolf* and singles out *The Glass Bead Game* (first translated under the title *Magister Ludi*), which Koch finds unreadable as "the masterful exception" in Hesse's oeuvre. But like Koch, Steiner is not really talking about Hesse at all. What bothers Steiner, straight from a visit to a hippie commune in Haight-Ashbury, is the fact that "The young have read little and compared less. Stringency is not their forte. Like prayer bells and beads, like pot and love-ins, Hesse seems to offer ecstasy and transcendence on the easy-payment plan." D. J. Enright, surveying new translations of Hesse's works for *The New York Review of Books* (September 12, 1968), excludes *Steppenwolf* from his general condemnation and calls *Narcissus and Goldmund* the best of Hesse's novels. Yet Enright's Anglo-Saxon sensibilities are offended by Hesse's "German" qualities: the theme of dualism that is pervasive in his works, his Romantic traits, and his philosophical idealism. "A highly cultivated person, he is the ideal second-order writer for the sort of serious-minded reader desirous to believe that he is grappling successfully with intellectual and artistic profundities of the first order."

As a final example of critical hostility, let us consider Jeffrey L. Sammons's "Notes on the Germanization of American Youth" in *The Yale Review* (Spring 1970). Sammons begins with the usual concessions. "In one respect, to be sure, it is churlish to speak ill of him, for he is certainly the nearest thing to a saint that modern German literature has produced." Sammons realizes that "the purity of Hesse's high-mindedness and character undoubtedly accounts in part for his appeal to young Americans, who in literary matters have a great opinion of a quality they call 'sincerity.'" But then he gets down to business. Like other critics, Sammons declares that *Steppenwolf* is Hesse's "best, or least silly, book." However, he is quite stern, pronouncing Hesse's works to be little more than "a child's introduction to Nietzsche and Jung," while *The Glass Bead Game* strikes him as being "a repository of superannuated German intellectual patterns, most of them a century old or more." Sammons sanely cautions that "it would be foolish to become too upset at the adolescent enthusiasm for Hesse"; but he wishes that Hesse's more devoted readers could be provided with "an awareness of the cultural heritage in which he foundered"—something, he reluctantly admits, that "American education is not prepared to do yet."

It should be readily evident that Hesse criticism cannot be dissociated wholly from the Hesse cult among the young, for to a conspicuous extent much recent criticism is a direct response to that cult—to a sociological situation, not a literary one. I have discussed these articles at some length because I have not included any of them in this volume.[2] First, they are not really about Hesse at all, but about the youth cult and the deficiencies of American education. Second, to the extent that these reviews are a reaction against the excessive adulation of the youth cult, they constitute part of the problem rather than a solution to it. For their criticism often amounts to little more than the expression of a cluster of antipathies—against "irrationalism," "romanticism," "mysticism"—which they as writers project upon a scapegoat (or Jungian "shadow"?) that they conveniently label "Hesse." Third, when the critics do talk about Hesse, they are concerned with him not as a writer, but as a "second-rate" thinker. Largely ignoring his literary characteristics, they also fail to account for the fact that Hesse's ideas appealed to a group of twentieth-century intellectuals that included T. S. Eliot, André Gide, Romain Rolland, and Martin Buber. Between the extremes of a Hessophilia that has mindlessly "co-opted" him and a Hessophobia that seizes upon the writer as the pretext to vent its grievances on a variety of matters, there exists the need for a third mode: a reasonably objective criticism that deals responsibly with Hesse as a writer and thinker on the basis

---

[2] Their critical point of view is represented, however, by Jeffrey L. Sammons's more recent piece, "Hermann Hesse and the Over-Thirty Germanist," which is included in this volume.

of a thorough acquaintance with his oeuvre (and not merely a few novels in translation) as well as with the cultural and intellectual background from which he emerged. This volume aims to fill that need.

At first glance the problem of selection seems to be overwhelming. Helmut Waibler's bibliography, published in the year of Hesse's death, lists over two thousand items on Hesse's life and works.[3] The more significant of these contributions are surveyed in Joseph Mileck's valuable analysis of Hesse criticism up to 1957.[4] On closer examination, however, hundreds of items turn out to be useless for our purposes, falling as they do into the category of brief reviews or congratulatory messages on the occasion of birthdays and awards. Moreover, many of the pieces tend to adopt one of the two poses that characterize the situation today: uncritical adulation or an equally unselective attack. Even though Hesse's literary career goes back to the turn of the century, serious criticism of his works is essentially a product of the past twenty-five years.

## II

Hesse's first two books appeared in 1899—a volume of poems, *Romantic Songs,* printed at the author's own expense, and a collection of nine *poèmes en prose* entitled *An Hour beyond Midnight.* Although only six hundred copies of the latter were published before Hesse withdrew it from circulation, it was reviewed sympathetically by another young poet, Rainer Maria Rilke.[5] Arguing that the beginning of all art is reverence, Rilke observed that Hesse's very words "kneel"—out of reverence for Dante, whom Rilke recognized as the guiding spirit behind Hesse's *vita nuova,* and out of reverence for the Beatricelike woman who seemed to have inspired the work. Rilke was pleased by the "metallic" words and images of certain passages, but in other places he found that the language became too abstract. He concluded his brief appraisal with the verdict

[3] Helmut Waibler, *Hermann Hesse: Eine Bibliographie* (Bern and Munich: Francke, 1962).

[4] Joseph Mileck, *Hermann Hesse and His Critics: The Criticism and Bibliography of Half a Century* (Chapel Hill: University of North Carolina Press, 1958).

[5] In *Der Bote für deutsche Litteratur,* 2 (1898–1899), 388; reprinted in Rainer Maria Rilke, *Sämtliche Werke,* ed. Ernst Zinn (Frankfurt am Main: Insel, 1965), V, 466–68.

that Hesse's early effort was "unliterary"—a vocable of praise in Rilke's vocabulary—and that "it stands on the periphery of art."

Despite their generally friendly tone, the scattered reviews of these two early works and Hesse's first novel, *Hermann Lauscher* (1901), did little to enhance his reputation. However, *Hermann Lauscher* caught the attention of the noted publisher Samuel Fischer, who urged Hesse to submit his next manuscript to his firm. *Peter Camenzind* (1904) turned out to be an instant success: widely reviewed by reputable critics, the novel went through thirty printings in the first two years. Giving up his job in a Basel bookstore, Hesse was able henceforth to support himself through his writing. Popular biographies of Boccaccio and Saint Francis emerged from several trips to Italy. Hesse contributed frequent essays and reviews to many journals, including *März*, which he coedited from 1907 to 1912. His stories and poems were collected in volumes that were commercially as successful as his longer works: the schoolboy-novel *Beneath the Wheel* (1906), the musician-novel *Gertrude* (1910), and the painter-novel *Rosshalde* (1914). A trip to the East Indies in 1911 produced essays, poems, and stories that went into the book *Out of India* (1911). Hesse was widely read, a pleasing *littérateur*, yet despite his activity his works were rarely discussed seriously. The reviews generally contented themselves with facile allusions to such models as the Romantic poet Eichendorff and the nineteenth-century Swiss novelist and storyteller Gottfried Keller.

World War I brought a sharp change in Hesse's fortunes. As a German citizen living in Switzerland, he put himself at the service of the German consulate in Bern and devoted himself selflessly to relief work for German internees and prisoners of war, for whom he edited a newspaper as well as series of books. Despite his own pronounced pacifism, Hesse felt that the war was the inevitable product of a European spiritual crisis. But he shared Romain Rolland's conviction that the writers and intellectuals of all nations should remain *au-dessus de la mêlée* in order to work toward a new and cosmopolitan Europe of the spirit. These feelings prompted Hesse to write a series of articles on war and politics that won him a few allies but ruined his reputation with the generally conservative and nationalistic public that had bought his books up to that time. Readers noted with chagrin that they had been nourishing a viper at their breasts; indignant bookdealers notified Hesse that they would no longer carry the writings of a coward and traitor.

In order to gain a hearing in the face of this hostility and the conspiracy of silence, Hesse published his next novel, *Demian* (1919), as well as several essays—notably an address to German youth entitled "Zarathustra's Return"—under the pseudonym Emil Sinclair. The ruse worked for almost a year, fooling even many of Hesse's friends. The novel was hugely successful among young Germans returning from the war. It was awarded a distinguished prize for first novels (which Hesse subsequently returned). For a short time Hesse had won a new audience to replace the old one. In 1920—in a remarkable foreshadowing of the situation in the United States today—Hesse told Romain Rolland that his writings had elicited the sympathy of a large segment of German youth but that his old friends were turning against him because they feared the influence of his works on the young.[6] Yet the excitement surrounding *Demian* gradually subsided, and it turned out that even many younger readers did not always appreciate his message. In an essay, "Hate Letters" (1921), Hesse quotes from a typical communication that he received from a German student. "Your art is a neurasthenic-voluptuous wallowing in beauty, an enticing siren-cry above steaming German graves that have not yet closed. We hate writers—even if they offer us an art that is tenfold mature—who try to make women out of men, who want to internationalize us and pacify us and make us shallow."[7] During these same years Hesse's works earned him a new and deeper respect in Germany and abroad among such colleagues as Thomas Mann, Stefan Zweig, Theodor Heuss, C. G. Jung, Martin Buber, and André Gide. In 1922 T. S. Eliot wrote to Hesse to express his admiration for the volume of essays *Blick ins Chaos* (*In Sight of Chaos,* 1920), which he later cited in his Notes to *The Waste Land.* "I find in your book a concern with serious problems that has not yet penetrated to England, and I should like to spread its reputation."[8] Yet this impact on a small group of peers had no repercussions in the public at large. In 1923, shortly after the publication of *Siddhartha,* Hesse wrote to Rolland

[6] Hermann Hesse and Romain Rolland, *D'Une Rive à l'Autre: Correspondance, fragments du Journal et textes divers,* ed. Pierre Grappin (Paris: Albin Michel, 1972), p. 69.

[7] "Hassbriefe," *Vivos voco,* 2 (1921–22); reprinted in *Materialien zu Hermann Hesses 'Der Steppenwolf',* ed. Volker Michels (Frankfurt am Main: Suhrkamp, 1972), pp. 224–28.

[8] Quoted in *Hermann Hesse: Eine Chronik in Bildern,* ed. Bernhard Zeller (Frankfurt am Main: Suhrkamp, 1960), p. 109.

that none of his works had ever fallen into such a profound silence. Even former friends did not bother to acknowledge the book.

When *Steppenwolf* (1927) appeared, the timing seemed to be auspicious for a new evaluation. It was the year of Hesse's fiftieth birthday, and a flurry of general appreciations showed up—including notably Hugo Ball's highly readable biography, the first book on Hesse's life and works. The novel was widely reviewed, and it had to be reprinted to meet the popular demand. But many readers were offended by what they considered to be the book's glorification of drugs, sex, and jazz; while the reviews, as Hesse complained, consistently misunderstood his deeper meaning and played up the more sensational aspects. Hesse's readers were mollified in part by the seemingly more "harmonious" quality of his next novel, *Narcissus and Goldmund* (1930). But political events soon nullified this gradual rehabilitation. Although Hesse's books were not officially proscribed until 1943, his major works were generally unavailable in Nazi Germany. To be sure, almost half a million copies of various titles were printed between 1933 and 1945; but well over half of these comprised a single anodyne short story and an edition of selected poetry. In contrast, Hesse's major work, *The Journey to the East* (1932), after an initial printing of nine thousand copies, was not reissued until after the war.

Meanwhile, Hesse again antagonized many Germans by his "unpatriotic" attitudes. As early as 1935 we find the following typical reaction by Will Vesper, a party spokesman on literary affairs.[9] After a hysterical paragraph denouncing the international "Judaism of the Press" that allegedly dominates cultural life in Germany and abroad, Vesper turns his attention to a survey of German literature that Hesse had recently published in the Swedish literary journal *Bonniers Litterära Magasin*. Vesper finds it unpardonable that Hesse, "a true poet and an Aryan," had stooped to praise not only an émigré like Thomas Mann, but even such Jewish writers as Kafka and Zweig—not to mention the Marxist, Ernst Bloch. To make matters worse, Hesse had attacked the current (Nazi) writers, whom he accused of a "tendency to primitive dogmatism." Vesper concludes that Hesse "is betraying German literature of the present to the enemies of Germany and to Judaism." "The German writer Hermann Hesse has taken over the traitorous role of the Jewish

9 "Unsere Meinung," *Neue Literatur*, 36 (1935), 685–86.

critics of yesterday. To oblige the Jews and the culture-bolsheviks
he is helping to disseminate false notions that harm his fatherland."
It goes without saying that such obloquy did not encourage any
serious critical appraisal of Hesse in Germany. At the same time,
there was little interest abroad—first, because few of his works were
available in translation; and second, because he was being attacked
simultaneously from another quarter, namely, by German émigrés
who resented the apolitical stance that Hesse tried to maintain in
neutral Switzerland. In 1936 Hesse wrote to Rolland that he once
again found himself caught between two hostile camps, having become "the focal point for an obstinate press campaign involving
calumny, falsified biographical information, and so forth." It is
symptomatic of this neglect in Germany and abroad that for the
first three years after its publication Hesse's *opus magnum, The
Glass Bead Game* (1943), was reviewed almost exclusively in Swiss
newspapers and magazines.


III


   The first serious and sustained criticism began, principally in Germany and among professional Germanists abroad, after Hesse received the Nobel Prize in 1946. In retrospect it is clear that many of
the early acknowledgements had secondary aims in mind. Hesse was
the first German-language author to receive the Nobel Prize since
it was bestowed upon Thomas Mann in 1929. According to the
terms of the award, Hesse was "besides Thomas Mann the best
custodian of the German spiritual heritage in contemporary literature." By giving the award to a German-born writer, the Swedish
Academy was able to make a gesture toward international understanding. At the same time, since Hesse had lived in Switzerland
since 1912 and held Swiss citizenship since 1923, the Academy
avoided the dilemma of honoring a German writer associated in any
way with the Third Reich. (As a matter of record, the Nobel Prize
was not presented again to a German citizen until Heinrich Böll
accepted it in 1972.) Similar semipolitical overtones are clearly
evident in the first appreciations.
   Both Thomas Mann and André Gide, concerned above all else
with the rehabilitation of a Germany whose image had been
tarnished by the National Socialists, present Hesse as the preserver

of "German" qualities in the finest sense of the word. Mann, as a fellow German keenly aware of his spiritual kinship with Hesse, pays particular attention to Hesse's debt to the German Romantic heritage and detects in Hesse a representative of all that is "Germanic in the old, happy, free, and intellectual sense to which the name of Germany owes its best repute." At the same time, conscious of the cosmopolitan impulse that prompted Hesse to oppose "stifling provincialism," he praises the great service that Hesse rendered to German culture through his many translations, anthologies, editions, and critical essays—an aspect of Hesse's literary activity that is still too little understood and appreciated. Gide, a well-informed observer of German culture, speaks shrewdly of the readiness (*disponibilité*) with which the German character often commits itself to various emotional and intellectual appeals. Though Hesse displays this character almost typologically, his irony saves him from any facile commitment and distinguishes him from most German writers, who in Gide's Gallic opinion take themselves far too seriously. It is Germans like Hesse—their characters tempered by irony and the *Eigensinn* that Gide defines—with whom the European intellectual community, in the dark days following World War II, needs to reestablish rapport. Martin Buber's address was written— a decade after the pieces by Mann and Gide—to celebrate Hesse's eightieth birthday (1957). But now the problems have changed: with a prosperous Germany once again integrated into the European community it is no longer the semipolitical question of the German character that obsesses men. Buber is concerned, instead, with the much broader crisis of the spirit afflicting Western civilization as a whole. He greets Hesse as one of those who, amidst the turmoil of the twentieth century, have helped to preserve the value and meaning of the human spirit in general—and not simply "German" values.

The professional scholars and critics who began to look seriously at Hesse's works around 1950 were all faced with the same problem: they had to introduce Hesse, once again a virtually unknown writer, to their audiences in Germany and abroad; and they took it upon themselves to locate Hesse, known primarily as a "German" writer, in the greater context of world literature. Ernst Robert Curtius approaches Hesse with the sensibilities of a critic who had played an important role as cultural mediator in the twenties, introducing contemporary French and English literature to German readers, and with the sophisticated tools of historical analysis befitting a distinguished medievalist. His academic bias is evident, perhaps, in his admiration for the "medieval" novel, *Narcissus and Goldmund,* yet he comes close to Mann and Gide in his appreciation of the "Western" qualities in Hesse's work, notably *The Glass Bead Game.* Curtius is keenly aware of Hesse's shortcomings, notably in linguistic vigor and epic thrust, but in his attention to Hesse's techniques and imagery (wolf, fish, water, etc.) he points the way for subsequent studies, which have subjected Hesse's works to rigorous scholarly analysis.

Like Curtius, Oskar Seidlin also regards Hesse from a comparative point of view, but his focus is quite different. Whereas Curtius was concerned primarily with the analysis of theme and technique, Seidlin was one of the first to stress the sense of metaphysical anxiety underlying Hesse's works. Following Seidlin's brilliant lead, subsequent critics have begun to analyze the existential elements in Hesse's thought, distinguishing them from the "Romantic" traits with which they are often confused. Still others, taking up Seidlin's well-founded objections to a Freudian interpretation of Hesse, have investigated the mythic dimensions of his works as well as the fascinating parallels and relationships between Hesse and Jung, which are only now beginning to come to light.

Hans Mayer is also opposed to a Freudian interpretation—but for wholly different reasons. Hesse's "humanism" has long made him an attractive figure for Marxist critics and readers. As early as 1952 a bibliography could be published in the German Democratic Republic containing only East German editions of Hesse's works and studies of Hesse by East German scholars and critics. Around the same time several of his novels were reprinted in the series, "Progressive German Writers"; and as recently as July, 1972, *Narcissus and Goldmund* was at the top of the best-seller lists in East Germany. Hans Mayer's essay, which exemplifies the thoughtful Marxist approach, opened the way for a number of studies devoted to Hesse's criticism of society and technology, a central preoccupation in his work from start to finish. G. W. Field, finally, in one of the earliest of a series of articles leading up to his recent book on Hesse (1970), deals with two matters that have evoked much comment: Hesse's use of music in his works (both as theme and as structural pattern) and his relationship to Thomas Mann—an affinity of which both Hesse and Mann were acutely aware. These four essays are included here for at least two reasons. As general appraisals and summings-up, they represent the best Hesse criticism from the early years when the critic still had to identify Hesse and justify his consideration. At the same time, in their thematic and methodological variety they anticipate several of the most rewarding approaches that Hesse studies in the next two decades were to take.

Hesse's postwar popularity lasted for about ten years in Germany, and the immense success of his works provided the financial basis for the Suhrkamp Verlag during its early years.[10] The reasons for the decline in his popularity, which continues today, are complex: in part Hesse simply suffered the fate of many older writers whose works helped to fill the literary vacuum in Germany immediately after the war, but who were pushed aside as a younger generation of postwar writers emerged. In any case, the end of Hesse's German vogue was signaled, though not caused, by Karlheinz Deschner's widely publicized "literary polemic" *Kitsch, Konvention und Kunst* (1957), which in its harshness puts even Hesse's severest Anglo-American critics in the shadow. After a long stylistic analysis of *Narcissus and Goldmund*—chosen, no doubt, because it was Hesse's most popular work—Deschner concluded that the novel contains "not a single image, not a single twist that has not already been often encountered in earlier writers." Deschner is appalled by the very traditionalism that appealed to Mann and Buber. "If we apply strict criteria," he sums up, "then in most of his works Hesse is not even second-rate because, as he himself says, he is 'epigonal.' "

By a curious coincidence, just as Hesse's fortunes were declining at home, an astonishing growth of interest was taking place abroad. Although Hesse has won a large following in India, Japan, and South America, this success has been most conspicuous in the United States.[11] Up to 1945 only eight articles had been published on Hesse in this country. In 1949 *Time* magazine, in a review of *The Glass Bead Game (Magister Ludi)*, commented almost condescendingly that Hesse was virtually unknown in America. And his reputation was certainly not well served by the quality of the early translations.

[10] See Siegfried Unseld's Afterword to his edition of the Hesse-Suhrkamp *Briefwechsel 1945–1959* (Frankfurt am Main: Suhrkamp, 1969), esp. p. 484.

[11] See Eugene F. Timpe, "Hermann Hesse in the United States," *Symposium* (Spring 1969), 73–79; Theodore Ziolkowski, "Hesse's Sudden Popularity with Today's Students," *University: A Princeton Quarterly* (Summer 1970), 19–25; and Egon Schwarz, "Hermann Hesse, the American Youth Movement, and Problems of Literary Evaluation," *PMLA*, 85 (October 1970), 977–87.

In 1952 his American publisher wrote him that it would be necessary to remainder his books because there was no demand for them. If the situation changed within a decade, it was due in part to two rather idiosyncratic works. In his controversial but widely discussed study of alienation entitled *The Outsider* (1956), Colin Wilson cites Hesse as the prime example of what he calls "The Romantic Outsider." Surveying several of Hesse's novels, he gives his particular attention to *Steppenwolf*, "one of the most penetrating and exhaustive studies of the Outsider ever written." Wilson recognizes that Hesse does not possess the epic or dramatic imagination of a Tolstoy or a Shakespeare. But "considered as a whole, Hesse's achievement can hardly be matched in modern literature; it is the continually rising trajectory of an idea, the fundamental religious idea of how to 'live more abundantly.'" These heady notions made a great impact when *The Outsider* appeared, and it is probably safe to say that Wilson's book, along with his subsequent lecture tours in the United States, did more to make Hesse's name known than all the reviews and articles that had appeared in English up to that point.

Timothy Leary and Ralph Metzner grope for similar superlatives in their presentation "Hermann Hesse: Poet of the Interior Journey," in *The Psychedelic Review* (Fall 1963). "Few writers have chronicled with such dispassionate lucidity and fearless honesty the progress of the soul through the stages of life." The authors note that Hesse is "one of the great writers of our time" and claim that he "wrote *Finnegans Wake* in several German versions." But previous critics, we learn, have missed the real message. "At another level Hesse is the master guide to the psychedelic experience and its applications." They urge their audience to read *Siddhartha* before their next LSD session. "The last part of *Steppenwolf* is a priceless manual."

Both of these works contributed substantially, though in a manner that cannot be accurately measured, to the Hesse craze that was beginning to intensify in the United States. Appealing, respectively, to the nascent religious impulse and the drug cult among the young, they represent an ecstatically affirmative counterpart to the negative critical voices that we listened to earlier. But I have not included the pieces for two reasons. Neither of the discussions adds to our understanding of Hesse either as writer or thinker because they adduce Hesse merely as an example to illustrate a theme and to back up an argument. In my opinion, Leary and Metzner are simply wrong—both factually and critically. It has not been demonstrated that Hesse himself experimented with drugs; and his novels are certainly not simply drug manuals. Colin Wilson points to an important tendency in Hesse's work and character; but he stresses it so one-sidedly that the total impression is distorted. For the sense of community, which balances the theme of the Outsider from the very beginning, ultimately emerges as the principal responsibility of the individual in the later novels. In addition, both pieces consist largely of lengthy plot recapitulations. They remain crucial texts, however, for anyone investigating the sociological phenomenon of the Hesse cult. In fact, many of the recent critical attacks on Hesse —notably those of Koch and Steiner—should properly be addressed to the image of Hesse as presented by Wilson and Leary, rather than to Hesse himself.

Since 1960 the balance of scholarly and critical interest in Hesse, as evidenced by an outpouring of books, articles, and dissertations, has clearly shifted to the United States. (With few exceptions, recent German books on Hesse have been either naïvely impressionistic or calculatingly journalistic, lagging far behind the critical sophistication of the better American studies.) For reasons of space I have had to omit many useful contributions. I decided not to include chapters from any of the recent books on Hesse (see the Selected Bibliography) because the books, many of them in paperback editions, are easily obtainable. And I have not reprinted studies, however valuable, that are largely of specialized appeal or that depend upon an analysis of the German text. To represent the current state of Hesse criticism I have selected three recent pieces, two of them hitherto unpublished. Jeffrey L. Sammons's article is in my opinion the most intelligent and best-informed statement of certain serious reservations shared by many scholars and critics. In contrast to his earlier article (mentioned above), this one is devoted wholly to Hesse, and the criticism is based upon a careful study of Hesse's entire oeuvre.

To date, the most interesting Hesse criticism has been concerned in large measure with a complex of attitudes defined as "Hesse." As a result, most of the essays in this volume are of a fairly general nature, dealing with topics—e.g., his humanism or his service to the spirit—that manifest themselves throughout Hesse's life and work. The most recent studies, in contrast, seem to be moving in two different directions. My own contribution is representative, I think, of an increasing number of articles devoted to Hesse as a writer— to the interpretation of specific texts as aesthetic structures within a literary tradition rather than to the discussion of his ideas, taken out of the context of the works and their cultural background. And Ralph Freedman's essay reveals how much we stand to learn—about Hesse's life as well as his works—from the wealth of new material that is beginning to be published by the Suhrkamp Verlag with the collaboration of Hesse's heirs and the various Hesse archives. I do not venture to hope that new documentary evidence will significantly affect the adulation of Hesse's admirers or the contempt of his detractors because, as the record shows, for over fifty years the response to his works has tended to be polarized into extremes. But the coming decade promises to produce a more consistent and responsible understanding of Hesse and his works, based on evidence rather than speculation and continuing the critical tradition established by many of the essays in this volume. And this new image is beginning to assert its place alongside the legend of "Hesse" that has obsessed critics and cultists alike for the past half century.

# Introduction to *Demian*

## *by Thomas Mann*

A full decade has passed since I last shook Hermann Hesse's hand. Indeed the time seems even longer, so much has happened meanwhile—so much has happened in the world of history and, even amid the stress and uproar of this convulsive age, so much has come from the uninterrupted industry of our own hand. The outer events, in particular the inevitable ruin of unhappy Germany, both of us foresaw and both lived to witness—far removed from each other in space, so far that at times no communication was possible, yet always together, always in each other's thoughts. Our paths in general take clearly separate courses through the land of the spirit, at a formal distance one from the other. And yet in some sense the course is the same, in some sense we are indeed fellow pilgrims and brothers, or perhaps I should say, a shade less intimately, confreres; for I like to think of our relationship in the terms of the meeting between his Joseph Knecht and the Benedictine friar Jacobus in *The Glass Bead Game* which cannot take place without the "playful and prolonged ceremony of endless bowings like the salutations between two saints or princes of the church"—a half ironic ceremonial, Chinese in character, which Knecht greatly enjoys and of which, he remarks, Magister Ludi Thomas von der Trave was also past master.

Thus it is only natural that our names should be mentioned together from time to time, and even when this happens in the strangest of ways it is agreeable to us. A well-known elderly composer in Munich, obstinately German and bitterly angry, in a recent letter to America called us both, Hesse and me, "wretches" because we do not believe that we Germans are the highest and noblest of

"Introduction to Hermann Hesse's *Demian*," by Thomas Mann. From Hermann Hesse, *Demian: The Story of Emil Sinclair's Youth* (New York: Holt, Rinehart and Winston, Inc. 1948), translated by N. H. Puday. Copyright 1948 by Holt, Rinehart and Winston, Inc. Reprinted by permission of Holt, Rinehart and Winston, Inc.

15

peoples, "a canary among a flock of sparrows." The simile itself is
peculiarly weak and fatuous quite apart from the ignorance, the incorrigible arrogance which it expresses and which one would think
had brought misery enough to this ill-fated people. For my own
part, I accept with resignation this verdict of the "German soul."
Very likely in my own country I was nothing but a gray sparrow of
the intellect among a flock of emotional Harz songsters, and so in
1933 they were heartily glad to be rid of me, though today they
make a great show of being deeply injured because I do not return.
But Hesse? What ignorance, what lack of culture, to banish this
nightingale (for, true enough, he is no middle-class canary) from its
German grove, this lyric poet whom Mörike would have em-
braced with emotion, who has produced from our language images
of purest and most delicate form, who created from its songs and
aphorisms of the most profound artistic insight—to call him a
"wretch" who betrays his German heritage simply because he holds
the idea separate from the form which so often debases it, because
he tells the people from whom he sprang the truth which the most
dreadful experiences still cannot make them understand, and because the misdeeds committed by this race in its self-absorption
stirred his conscience.

If today, when national individualism lies dying, when no single
problem can any longer be solved from a purely national point of
view, when everything connected with the "fatherland" has become
stifling provincialism and no spirit that does not represent the
European tradition as a whole any longer merits consideration, if
today the genuinely national, the specifically popular, still has any
value at all—and a picturesque value may it retain—then certainly
the essential thing is, as always, not vociferous opinion but actual
accomplishment. In Germany especially, those who were least content with things German were always the truest Germans. And who
could fail to see that the educational labors alone of Hesse the man
of letters—here I am leaving the creative writer completely out of
account—the devoted universality of his activities as editor and col-
lector, have a specifically German quality? The concept of "world
literature," originated by Goethe, is most natural and native to him.
One of his works, which has in fact appeared in America, "published
in the public interest by authority of the Alien Property Custodian,
1945," bears just this title: *Library of World Literature*, and is proof
of vast and enthusiastic reading, of especial familiarity with the

temples of Eastern wisdom, and of a noble humanistic intimacy with the "most ancient and holy testimonials of the human spirit." Special studies of his are the essays on Francis of Assisi and on Boccaccio dated 1904, and his three papers on Dostoevski which he called *Blick ins Chaos (In Sight of Chaos).* Editions of medieval stories, of novelle and tales by old Italian writers, Oriental fairy tales, *Songs of the German Poets,* new editions of Jean Paul, Novalis, and other German romantics bear his name. They represent labor, veneration, selection, editing, reissuing and the writing of informed prefaces—enough to fill the life of many an erudite man of letters. With Hesse it is mere superabundance of love (and energy!), an active hobby in addition to his personal, most extraordinarily personal, work—work which for the many levels of thought it touches and its concern with the problems of the world and the self is without peer among his contemporaries.

Moreover, even as a poet he likes the role of editor and archivist, the game of masquerade behind the guise of one who "brings to light" other people's papers. The greatest example of this is the sublime work of his old age, *The Glass Bead Game,* drawn from all sources of human culture, both East and West, with its subtitle "A Tentative Sketch of the Life of Magister Ludi Joseph Knecht, Together with Knecht's Posthumous Writings, Edited by Hermann Hesse." In reading it I very strongly felt (as I wrote to him at that time) how much the element of parody, the fiction and persiflage of a biography based upon learned conjectures, in short the verbal playfulness, help keep within limits this late work, with its dangerously advanced intellectuality, and contribute to its dramatic effectiveness.

German? Well, if that's the question, this late work together with all the earlier work is indeed German, German to an almost impossible degree, German in its blunt refusal to try to please the world, a refusal that in the end will be neutralized, whatever the old man may do, by world fame: for the simple reason that this is Germanic in the old, happy, free, and intellectual sense to which the name of Germany owes its best repute, to which it owes the sympathy of mankind. This chaste and daring work, full of fantasy and at the same time highly intellectual, is full of tradition, loyalty, memory, secrecy—without being in the least derivative. It raises the intimate and familiar to a new intellectual, yes, revolutionary level —revolutionary in no direct political or social sense but rather in a psychic, poetical one: in genuine and honest fashion it is prophetic of the future, sensitive to the future. I do not know how else to describe the special, ambiguous, and unique charm it holds for me. It possesses the romantic timbre, the tenuousness, the complex, hypochondriacal humor of the German soul—organically and personally bound up with elements of a very different and far less emotional nature, elements of European criticism and of psychoanalysis. The relationship of this Swabian writer of lyrics and idyls to the erotological "depth psychology" of Vienna, as for example it is expressed in *Narcissus and Goldmund,* a poetic novel unique in its purity and fascination, is a spiritual paradox of the most appealing kind. It is no less remarkable and characteristic than this author's attraction to the Jewish genius of Prague, Franz Kafka, whom he early called an "uncrowned king of German prose," and to whom he paid critical tribute at every opportunity—long before Kafka's name had become so fashionable in Paris and New York.

If he is "German," there is certainly nothing plain or homely about him. The electrifying influence exercised on a whole generation just after the First World War by *Demian,* from the pen of a certain mysterious Sinclair, is unforgettable. With uncanny accuracy this poetic work struck the nerve of the times and called forth grateful rapture from a whole youthful generation who believed that an interpreter of their innermost life had risen from their own midst—whereas it was a man already forty-two years old who gave them what they sought. And need it be stated that, as an experimental novel, *Steppenwolf* is no less daring than *Ulysses* and *The Counterfeiters?*

For me his lifework, with its roots in native German romanticism, for all its occasional strange individualism, its now humorously petulant and now mystically yearning estrangement from the world and the times, belongs to the highest and purest spiritual aspirations and labors of our epoch. Of the literary generation to which I belong I early chose him, who has now attained the biblical age, as the one nearest and dearest to me and I have followed his growth with a sympathy that sprang as much from our differences as from our similarities. The latter, however, have sometimes astounded me. He has written things—why should I not avow it?—such as *A Guest at the Spa* and indeed much in *The Glass Bead Game,* especially the great introduction, which I read and feel "as though 'twere part of me."

I also love Hesse the man, his cheerfully thoughtful, roguishly kind ways, the beautiful, deep look of his, alas, ailing eyes, whose blue illuminates the sharp-cut face of an old Swabian peasant. It was only fourteen years ago that I first came to know him intimately when, suffering from the first shock of losing my country, my house and my hearth, I was often with him in his beautiful house and garden in the Ticino. How I envied him in those days!—not alone for his security in a free country, but most of all for the degree of hard-won spiritual freedom by which he surpassed me, for his philosophical detachment from all German politics. There was nothing more comforting, more healing in those confused days than his conversation.

For a decade and more I have been urging that his work be crowned with the Swedish world prize for literature. It would not have come too soon in his sixtieth year, and the choice of a naturalized Swiss citizen would have been a witty way out at a time when Hitler (on account of Ossietzky) had forbidden the acceptance of the prize to all Germans forevermore. But there is much appropriateness in the honor now, too, when the seventy-year-old author has himself crowned his already rich work with something sublime, his great novel of education. This prize carries around the world a name that hitherto has not received proper attention in all countries and it could not fail to enhance the renown of this name in America as well, to arouse the interest of publishers and public. It is a delight for me to write a sympathetic foreword of warm commendation to this American edition of *Demian,* the stirring prose-poem, written in his vigorous middle years. A small volume; but it is often books of small size that exert the greatest dynamic power—take for example *Werther,* to which, in regard to its effectiveness in Germany, *Demian* bears a distant resemblance. The author must have had a very lively sense of the suprapersonal validity of his creation as is proved by the intentional ambiguity of the subtitle "The Story of a Youth" which may be taken to apply to a whole young generation as well as to an individual. This feeling is demonstrated too by the fact that it was this particular book which Hesse did not wish to have appear over his own name which was already known and typed. Instead he had the pseudonym Sinclair—a name selected from the Hölderlin circle—printed on the jacket and for a long time carefully concealed his authorship. I wrote at that time to his publisher, who was also mine, S. Fischer in Berlin, and urgently asked him for particulars about this striking book and who "Sinclair" might be. The old man lied loyally: he had received the manuscript from Switzerland through a third person. Nevertheless, the truth slowly became known, partly through critical analysis of the style, but also through indiscretions. The tenth edition, however, was the first to bear Hesse's name.

Toward the end of the book (the time is 1914) Demian says to his friend Sinclair: "There will be war. . . . But you will see, Sinclair, that this is just the beginning. Perhaps it will become a great war, a very great war. But even that is just the beginning. The new is beginning and for those who cling to the old the new will be horrible. What will you do?"

The right answer would be: "Assist the new without sacrificing the old." The best servitors of the new—Hesse is an example—may be those who know and love the old and carry it over into the new.

# Preface to *The Journey to the East*

## *by André Gide*

While the world conference was taking place at Geneva, that I was afraid would be too tiring for me to take part in, I answered the appeal of young teachers and students of various nationalities gathered together in the vicinity of Innsbruck.

Nothing less solemn, more simply cordial than that assembly initiated by the French. I took the floor to repeat almost exactly what I had previously said in Alexandria, Beyrouth, then in Brussels: that our occidental culture appeared to me in grave danger; besieged on the right and the left by totalitarian doctrines into which all individuality had been reabsorbed.

"I believe in the virtue of a small number. . . . The world will be saved by a few." It is on the confession of a like conviction, expressed in almost the same words that the last book of Hesse ends: *Krieg und Frieden*,[1] of which the last chapter alone is recent. The large number of articles he groups together is inspired by the other war and its consequences. From the beginning of Hitlerism, he foresaw the dangers of that sinister adventure into which Germany, with blind-folded eyes, was about to let herself be led.

In Pertisau, during the course of a little unofficial congress, someone asked how it happened that not a voice in Germany was raised in time to denounce the danger, and, perhaps, by denouncing it, to prevent it. "He who remains silent, approves. Germany, unanimous in its error, should be unanimously condemned." I protested that that was to fail to recognize the many clandestine efforts and the heroic opposition of the churches, both Catholic and Protestant. One had to see in this general silence not so much indifference or

"Preface to *The Journey to the East*," by André Gide. From André Gide, *Autumn Leaves* (New York: Philosophical Library, Inc., 1950), translated by Elsie Pell, pp. 227–34. Reprinted by permission of the Philosophical Library, Inc.

[1][*War and Peace*, a collection of essays on war and politics, published in translation under the title: *If the War Goes On* (1971)—ED.]

submission, as muzzling. Totalitarianism, in this case as almost always, obtained only precarious results, and by what cruel means: censorship of writings, death, prison, exile, for those who would have liked to speak. May we in France never know a time when the dissenters would be reduced to silence in such a way! Merit is on the side of the small number; on the side of those who do not belong to a party, or, at least, who, even if they are enrolled (and that is then called "voluntary enlistment") keep their consciences clean, their minds free and speak openly. They are rare; but the importance of their voices can be recognized by that very dissonance. It is it, it is they, who will be listened to later.

During the entire Hitlerian period, Hesse's writings were banned in Germany. Even to-day printed in Switzerland, they have acquired, through repression, a power of expansion all the greater. Some of his books, translated into French, had appeared well before the war, but had remained little noticed. In our time, one scarcely pays heed to anything except explosives, and restrained writings hang fire. When they have real merit, it is rarely until several years after that their furrow spreads and widens.

With Hesse the expression alone is restrained, not the feeling or the thought; and what tempers the expression of these is the exquisite feeling of fitness, reserve and harmony, and, with relationship to cosmos, the interdependence of things; it is also a certain latent irony, of which few Germans seem to me capable, and whose total absence so often spoils so many works by so many of their authors, who take themselves terribly seriously. It is difficult to explain this, for we in France, to be sure, fall willingly into the opposite excess, and I am far from making the apology for our faults. For the narrow-minded convictions of Rousseau, I would often yield the most amusing maliciousness of Voltaire; but with Pascal, for instance, how much the laughter in the *Provinciales* deepens for me the gravity of the *Pensées!*

Schumann had this irony, with or without Heine, and I love the title he gives to one of his "Scenes of Children": "Fast zu ernst!" [2] What I have especially retained from *Wilhelm Tell* (apart from the springtide song that opens the play) is, at the beginning of Act 2, the first words of Walter Furst's wife, when she sees her husband all weighed down by cares that he has not yet related: "So ernst, mein Freund!" "So serious, my dear!" I shall have to reread that play. . . .

[2] "Almost too serious."

Serious, does Schiller know how not to be so always?—and that is
too much.

There are bitter ironies where bile and peccant humors pour out;
but Hesse's, so charming in quality, seems to me to depend on the
faculty of leaving himself behind, of seeing himself without looking,
of judging himself without complacency;[3] it is a form of modesty
that becomes all the more attractive because more gifts and virtues
accompany it.

Hesse is a painter almost as much as a poet. In certain of his
collections of verse, the reproduction of a watercolor accompanies
the poem as an illustration; it is of an almost childlike docility; so
natural and translating a communion with the outer world, so
harmonious and so perfect that no disturbance of the soul can
find an access to it. It is a work of art. However diverse (in subject
matter if not in tendency) may be Hesse's books that I have read, I
recognize in each of them the same pagan love of Nature: a sort of
devotion. The open air circulates through their pages that quiver
with panicky breaths, like the leaves of forest trees. In each of them,
too, I refind the same indecision of soul; its contours are illusive
and its aspirations, infinite; it is infatuated with vague sympathies,
ready for the reception of any chance *imperative;* little determined
by the past to find in submission itself an aim, a reason for living,
an anchor for his floating impulses. Such, moreover, is the German
soul of which Hesse, in spite of his resistance (which is explained by
other and very rare virtues), remains one of the most representative witnesses. For something primitive lingers in the Germanic soul
when not ameliorated by culture; a sort of functional availability;
subject to the call of the seasons, of encounters and a proposed
ideal to which to devote themselves without critical examination or
haggling. From then on you understand easily what facile prey
these souls will be, spontaneously disposed to abnegation. Indolently
they allow themselves to be seized by a sort of voluptuousness
brought about by non-resistance, the almost feminine abandon to
the invitation of anything at all triumphant: enthusiasm, vague
effusions, thirst for conquest and limitless expansion. . . . Let us
add this to, as a corollary: a somewhat gregarious need to group
themselves, to form *Bund,* a more or less secret society, and to wend

[3] Such also is the humor of which he speaks in his *Steppenwolf:* "You have to
learn to laugh. To attain a higher form of humor, cease first to take yourself too
seriously."

their way in company toward an end often ill-defined, in appearance all the more noble because it is colored by mysticism and
remains rather mysterious. That is, strictly speaking, the subject
even of this book; and so it seems to me, in spite of its specious form,
strangely revealing.

And everything that I say here would predispose Hesse to acceptance, would have offered him as a docile and easy victim to
this totalitarian mirage that charms, even to-day, so many of the
indecisive and so many "voluntary recruits"—had it not been for
the singular virtue he advocates, that he declares he cherishes above
all, that he considers superior to all other virtues, and which he
deeply regrets that the German soul so often lacks lamentably; he
calls it *Eigensinn,* a word that means at the same time confidence in
oneself and consciousness of oneself. In a writing dated 1919 which
he has just brought out again, he speaks of it excellently. All the
human virtues (about the way he expresses it) are embodied in a
single nomenclature alone: obedience. But it is a question of knowing to what. The *Eigensinn* itself is assimilated into obedience; but
while all the other virtues, the most preached and the most beloved,
go back or refer to laws that men have invented, this supreme vir-
ture alone heeds and respects only *itself.* That this virtue isolates
you goes without saying; and opposes you to the masses, and points
you out to the fury of the chiefs and directors of the herd. Hesse
paid with exile; and others with imprisonment and death.

Again he says in a short writing that all creatures under the sun
live and develop as they wish and according to their own laws; man
alone allows himself to be fashioned and bent by the laws that others
have made. The entire work of Hesse is a poetic effort for emancipation with a view to escaping imitation and reassuming the genuine-
ness compromised. Before teaching it to others, it is necessary to
preserve it in oneself. Hesse arrives at it through culture. Although
profoundly and fundamentally German, it is only by turning his
back on Germany that he succeeds. Those in his country who were
able to remain loyal to themselves, and not to allow themselves to
be deflected are rare; it is to them he addresses himself and says:
however few you may be, it is in you, and you alone, that the virtue
of Germany has taken refuge and it is on you that her future depends.

With them we can come to an understanding. With them we
should speak.

# Hermann Hesse in the Service of the Spirit

## by Martin Buber

### An Address on the Occasion of the Hesse Celebration in Stuttgart (1957)

## I

When I was invited to speak on the occasion of the eightieth birthday of my friend, Hermann Hesse, I felt that I was not capable of providing what is expected of such talks: the assessment of a total literary oeuvre. What I did believe that I could do—and hence my acceptance—was to hint at the significance of the central portion of that oeuvre—the series of great narratives undertaken when Hesse reached the "Swabian Age" of forty—within the endeavors of our age to clarify the position of the spirit. When the separate stages of Hesse's own road toward this goal are made evident, they display an exemplary pattern.

It is essential to keep in mind the fact that we are talking about narrative works. The born narrator experiences and records all being as event. Landscape, intellectual utterance, even the very stirrings of the soul must express themselves as unfragmented happening. In 1917, after a number of books that took pleasure in their own narrative virtuosity and that were happily received as such, Hesse entered the service of the spirit. He now had to render in the form of temporal event a spiritual conception of spirit, which he had experienced in the realm of temporal events. The hand of the spirit had wrested the writer Hesse, in the middle of his life,

"Hermann Hesse in the Service of the Spirit," by Martin Buber. From Martin Buber, *A Believing Humanism: My Testament, 1902–1965* (New York: Simon and Schuster, 1967), pp. 70–79. (Originally in *Neue deutsche Hefte*, 4 [1957–58], 387–93.) Copyright © 1967 by Simon and Schuster. Reprinted by permission of Simon and Schuster and Rafael Buber. Newly translated by Theodore Ziolkowski.

out of his carefree storytelling and had compelled him to report its
(the spirit's) struggles, its perils and ventures, in epic fashion—that
is, as occurrences in the lives of people engaged with other people.
In the process and from one work to the next, this concern became
ever more specifically a spiritual one. At the same time his mastery
of narrative, the power of transforming problem into event, became
increasingly perfect. Finally, by the time when Hesse wanted to
give his account of an imaginary realm of the spirit enclosed within
itself, no other language was audible than the language of events.
The destiny of the spirit entered the world of appearance as a
process displayed to our senses.


# II


Destiny of the spirit—what that means in our age is principally
the crisis of the spirit or, more precisely, this crisis in its relation to
life. The signs of this crisis had already revealed themselves in the
heavens of philosophy. Overcome by the storms and demands of
life, the spirit denied its proper office of truth-finder and law-
speaker. Liberating life from its constraints, it aspired to be nothing more than life's interpreter—either dithyrambic or prag-
matically instructive, according to the circumstances. We subsequently learned to our full satisfaction what life, thus liberated by
the spirit, was capable of perpetrating. But before it became unmistakably clear, life echoed its response to the summons of the
spirit. Or more precisely: now the poetically creative spirit spoke
in the name of irrepressible life, became indignant at the tyranny
of any absolute morality, and praised sovereign individuation. And
this is where we encounter the first in that series of Hermann Hesse's
works that reflect the crisis of the spirit—the inflammatory novel
*Demian* from the time of World War I, in which the author advocates the rights of an authoritarian Cain against a submissive
Abel, an attitude that already in Byron's age was a prerogative of
poets who sought freedom from the law.

It is no accident that Hesse supplemented this anthropological
postulate with a theological one and that the god he proclaimed
was none other than that gnosticizing being, Abraxas. According to
Hesse, this being (which is also known to us from an early writing
of the psychologist C. G. Jung) "has the symbolic responsibility of

uniting the divine and the satanic." It therefore possesses in eternal perfection what psychologistic theory exhorts its adepts to achieve under the label "integration of evil."

It seems as though here an insurrection were being mounted against that power of the *creator spiritus* which distinguishes not merely between light and dark but also between salvation and perdition. And yet this first work of the series initiates the endeavors of the writer, Hesse, in the service of the spirit. For the course of the human spirit invariably begins with a bold breakthrough, and every breakthrough is preceded by a daring breaking-off. All that matters is where the road now leads. You cannot go back, and you cannot simply remain standing where you have arrived. Anyone who is content merely to break with the past loses the life of the spirit. In the search for the living god you must sometimes shatter images that have become unworthy in order to create room for a new one. But Abraxas is not the image of a god: it is a complex concept, the concept of an ultimately valid coalescence of good and evil. You must turn your back on this being if you want to make further progress. For a being that represents and legitimatizes nothing but ourselves, even when raised to the absolute power, is not of divine nature.

After the breakthrough of *Demian* Hesse, not aiming for a reconciliation, remained on the side of rebellious life. But the very next step leads him to a stage of greater illumination.

## III

The next narrative in the series, *Siddhartha,* is designated as an "Indic Poem." A product of the first postwar years, it gives a new and significant twist to the great question pervading all these works by Hesse—the question concerning the goal of the spirit.

Siddhartha, a contemporary of Buddha, resists the teaching of the master because, like all teachings, it is one-sided. In Siddhartha's opinion no single teaching can do justice to the reality of being, for they all necessarily affirm one thing and deny the other. Siddhartha has no desire to probe and split the world by discriminations, by saying Yea and Nay, for in the real world sin and grace reside close together. Instead, he wants only to love the world, love it as it is, a world existing in and of itself.

In *Demian* Hesse had advocated the claims of urgent life against the dictates of the spirit; in *Siddhartha* no further claims are regarded as valid. In the earlier novel the goal was perfect individuation; now it is love for a world that is irreproachable in its existence. In both cases, ultimately, spirit stands opposed to spirit—in the one case, for the sake of the liberation of elemental forces suppressed by the spirit, and in the other for its own sake, for the sake of spirit. *Siddhartha* permits no prescriptions concerning what one is supposed to love in the world and what one is supposed to despise. Between the two novels stands the beginning of the gruesome experience of the age: that life, when it is no longer obedient to the spirit, rages self-destructively against itself. As long as Siddhartha remains in constant meditation, he can embrace sin and grace simultaneously. But when he is dealing no longer with "sin" in general, but with a concrete act of violence taking place before his very eyes, with the mistreatment of the weak by the strong, with the misuse of those who are dependent by those who are in power, then Siddhartha will renounce his all-embracing love and take action against evil. In the dimension of reality, if human evil is not to become overwhelming, the spirit must time and again make the most rigorous distinctions within the human world. Hesse himself, as a human being, became ever more intimately acquainted with this dilemma of the world-loving man. In a time in which the representatives of the spirit so frequently enslaved themselves to rulers, he intrepidly maintained the free steadfastness of the spirit.

## IV

The novel *Steppenwolf*, which according to sequence ought to be taken up at this point, belongs only peripherally to our theme: service of the spirit. For all its unrestrained topicality, it is still a profoundly Romantic work and points back in a curious way to the phase when Hesse was still breaking with the past. It is as though the author felt himself hindered in his progress by something that, though of fundamental significance, had remained unsaid a decade earlier. The book purports to be the "inner biography" of a man who is destined by "his high degree of individuation," as Hesse puts it, to be an outsider, alienated from the bourgeois world. *Siddhartha* had gone a significant step beyond this basic view, but

at the same time it had ignored something that now clamored to
be appended retrospectively.


## V


But immediately after this *intermezzo appassionato* we are presented with a new step to be climbed.

*Narcissus and Goldmund,* a severe and inherently melancholy
work, is the cleanest and most rounded narrative from the standpoint of the classical tradition. In contrast to the earlier books of the
series, here the rebellious spirit, embodied in the main character,
is complemented by a counterpart who is his equal in every respect.
And between the two—the spirit that is always on the move, roaming, seizing, and shaping what has been grasped into images and
the ascetic spirit, dedicated to thought and answering life with the
idea—there prevails a grandly conceived relationship of dialogue.
The authenticity of the spirit is inherent in both: both are spirit,
both together constitute the spirit. Here for the first time Hesse embodied the conflict of the spirit in the duality of these two men who
do not contest each other, but who exist on opposite sides and yet
together. The thinker (Narcissus) is wrong when, speaking of his
own being, he tells his antagonist and friend (the sculptor Goldmund) that the spirit cannot live in nature but only in opposition
to it, as its counterpart. Only the two of them together—the one
allowing himself to be swept along by nature and the other defying
nature—constitute spirit. In history, the conflict of spirit inevitably
and in a unique conjunction with historical factors explodes in
crises. But here this conflict has been comprehended and rendered
symbolically in the opposition and coexistence of two human beings.

To be sure, only one of these lives, the artist's, is actually narrated.
The monk Narcissus speaks to us, but even as he does so he remains immutable; we scarcely learn what happens to him. Later
Hesse was to realize profoundly that he had failed to do justice to
the reflective spirit, and he compensated for this shortcoming splen-
didly in the last work of the series, *The Glass Bead Game.*

In another notable connection, which concerns us particularly
here, *Narcissus and Goldmund* provides a bridge to the later novel.
Narcissus says of himself: "The goal is this: always to place myself
where I can best serve. . . . Within the scope of my capacities I

want to serve the spirit as I understand it." On the next level this desire is reflected in the mysterious fact that Leo, the "servant" of the league of Journeyers to the East, reveals himself to be its highest master. And the same motif resounds in the name of Joseph Knecht ("servant"), whose life story is recounted in *The Glass Bead Game*. The law that prevails here is called by Leo "the law of service."

## VI

In these last two works of the series, the theme developed in the earlier novels, the conflict of the spirit, is seemingly no longer present. Here the spirit is not fighting for the rights of life nor does it oppose an all-affirming love to the analytical power of cognition. Nor, incarnated in two persons, does the adventuresome and creative spirit stand opposed to the spirit that is self-contained. Yet the sense of community documented in *The Journey to the East* and the great peace that prevails in *The Glass Bead Game* would surely not have been reached other than by walking through the fire of opposites, and deep within the Journey and the Game this transformed fire continues to glow.

The fantastic allegory of *The Journey to the East*—permeated by a late and whimsical Romanticism but fundamentally con-temporary—is the successful attempt to comprehend and narrate as a single mutual venture the dream-voyages of all men who have the power of expressing their wishes as vivid images. I call the attempt successful because Hesse has succeeded in reporting the unthink-able—a trip through space and time simultaneously, the journey of a great troop and at the same time of smaller groups of those more intimately associated, but in the last analysis the journey of each individual toward the unattainable goal of his life wish—as though it were actually a process.

The troop consists not merely of people living at the same time, but also of saga-enshrouded heroes of the past; the historical figures are joined by figures from ancient and modern epics; and even pseudonyms of the author himself venture to mingle in the crowd. They are all united in a *Bund*, the League of Journeyers to the East, who are traveling separately and together to the longed-for goal-land of their imaginations. This leaguelike association, impossible and yet real, has replaced the struggling solitudes of Hesse's earlier narratives. With this League and the Order, which here and in *The Glass Bead Game* give structure to the events, the category of "We" has entered Hesse's works. Accordingly the turning point of *The Journey to the East* occurs when the League-member who relates the story, designated with no attempt at self-concealment as H. H., succumbs to doubts regarding the reality of the League. And it is the highpoint of the story when he regains his faith, and thereby reality itself, on a higher level. It is the reality of the spirit, which constructs new worlds out of the materials of this world. And this spirit is in the last analysis a collective one.

*The Journey to the East* has no proper ending. The narrator simply breaks off his tale; and yet the perspicacious reader does not feel that this conclusion is fragmentary. The double figure consisting of a "half-real" H. H. and a wholly real Leo, which is displayed to us here, permits us to sense how the spirit, by way of flesh and blood, enters into the statue. The story has fulfilled its obligation as a confession, and in doing just that it has become an allegory.

## VII

We can regard *The Journey to the East* as a prelude to the last and most impressive work of the series, *The Glass Bead Game*. In neither do we perceive anything more of those storms of the spirit which raged through the earlier works. But *The Journey to the East* still depicts the failure of man in the tribulations of the spirit; in *The Glass Bead Game* there prevails a great peace between the two. All that happens here takes place in the old, accustomed dimensions of human existence, albeit in a future phase of this existence; and yet it seems as though the spirit were really at home here in its human domicile.

Here, this state of being-at-home, this homecoming of the spirit, assumes the form of a game; and only in this form could deeds of the spirit be narrated so deliberately. This self-contained game with its own strict rules, this consistently regulated play "with all the contents and values of our culture," related equally to music and mathematics, to art and science alike, this perfection of *homo ludens* emerging from supreme cultivation of the spirit—all this is served by the Castalian Order of the Glass Bead Game Players,

which appears Joseph Knecht as its *magister ludi*. Knecht works
for the spirit, manifested here in its late and final form, with a
great and unflagging devotion and in a mood of serenity that
nothing can dampen. He succeeds in bringing the educational function of the Order to even greater perfection. But at the same time
he realizes with increasing clarity and inexorability that, for all
this, the spirit has neglected rather than carried out its responsibility
for the world of living and suffering humanity that has been en-
trusted to it. Since the spirit has been summoned as the helper of
life that is infinitely exposed and infinitely threatened by itself, one
serves the spirit most effectively by assisting life. Joseph Knecht
gives up his office and leaves the Order with the intention of beginning anew somewhere in the country as a teacher in an ordinary
school. First he wants to tutor the son of a friend. In order to win
the full confidence of the youth, he follows him in a hazardous
swimming race and drowns. Whenever I read the conclusion of this
magnificent work, I am curiously reminded of the sacrificial death
that the Rainmaker of a matriarchal tribe (in Knecht's own story
about a fictional earlier life) takes upon himself because he has
failed to prevent a cosmic catastrophe.


## VIII

The spirit did not spring into being as a curious byproduct of
the natural process of evolution: it revealed itself to a singular
natural being, called man, and entered into him. Paracelsus and,
following him, a poet of our own time, Hofmannsthal, have said
that the spirit does not reside in us. But I rather believe that it
both does and does not. We are indebted to the spirit for Prome-
thean gifts, and it has suffered like Prometheus. To aid the life of
man, the spirit has fought against monsters of every sort. But at
odds with itself, it denied itself, and at that point it was no longer
able to be our reliable helper. We have come into dire need, and it
has succored us. Yet it has also betrayed us, for it was no longer
a whole and integral spirit. Today it is in a state of crisis. Its crisis
is ours. It can become whole and integral only if it takes a stand in
support of our unity.

Hermann Hesse, in his capacity as writer, has served the spirit by
telling of the conflict between spirit and life and of the struggle of

the spirit against itself. Thereby he has rendered more tangible the obstacle-ridden road that can lead to a new wholeness and unity. But in his capacity as human being, as the *homo humanus* that he is, he has performed the same service by always taking a stand, whenever it was important, for the wholeness and unity of the human condition.

It is not just the Journeyers to the East and the Players of the Bead Game all over the world who salute you today, Hermann Hesse. All those who serve the spirit, throughout the entire world, unite in a great greeting of love. Wherever the spirit is served, you are loved.

# Hermann Hesse

## by Ernst Robert Curtius

November 1918. . . . Leaden despair weighs upon men. For the old generation, Germany is shattered, because to them Germany means the empire of the Hohenzollern. There are dignitaries of the fallen regime who do not wish to survive the entry of the occupying forces. But the younger generation do not mourn the passing of this unreal world. To them Germany was, in George's words, "the land still imbued with great promise." Through the collapse of the regime all the progressive forces had been set free. In the German universities great teachers were functioning at the height of their powers: Ernst Troeltsch in Berlin, Max Weber in Munich, Max Scheler in Cologne, Wilhelm Worringer in Bonn, Alfred Weber and Friedrich Gundolf in Heidelberg. A springtime of the mind, lavish in its wealth, had begun to blossom. Students, still wearing their field-gray uniforms, crowded into the lecture halls, the most open-minded student generation since the summer of 1914. In many of them the spirit and the traditions of the *Freideutsche Jugend* were still alive. Their sacred texts were the parables of Chuang-Tsu, Plato, Hölderlin, Nietzsche, and George. Their attitude was a wonderful cosmopolitan openness, an awakening to a new day.

It was this generation that Hermann Hesse addressed in the periodical that he edited in collaboration with Richard Woltereck, *Vivos voco*. It bore witness to a new spirit, a spirit striving to overcome the evil forces of national hatred. In 1920, I had the opportunity to report on "a voice from the youth of America" in its pages. Hesse's literary work had made no impression upon the young. That was to change as by magic with the appearance of

"Hermann Hesse," by Ernst Robert Curtius. From Ernst Robert Curtius, *Essays in European Literature (Kritische Essays zur europäischen Literatur)*, translated by Michael Kowal (Princeton, N. J.: Princeton University Press, 1973). Reprinted by permission of Princeton University Press.

*Demian* in 1922.[1] This work spoke directly to the students in field-gray. Here were the sufferings of school; the perplexities of sex; the experience of myths and mysteries; the War, felt as a premonition, endured, paid for in death. The dying Demian to his wounded friend: "Little Sinclair, pay attention! I shall have to go away. Perhaps you will need me again some time. . . . If you call me then, I shall not come again, riding on a horse so rudely or on the train. You must listen to what is inside yourself, then you will see that I am within you." A message as simple as it is profound. Nothing else in Hesse's work attains the level of this utterance. You say something like that only once.

In the same year, 1922, I was surprised by a letter from T. S. Eliot. His friend Hermann Hesse had brought me to his attention. Whether I would like to contribute to *The Criterion?* The first number (October 1922) contained Eliot's *The Waste Land*—and an essay by Hermann Hesse on "New German Poetry." In the notes to *The Waste Land* we read that several lines were inspired by Hesse's *Blick ins Chaos [In Sight of Chaos]*. A single crossing of the paths. But how many paths and encounters there were in the spiritually relaxed Europe of the time! Rilke translated poems by Valéry, who showed them to me in manuscript. At Scheler's house I saw the first issue of Ortega's *Revista de Occidente*. Valery Larbaud introduced Joyce in France. Sylvia Beach's bookstore, "Shakespeare and Company," was an international meetingplace as was that of her friend Adrienne Monnier diagonally opposite. From 1922 on the "Decades" at Pontigny were taking place again. The Pen-Club was founded. . . . A Europe of the mind—above politics, in spite of all politics—was very much alive. This Europe lived not only in books and periodicals but also in personal relations. One visited the venerable Ivanov in Rome. In Heidelberg, one saw Thomas Mann and André Gide during the same week. "European Conversations" (*Europäische Gesprache,* the title of a Hamburg periodical) were conducted in those days. . . .

Hermann Hesse no longer took part in them. It was not his way. He was the hermit of Montagnola: gardener, dreamer, painter and writer—"the literary man Hermann Hesse" (as he styles himself in *Kurgast [Guest at the Spa]*); "an idler, a timewaster, an easygoing, work-shy man, to say nothing of his other vices" (*Nürnberger Reise*)

---

[1] [Curtius gives the wrong date; *Demian* actually appeared in 1919.—Ed.]

[*The Journey to Nuremberg*]. Meanwhile he turned fifty (July 2, 1927). For this date an official biography appeared from the pen of Hugo Ball (1886–1927), that profound and solitary spirit, who had found his way back from Dadaism to *Das Byzantinische Christentum* (1923) and the Roman Catholic Church. His *Kritik der deutschen Intelligenz* (1919) was an apocalyptic cry of alarm which has not even now reached its destination. Ball's biography may be called official because it is illustrated "with fourteen photographs from the family collection," and is based on a great deal of information furnished by the poet himself. The account of Hesse's home and family, of his Germano-Russian and his Swabian grandfather (two splendid characters), of the Hindu-Pietistic atmosphere of the Basel mission, is vivid cultural history. At thirteen, the gifted boy broke out of this protected world. It is the decisive break, which the poet himself, in a later retrospect (*Kurzgefasster Lebenslauf* [*Life Story Briefly Told*], *Neue Rundschau* [1925]) merely notes, without explaining it. "When I was thirteen, and that conflict had just begun, my behavior at home and at school left so much to be desired that I was exiled to the Latin school of another town. One year later I became a pupil in a theological seminary, learned to write the Hebrew alphabet, and was well on the way to grasping what a *dagesh forte implicitum* is, when inner storms suddenly broke over me, leading to my flight from the monastery school, my confinement in the 'dungeon,' and my expulsion from the seminary. For a while I made an effort to continue my studies at a Gymnasium, but the outcome, confinement and dismissal, was the same there too. After that I was a shopkeeper's apprentice for three days, ran away again, and to my parents' great consternation disappeared for several days and nights. I was my father's assistant for half a year, then, for a year and a half, a locksmith in a machine shop and tower-clock manufactory. In short, for more than four years everything they tried to do with me went awry—no school would keep me, and I couldn't stand any apprenticeship for long. All attempts to make a useful person out of me ended in failure, sometimes in ignominy and scandal, at other times in escape and expulsion. And yet people were ready to grant that I had ability and even a certain amount of sincere good will!"

Conflict with the school is a normal experience and since 1900 had become a popular subject for literature. *Flachsmann als Erzieher*

[*Flachsmann as Educator*] by Otto Ernst (1901) and Wedekind's *Frühlings Erwachen* [*Spring's Awakening*] ran to full houses. Emil Strauss (*Freund Hein*, 1902), Hermann Hesse (*Unterm Rad* [*Beneath the Wheel*], 1905), Heinrich Mann (*Professor Unrat*, 1906), Robert Musil (*Die Verwirrungen des Zöglings Törless* [*Young Törless*], 1906) were the classics of the *Schülerroman*, the novel of student life. Even *Buddenbrooks* concluded with the catastrophe of little Hanno's schooldays. Thomas Mann himself got no further than the "Einjährig-Freiwilliger-Examen" (high-school-leaving examination),[2] with which one could bid school farewell at the end of the sixth year. But the rare combination of talent, determined application, and luck led him rapidly to success, esteem, prestige. "Gustave Aschenbach, or von Aschenbach, as his name has been officially known since his fiftieth birthday"—thus begins *Der Tod in Venedig* [*Death in Venice*] (1913). This Aschenbach, "the author of the lucid and powerful prose epic on the life of Frederick the Great of Prussia," at the age of forty already had "to cope daily with post that bore the stamps of every country in the world." The school authorities have included selections from his writings "in their pre-scribed textbooks." Early in life he had chosen Munich for his place of residence, "and lived there amid such civic honor as the in-tellect may in rare instances be privileged to enjoy." When Thomas Mann was fifty years old in 1925, there was a banquet in the Munich Town Hall and many other corroborations of civic honor. Thomas Mann knew the value of representation as well as Senator Buddenbrook.

Hermann Hesse's fiftieth birthday passed without ceremony. He would not have had it any other way. As a "reply to the greetings" he published, in 1928, the angry volume *Krisis*, forty-five poems only fifteen of which were later included in the collected edition (*Gedichte* [*Zurich*, 1942]). These verses give utterance "to one of those stages of life where reason becomes weary of itself, abdicates its authority, and leaves the field free to nature, chaos, and the animal instincts." Animal instincts, in this context, mean the shimmy, whisky, cognac, bars, and hangovers. *Armer Teufel am Morgen nach dem Maskenball* [*Poor devil the morning after the costume ball*] ends:

[2] Literally, examination for one-year volunteers. It enabled the holder of the certificate to reduce his military service to one year.—TR.

Ach wäre dieser Sonntag schon vorbei
Und ich und du und dieses ganze Leben.
Ich höre auf, ich muss mich übergeben.

[If only this Sunday were over at last, and you and me and this
whole dreary life. I've got to stop, I'm going to be sick.]

But that is still too tame. Everything must come out, though it
were in the diction of a schoolboy:

Das Leben ist darum so beschissen,
Weil wir doch alle sterben müssen.

[The reason why life is so shitty is that we all must die.]

Even in the charming *Nürnberger Reise* we hear of the "peculiar
sadness and, pardon the expression, shittiness of life." In such
moods Hesse crossed the threshold of his sixth decade, "more concerned with the fear of aging and dying than with the pleasure of
celebrating" (*Krisis,* postscript). *Krisis* is the birthday child's sullen
requital: a document of emotional stresses but a gesture of provoca-
tion as well. The revolt of the thirteen-year-old has turned into a
defiance of social conventions. It makes the aging man into an
"unsociable hermit . . . , who is deeply pained when he has to
obtain a certificate of residence from the local authorities or even
to fill out a census slip" (*Kurgast,* 1925).

Hugo Ball informs us that in Switzerland, in 1916, Hesse suffered
an acute nervous crisis. Psychoanalytic treatment, administered by
a student of C. G. Jung, provided relief. Between May 1916 and
November 1917 there were more than seventy sessions. The fruit of
this period was *Demian:* release of new creative power and depth
perception. Psychoanalysis, as we have seen, was unable to resolve
the tensions in Hesse's nature, or even to prevent their recurrence.
But neurotic conflicts are not operable injuries or unmitigated
disasters. They are part of the very substance of life and therefore
part of the material and the problems to be shaped by life. That this
is true was demonstrated in Hesse's finest book, *Narziss und Goldmund* [*Narcissus and Goldmund*] (1930). We know that Hesse's
early novel *Unterm Rad* depicts his escape from the monastery
school at Maulbronn. After a quarter of a century the poet returned
to this theme, but transposed now to a timeless Middle Ages, and
purged of all the passions of youthful revolt. Goldmund, a student
at the monastery, admires his teacher, the ascetic young monk

Narcissus, with a shy and worshipful love. He wants to devote his entire life to the Order. But Narcissus explains to him that that is not his destiny. "You are an artist, I am a thinker. You sleep at the mother's breast, I watch in the desert. For me the sun shines, for you the moon and the stars. Your dreams are of girls, mine of boys." Narcissus awakens Goldmund to a knowledge of his own nature. Instead of study, monastic discipline, and virtue, powerful instincts take possession of Goldmund: sex, love of women, longing for independence, travel. He roams through woods, mountains, towns, cities; women's favors accompany him on his journey. He knows how to fend off treacherous companions with a knife. He sees whole territories laid waste by plague; orgies of brutality and lust at the edge of the grave. He becomes a woodcarver and is about to be inducted with honor into the guild. But restlessness drives him to seek new adventures. He is on the point of losing his shirt and his head when Narcissus, the powerful abbot, intercedes for his release and brings him back to the monastery. The whole thing is a wonderfully colored picture out of the German Middle Ages, in which romanticism and realism are blended. Fruity, fragrant, round, self-contained, neither didactic nor problematical; a variegated tapestry of the everlasting powers of life, steeped in magical essences that recall Arnim, Tieck, Novalis—but as a result of a secret affinity of blood, not of literary borrowings or an overlay of antiquarianism. No single work of Hesse's has a greater claim to a place in the heritage of German literature. It is a completely German book, unaffected by the lure of the Orient to which the poet was succumbing even then.

Hesse's maternal grandfather, Dr. Hermann Gundert, was one of the first pioneers of the German evangelical mission in India. Upon his return he worked for thirty more years on a dictionary of one of the Indian dialects, on behalf of the Basel mission. He had married in India; Hesse's mother was born there. All the thoughts of his parents and of their friends from the mission revolve around the fabulous land. So it is not surprising that in 1911 Hesse embarks on a journey to India. He has personal reasons for going, were it only the need to see India with other eyes than those of his parents. His book *Aus Indien* [*Out of India*] appears in 1913. Around the same time Waldemar Bonsels (*Indienfahrt* [*Voyage to India*], 1916) and Graf Keyserling (*Reisetagebuch eines Philosophen* [*Travel Diary of a Philosopher*], 1919) had visited India. Thus, with his book on India, as with his school novel and psychoanalysis,

Hesse had unwittingly and unintentionally set foot on a terrain that was soon to become a playground of intellectual fashion (Rabindranath Tagore's *Gitanjali* had appeared as early as 1914). Hesse's encounter with India proved a disappointment. He thought that he would find there the innocent and simple children of paradise. "But," the travel book concludes, "we ourselves are different. We are strangers here and have no rights of citizenship. We lost our paradise long ago and the new one that we wish to have and build is not to be found on the equator or beside warm Eastern seas. It lies within us and in our own Northern future."

The next book about India, *Siddhartha* (1922), is merely a transposition of Hesse's revolt against his pietistic home to an Indian setting. Siddhartha, the devout son of a Brahmin, can find peace neither in the teachings of his ancestors nor in asceticism nor in sensual pleasure. Nor can he accept Buddha's doctrine: "No, a seeker after truth cannot accept any doctrine, not if he truly wishes to find. One who has found, however—he can approve of every doctrine." In the end the seeker finds peace by listening to the great stream, "surrendering himself to its streaming, at one with Oneness." A rather more novelistic than philosophical solution to the problems posed. A stage, of which there are many in Hesse's work, destined to be superseded by more impressive elaborations. *Die Morgenlandfahrt* [*Journey to the East*] (1932) is pretty much along the same lines. The East here is "not only a country and a geographical location but rather the homeland of the soul's youth, the everywhere and nowhere," "the union of all the ages." The travelers to the East are an Order;[3] all disclosures regarding the secrets of the Order are forbidden. The journey takes place for the most part in Europe (a proceeding justified by the indication "everywhere and nowhere"). The narrative is confused, with no attempt at construction. "How to make the story of our Journey to the East tellable? I don't know." A significant admission. In this instance Hesse availed himself of the literary puzzle in the manner of E. T. A. Hoffmann in order to legitimate the irreality of his account. The narrative ends in Basel, where it turns out that Leo, "the perfect servant," is at the same time the head of the Order. The "servant" might easily be a preliminary version of Joseph Knecht of *Das Glasperlenspiel* [*The Glass Bead Game*], whose name

[3] Cf. *Demian*, p. 143: "the first fulfillment of my life and my admission to the Order."

means squire or servant. Hesse likes name symbolism, and he also likes to play hide-and-seek with names. One of the officials in *Das Glasperlenspiel* is called Dubois—like Hesse's grandmother. Her first husband, Isenberg, lent his name to Knecht's friend Ferromonte. Thomas Mann appears in the book as Meister Thomas von der Trave, Jacob Burckhardt as Pater Jacobus. Knecht's friend Designori ("of the nobles") is of patrician stock; his name is the antithesis of "Knecht." Such playing with names may be regarded as a system of correspondences invented by the writer for his personal use. It enables him to establish cross-connections between widely separated periods in his life and work. Its function is similar to the interweaving of themes that is so typical of Hesse's literary technique. In *Rosshalde* (1914), little Pierre wants to know what carnations are called in the language of the bees and what the robin redbreasts say to each other. On his wanderings through the woods Goldmund would have liked to become a woodpecker, perhaps for a day, perhaps for a month. "He would have spoken woodpecker language and extracted good things from the bark of trees." Among the travelers to the East is one who hopes to learn the language of the birds with the aid of Solomon's key. And now the same thought without the dress of fiction: "To feel life throbbing in me . . . to have a soul so nimble that by the play of hundreds of fancies it can slip into hundreds of forms, into children and animals, and especially into birds, that is what I want and need in order to live" (*Wanderung* [*Wandering*] 1920). To understand the language of the birds—eternal motif of fairy tale, of legend (cf. Wagner's *Siegfried*), of dream; the longing to be in harmony with all living creatures, not merely with the birds. One of Goldmund's wishes is never to find his way out of the forest, never to see people again, never to love another woman—to become an animal, "a bear or a stag." In the tale *Der Wolf* [*The Wolf*], the hero is the wounded animal: driven off and sad, on the heights of the snow-covered mountains, the wolf feels the approach of death and sees the red moon rise. The singer Muoth (*Gertrud,* 1910) "had been emaciated by solitude like a wolf." The motif is transformed and developed fully in the novel *Der Steppenwolf* (1927).

Fish too are fraught with symbolism for Hesse. Fishing in the Nagold, depicted by the painter Veraguth in *Rosshalde;* Goldmund at the fish market: there is always a mysterious correspondence to life. Fish and moisture—these are related like bird and air, wolf and wood. The fish-motif participates in the water symbolism, and water, as we know, signifies the unconscious in the language of dreams. Water is attraction and peril at the same time. The book that made Hesse famous, *Peter Camenzind* (1904), begins and ends by the Lake of Lucerne. The lake plays a prominent role in *Rosshalde*. Joseph Knecht will meet his death in an Alpine lake. Peter Camenzind's best friend drowns while bathing "in a ridiculously small South German stream." The monastery school pupil Hans Giebenrath (*Unterm Rad*) finds his death in the waves. Death by water—one of Hesse's basic themes.

Giebenrath and Heilner: a friendship that is tragically severed. Siddhartha and Govinda: a friendship that dissolves because the worthy Govinda runs out of breath. In *Demian* friendship ceases to be conflict, parallelism, or interrelation and becomes psychagogy. This pattern is repeated on a higher plane in *Narziss und Goldmund*. Here friendship mirrors the polarity of mind and life. The poet has embodied two dominant traits of his own character in the two figures. We are close to Novalis' theory of the "truly synthetic person": "Each person, though divided into several, is also capable of being one. The genuine analysis of the person as such brings forth persons. . . ."

These would be some examples of Hesse's themes, suggestions toward an analysis that could be carried much further. Thematic and technical analysis—that rarely practiced art—is the only adequate method for interpreting an author. As such, it is the preparatory course for all criticism that wishes to rise above verbiage, circumlocution, and inconsequentiality. Years ago I tried to explore Proust and Joyce by this method. The incentive was especially strong because both authors were using new techniques to render new aspects of life. They were artists in a sense of the word that can hardly be applied to Hesse. The epic writer makes a new aspect of the world visible. He constructs an objective reality. The opening sentence of *Ulysses* places us *in medias res*. Not personal experience but a series of images and characters detached from the writer is communicated. With Hesse this occurs only in *Narziss und Goldmund*. All the rest of his works are autobiographical ectoplasms, transposed life histories. The writer remains trapped in his own subjective sphere. He cannot contrive to set down an objective world and gain a footing in it. The conventions of art are as repugnant to him as those of society. In constantly renewed departures and variations he makes the reader privy to a development that begins in failure to master the tasks of life (*Peter Camenzind, Unterm Rad,* the novel of marriage *Rosshalde*), and then registers the attempts at a cure (psychoanalysis, India-cycle). Sometimes he will deviate into lyrical prose jottings (*Wanderung*), sometimes into diary-like reportage (*Kurgast, Nürnberger Reise*), occasionally into "magic theater" (*Steppenwolf*). Epic presentation is not one of his native gifts. It can happen that the form will grow brittle in his hand (as in the passage cited above from *Die Morgenlandfahrt*). He has a "mistrust of literature in general." "I can only consider the endeavors of contemporary German writers (my own included, naturally) to produce really articulated forms, genuine works of art, as somehow always inadequate and epigone." Literature having lost its certainty, he can grant it value only "insofar as it confessedly expresses its own poverty and the poverty of its age with the greatest possible candor" (all in *Nürnberger Reise*). The dichotomy in this evaluation is reflected by the slack diction, with its conversational jargon ("somehow"), self-conscious doublets ("real forms," "genuine works"), and turgidity ("confessedly," "with the greatest possible candor"). These sentences have no rhythm, no tautness, and are therefore not compelling. The writer not only mistrusts literature; he has no responsible commitment to the exigencies of his craft, to syntax and style. But is it his craft? In *Gertrud* and in *Das Glasperlenspiel* he is a musician, in *Rosshalde* a painter, in *Narziss und Goldmund* a woodcarver. In *Nürnberger Reise* he toys with the idea "that perhaps I might still manage to run away from literature and take up painting for a living, a craft I find more attractive." Is it unfair to lend weight to these utterances? Are they merely the result of passing moods? But the author did think them worth communicating, and they illuminate the problems of his art. They explain too why we were able to say something about Hesse's themes but very little about his technique. It is variable, often groping; now clumsy, now sedulous. The watercolors that Hesse added to a few of his books are done with a coloring box. His handling of language, too, gives the effect of careful daubing, now childlike, now amateurish. There is never any sparkle to this prose. But once in a while—as in Demian's farewell—a note is sounded that touches the heart with its magic.

The copious stream of Hesse's lyric poetry is also for long

stretches nothing but diligent rhyming. I choose a poem from *Das Glasperlenspiel:*

> Die ewig Unentwegten und Naiven
> Ertragen freilich unsre Zweifel nicht.
> Flach sei die Welt, erklären sie uns schlicht,
> Und Faselei die Sage von den Tiefen.
>
> Denn sollt' es wirklich andre Dimensionen
> Als die zwei guten, altvertrauten geben,
> Wie könnte da ein Mensch noch sicher wohnen,
> Wie könnte da ein Mensch noch sorglos leben?
>
> Um also einen Frieden zu erreichen,
> So lasst uns eine Dimension denn streichen!
> Denn sind die Unentwegten wirklich ehrlich,
> Und ist das Tiefensehen so gefährlich,
> Damn ist die dritte Dimension entbehrlich.

[The eternal die-hards and the naïve cannot, to be sure, bear our doubts. The world is flat, they declare simply, and the legend of depth mere drivel. For if dimensions other than the two good old familiar ones really did exist, how could a man still live without anxiety? So in order to reach a peaceful settlement, let us strike one of the dimensions. For if the die-hards are really sincere, and the view of depth is so dangerous, then the third dimension is dispensable.]

This poem looks like a sonnet and was perhaps on the way to becoming one. For this purpose, unfortunately, a line is missing. The rhyme scheme of the first quatrain is abandoned in the second. The rhymes are more miss than hit. "Die-hard" is the worst sort of newspaper jargon. The whole thing is versified prose with intrusive padding. For that matter, the weakness of Hesse's style generally has always been that he cannot leave anything out. In a preface to a collection of poems, *Die Harfe. Vierundzwanzig Gedichte* [*The Harp: Twenty-four Poems*], published in 1917, Alfred Kerr wrote: "Poets fill ten printed volumes. But a few islands finally project above the flood of time. Not to burden the world, I present the islands immediately." A few islands project above the flood of Hesse's lyric poetry too. They could fill one of those thin "Insel" volumes and in such a selection become a German possession.

This essay does not aim at a comprehensive evaluation of Hesse's work. That would be impossible in any case, if for no other reason than that many—and important—books are inaccessible. I have traced only a few of the main lines that conduce to an understanding of *Das Glasperlenspiel* (1943). The appearance of this work, impressive in content and scope, of the poet's old age, came as a happy surprise. When a writer in the seventh decade of life sums up his existence in a broadly-conceived work, it is noteworthy. But when it is a poet who has accompanied us from the days of our youth, whom we encountered in a new shape after the First World War, and who now speaks again across the abyss of calamitous years, we are moved and grateful. Something takes place in us that transcends everything literary: an exchange of greetings by the survivors of a catastrophe; the rediscovery of a familiar voice. Memories of long decades are stirred and give the work a resonance which vibrates with many destinies. The generations that awakened to maturity in the first decade of the twentieth century found their intellectual orientation in the writers born before and after 1870: George (1868), Hofmannsthal (1874), Rilke (1875), Thomas Mann (1875), Rudolf Borchardt (1877) in Germany; Romain Rolland (1866), André Gide (1869), Paul Claudel (1870) in France. Proust and Valéry (both born in 1871) did not achieve prominence till after 1918. Ten proud names radiating from one decade. Lives that intersected, attracting one another, repelling one another. And yet, from the perspective of the present, belonging to the same world. In the eighties a new generation emerges: the "moderns" of 1920: Joyce (1882), Ortega (1883), Eliot (1888). Between the first and the second row stands Hermann Hesse. He stands by himself, in scarcely more than fleeting touch with any of those named. We have referred to the slight contact with Eliot. Romain Rolland is mentioned once in a dedication; the *Nürnberger Reise* records a visit with Thomas Mann. But Hesse was never affected by the works of his great coevals. He shunned the living Europe of the twentieth century. France had nothing to give him. "Paris was ghastly," opines Peter Camenzind. "Nothing but art, politics, literature, and sluttishness, nothing but artists, literary men, politicians, and low women" (tautology as a stylistic device). The *Nürnberger Reise* informs us that the poet has "hitherto succeeded" in avoiding Berlin. Merely the journey to Nuremberg was a hazard. "It was beautiful and mysterious, but to me, as a south German, depressing and frightening as well. I thought to myself, if I should travel on, there would be more and more pines, and then more snow, and then perhaps

Leipzig or Berlin and pretty soon Spitzbergen and the North Pole. Good Lord, what if I had gone so far as to accept the invitation to Dresden! It was unthinkable." "Except for my native town in the Black Forest, I have felt really at home only in the region around Locarno."

Fortunately, between the Black Forest and Locarno there is a place called Switzerland—one of those friendly gifts of a durable kind that history has conferred upon our small, tormented portion of the globe. A country and a people secure in themselves; small enough to be protected from the troubles of their neighbors; large and varied enough to be a mirror of Europe. Years ago the Basel philosopher Karl Joël gave a lively description of the "Switzerizing" of Europe in the eighteenth century. Pestalozzi and Rousseau became the educators of the continent. Haller and Gessner transformed the natural sciences, Bodmer and Breitinger prepared the ground for the revolt against French Classicism. Voltaire lives near the Swiss border; Gibbon completes his history, conceived in Rome, at Lausanne. Goethe pledges fellowship with Lavater. In the nineteenth and twentieth centuries Switzerland becomes an asylum for those politically persecuted or disaffected in their own countries. Hesse, who had many ties with Basel, adopted Switzerland as his homeland. Transposed into the utopian "Castalia," it becomes the setting of *Das Glasperlenspiel.*

The work has been called a novel of education. That is one of its many aspects, but it does not touch the core of the book. We can approach it more closely by asking ourselves why Hesse picks up the theme of education again, and why he presents Joseph Knecht first as a student, then as a teacher, and finally as "magister ludi," the master of the game. *Unterm Rad* depicts the boy's failure in school. In *Das Glasperlenspiel* the delinquent pupil catches up on his schooling, as it were, and becomes a teacher himself (at a monastery school, like Narcissus). Thus a theme from Hesse's early period is taken up again in his latest, changed in value from negative to positive, and "reconciled on a higher level." Not just this theme alone. All the poet's themes (among which we found conflicts but also attempts at a cure) are taken up again and treated contrapuntally in this work. The *Versuch einer Lebensbeschreibung des Joseph Knecht* [*A Tentative Sketch of the Life of Joseph Knecht*] is the last and by this time definitely realized transposition and sublimation of all those personal histories in which Hesse

depicted himself as Camenzind, as Giebenrath, as Sinclair, as Siddhartha, as Goldmund. All those personal histories crystallized around
conflicts: conflict with the home and its pietistic atmosphere; with
the school; with the middle-class world; with society in general.
Finally, too, the conflict with the chosen profession—that of literature. As late as 1927 the poet notes: "As for myself, I am certain
that no respectable, hard-working person would ever shake my
hand again if he knew how little I value my time, how I waste
my days and weeks and even months, with what childish games I
fritter away my life." A fifty-year-old writer who cannot stop playing games and admits it with a bad conscience. But is the play-
instinct something to be ashamed of? Undetected and unanalyzed
residue of a bourgeois prejudice! Play and the capacity for play is
one of the most important functions of man's relation to the world.
A learned historian of culture has meticulously examined American
Indian games in order to confront *homo sapiens* with *homo ludens*.
Animals and men play, and so do the Gods, in India as in Hellas.
Plato views man as an articulated puppet fashioned by the Gods
perhaps for the sole purpose of being their plaything. What conclusion shall we draw? The play-instinct is to be affirmed. A negative
converted into a positive. To play one's own game with the deep
seriousness of a child at play. The highest achievement would be—
to invent a game of one's own. This the poet has succeeded in doing.
He is the inventor of the glass bead game. He has learned to master
it: the game of life, the game of the beads. Thus he has become
in two senses of the word *magister ludi* (in Latin *ludus* means both
"game" and "school"). The glass bead game is the symbol for the
successful completion of the school of life. The discovery of this
motif determined the conception: at once inspiration and stroke of
luck; the seed from which the golden blossom sprouted.

Motif and theme are two different things, and critics would do
well to distinguish between them. The motif is what sets the fable
(the "mythos" in Aristotle's *Poetics*) in motion and holds it together.
Motif belongs to the objective side. Theme comprises everything
that concerns the person's primary orientation toward the world.
The thematics of a poet is the scale or register of his typical reactions
to certain situations in which life places him. Theme belongs to the
subjective side.

It is a psychological constant. Motif is given by inspiration, discovered, invented—all of which amounts to the same thing. He who

has nothing but themes cannot attain to epic or drama. Or, for that matter, to the great lyric. Here we touch upon a law of aesthetics the best formulation of which I find in T. S. Eliot: "The only way of expressing emotion in the form of art is by finding an 'objective correlative'; in other words, a set of objects, a situation, a chain of events which shall be the formula of that particular emotion; such that when the external facts, which must terminate in sensory experience, are given, the emotion is immediately evoked." By means of the motif, the "objective correlative," the insufficiencies of personal experience are overcome. The motif is an organic, autonomous structure, like a plant. It unfolds, forms nodes, branches out, puts forth leaves, buds, fruit. Once the bead game was in existence, a whole world had to be built up around it. That could only be an imaginary world, i.e., a Utopia, or a Uchronia (Renouvier's concept). But this world had to be transferred to an era which was not too distant in time from our own. For elements of our own culture must still survive in Castalia. Hence a—somewhat labored—introduction is necessary to serve as a bridge between the twenty-second and twentieth century. This allows for a critique of our age, but, what is more important, it demonstrates that the glass bead game has precursors in every epoch of the European mind. This means, however, the integration of western tradition into Hesse's spiritual universe.

And the Orient? Like all the main themes of the poet it is crystallized on to the new structure. The work is dedicated to the "Travelers to the East." The psychic techniques of Yoga are practiced in Castalia. India reappears in *Indischer Lebenlauf* [*The Indian Life*]. Nevertheless, the role of guide has passed to China. Castalia has a "Chinese House of Studies," it even has, as in a rococo park, a Chinese hermitage called the "Bamboo-grove." There one finds goldfish ponds, yarrow stalks for consulting the oracle, brushes and water-color bowls: pretty Chinoiserie. But when the hermit is invited to Waldzell, there arrives in his stead only a daintily-colored Chinese letter containing the irrefutable assertion: "Movement leads to obstacles." Seneca, Thomas a Kempis, Pascal had stated something similar, if with less preciosity. Thus *Das Glasperlenspiel* also concludes and crowns the poet's Oriental cycle. And yet the world of the East is not the essential core of the book but rather the decorative background. Its effect is "antiquarian," as Demian says of Dr. Pistorius's Abraxas-mythology.

*Das Glasperlenspiel* is a western book. An ancestry is established for the bead game originating with Pythagoras and Gnosticism and continuing through Scholasticism and Humanism to the philosophy of Cusanus, the universal mathematics of Leibniz, and even to the intuitions of Novalis. Two names, however, with which only the fewest readers might be expected to be familiar, are mentioned with especial piety: Johann Albrecht Bengel (1687–1752) and Friedrich Christoph Oetinger (1702–1782), great Swabian theologians, in whom a strict belief in the Bible was united with apocalyptic doctrines, theosophy, chemistry, and Cabbala. They are intermediaries between Boehme, Swedenborg, and Schelling. Oetinger was pastor at Hirsau, near Calw, where Hesse was born. The prominence given these names implies the resolution of the conflict with the Swabian Pietism of his home and, by the same token, a rapprochement with Christianity. This rapprochement is further evidenced by Knecht's intimacy with Pater Jacobus and the Order of St. Benedict.

Castalia, too, is an order. So Hesses's oldest theme is drawn into the organization of the work: the theme of the monastery. It is most remarkable how this theme too is transformed by a newly-won freedom. As he has invented his own game, so the poet has invented his own order. Psychologically this means: he has become his own master. By his own full power he can impose the authority with which he will comply. What had, as a neurotic conflict, been a stumbling block becomes, through "anagogy," a building block. The revolt against all external authority is now recognized as the passionate search for an authority derived from his own inner law. Joseph Knecht passes through all the grades of the order, submitting voluntarily to its regulations. After long service, long mastership, he "awakens" (we recall that Goldmund was "awakened" by Narcissus). Knecht's inner law compels him to quit the order. His departure takes place in the prescribed ceremonial forms. To be sure, the administration of the Order cannot approve of this step. As he is about to leave, Knecht says to himself: "If only he had been able to explain and prove to the others what seemed so clear to him: that the 'arbitrariness' of his present action was in reality service and obedience; that it was not freedom he was going toward but new, unknown, and uncanny obligations; and that he was going not as a fugitive but as one who is summoned, not willfully but obediently, not as master but as sacrifice." So, after five decades, the boy's flight from the monastery school is repeated, only with its signs reversed from negative to positive; recast and purged of all slag it has come to be understood in its deeper significance: as a level of transcendence. In this work of the poet's old age, all the previous stages of his life have become transparent to him. It was conceived on the level of "illumination."

Where is the awakened teacher of the order summoned by his inner law? To the "world outside," the ordinary human world beyond Castalia's serene precincts. The "unknown obligation" toward which he is moving is—death. But this departure for the unknown, no longer of a wandering scholar but of a man who is "summoned," is the heroic setting-out of the Nordic man whom Oriental absorption does not restrain. Final confirmation of the return to the West; Protestant nonconformism; Düreresque knight-errantry.

One last point! We found that in Hesse psychoanalysis and Oriental wisdom were attempts at healing neurotic conflicts. In addition, a theme to which we have barely alluded, although it runs through all the books from *Peter Camenzind* on—the escape into alcoholic intoxication. *Das Glasperlenspiel* is the result and testimony of a self-cure, the only cure that is dignified and genuine because it proceeds from the very core of the person. Psychoanalysis, Yoga, Chinese wisdom, were only expedients. He who has been "awakened" no longer needs them. The conflicts are resolved in a blessed new period of creativity. It is brought on by the discovery of the bead game. This functions as the center around which the person and the productivity of the poet are reorganized. The resolution of discords is the great new experience. That is why music is so important in the work. It is a symbol of euphony and concord, of rhythmically articulated spiritualization—harmony with the All.

A more precise analysis, a more searching appreciation of the rich late work I must leave to others.

# Hermann Hesse:
# The Exorcism of the Demon

## by Oskar Seidlin

The conferring of the literary Nobel Prize for 1946 upon Hermann Hesse has brought into the international limelight, however briefly, a figure whose features were unfamiliar to the literary world at large. It has also illuminated the perplexing fact that our notions of literary greatness and fame are both arbitrary and relative in that an author, whose merits and standing are solidly confirmed at home, may be found "obscure" by foreign literary critics. The question that was being asked somewhat mockingly "Who, after all, *is* Hermann Hesse?" must be disquieting to anybody familiar with contemporary German literature. And the fact that second and third rate German novelists and biographers gained easy admittance into our country, while only a few of Hesse's books were translated (and are now being gradually re-issued), sets one thinking about the strange selective process at work in the establishment of a world-literature. This phenomenon would lose its awkwardness if Hesse's talent, themes and problems were such as to appeal primarily to a narrowly defined home audience. But this is not the case. One cannot easily dismiss the fact that two such discerning and different writers as Franz Kafka and André Gide have counted Hesse among their favorites, that a true citizen of the world, Romain Rolland, has not only found him worthy of personal friendship but considered him one of his most interesting literary contemporaries. This, and the adoration which Hesse's *Demian* (published anonymously in 1919) enjoyed among the élite of German youth who clasped this book as if it embodied a new Revela-

"Hermann Hesse: The Exorcism of the Demon," by Oskar Seidlin. From Oskar Seidlin, *Essays in German and Comparative Literature* (Chapel Hill, N. C.: University of North Carolina Press, 1961), pp. 203–27. (Originally in *Symposium*, 4 (1950), 325–48.) Reprinted by permission of the author and the University of North Carolina Press.

tion emerging from the apocalypse of the World War, may justify a closer analysis of Hermann Hesse's literary work. This evaluation will not deal with the obvious ties connecting Hesse with the poets of German Romanticism; it will not focus upon the socio-political concerns as expressed in his pacifist manifestos published during the first World War. Rather it will concentrate on Hesse's ruthless and self-tormenting exposure on the *condition humaine,* his metaphysical anxiety, his struggle with the demon and yearning for redemption which make him both a "modern" in the truest sense of the word and an ally of those who, by self-dissection, have made us painfully aware of the fate of man under the Sign of the Crisis.

## I. Awakening

"In the beginning was the myth"—these are the opening words of Hesse's *Peter Camenzind* (1904), the novel which carried an almost completely unknown author to fame, rather incongruous opening words; for the story of the Swiss peasant lad who, after years of struggles, disappointments, self-deceptions and frustrating experiences in the literary world finally returns to his native village, is much more closely related to the poetic realism of the late 19th century than to the myth-creating and myth-recreating efforts of our generation. Still, that these words introduce Hesse's first full-fledged literary achievement, that they stand as watch-words over his career, is no accident. The myth which is "in the beginning" will be forever the subsoil from which Hesse's works grow.

The myth is man's first answer to (or rather his first groping visualization of) the problems with which his own existence and his position in the cosmos confront him. It is man's awakening to himself, and it has all the landmarks of an awakening: the lingering on in the twilight region between night and day, the shock at the immediate directness of the new light, the courageous attempt to transpose experiences of a primeval nature into the language and symbols of reality. In just this way Hesse's stories are myths; his entire work seems an endless recording of the process of awakening. The very word fascinates him, and in his last work, the monumental *Glass Bead Game* (1943), published in this country under the title *Magister Ludi,* we find the protagonist's admission that "awakening was to me a truly magic word, demanding and pressing, consoling and promising." The process of waking in the morning was described with terrifying minuteness in *Kurgast* (*A Guest at the Spa*, 1925), as memorable as the similar analysis in Proust's *Du côté de chez Swann*, but intensified by the horror of facing the light again, by the deadly desire not to venture across the threshold of a new day. A painful exercise in trespassing the threshold: this, and nothing else, is the essence of Hesse's works.

In the early novels, *Peter Camenzind* and *Beneath the Wheel* (1906), this "exercise" was still so much shrouded in psychological realism that Hesse appeared to be one more of the many sensitive and delicate anatomists of puberty. Hans Giebenrath, hero of *Beneath the Wheel*, falls all too clearly into the well-established type of the languid adolescent: troubles with an antagonistic father, endless conflicts with a cruel and impersonal school-system, vague wanderings into the thoroughly bewildering realms of eros and sex, and finally the only half-intended suicide after some cheap carouse. Yet, in the light of Hesse's later development, it becomes quite obvious that the psycho-biological "case histories" of Peter Camenzind and Hans Giebenrath are only timid approaches to the painful process of awakening, timid even to the extent that both heroes shy away from passing through *la porte étroite*: Hans Giebenrath lets himself half-wittingly glide into the river, while Peter Camenzind returns to the quiet shelter of his home village where the "light of the day" does not penetrate. (The fact that in both cases the return to the dark is caused by failure to establish satisfactory sexual relations opens the door to psychoanalytic interpretations to which Hesse has been only too often subjected.) There is, in these early books, still a wall barring the adolescent hero from the open road, the same wall which separates young Hesse from the realization of his own inner self and of the problems which beset him and his time. A shock was needed to break down the barrier and bring an awakening which would force upon Hesse the reëvaluation of all values, and open the road before him. The shock came in the form of the first World War.

From this time on, the veil which so strangely shrouded Hesse's earlier productions is ruthlessly drawn away. No longer does the poet shrink from tasting the "forbidden fruit," from trespassing across the threshold between the stage of innocence and the acceptance of man's fate. No matter how painful this step might be, it has to be taken. In one of his short stories, *Klein and Wagner*, written immediately after the War (1919), we read: "In reality there was only one thing which man feared: letting himself fall, taking a step out into the Unknown, the little step beyond all existing securities. But who has once, just once abandoned himself, has just once given himself into the hands of fate, he is free." Klein, the hero of our story, has set himself free. After a secure life as a bank clerk he suddenly woke up and saw the humiliation caused by his daily routine, by his marriage to a woman he had never loved and finally learned to hate, by the suppression of all noble and strong desires. This awakening was his "original sin": the little bank teller, before embarking on his road to freedom, defrauded his institution of a considerable sum: he had fallen, but he was free. It would be hard not to see in this story, this little anecdote lifted from the every-day criminal register, a paraphrase of the story of the fall of man.

Protestant to the core, haunted by the consciousness of original sin, Hesse has circled again and again around man's tasting of the forbidden fruit of the tree of knowledge, his awakening amidst fear and trembling. The Forbidden which has to be faced exerts a dangerous but promising fascination. Already in *Beneath the Wheel* there was a dark and slimy alley which exuded "together with a strangely foul air a blissfully uncanny anguish, a mixture of curiosity, anxiety, bad conscience and heavenly premonitions of adventures." All of Hesse's heroes are simultaneously repelled and attracted by this dark alley, none more strongly than the young protagonist of *A Child's Soul* (1919) whose story becomes one of the most terrifying records of mental anguish in contemporary literature. Drawn to his father's room, where he has no business to be, he rummages in all the corners and drawers of the study "only to follow a compulsion which almost choked me, the compulsion to do evil, to hurt myself, to load myself with guilt." When the Serpent whispers, Adam will not resist, the sin has to be committed. And so the youngster in *A Child's Soul* steals fruit from his father's drawer, not an apple but a few dried figs (and that the fig-tree is introduced makes the "mythical" impact of the story perhaps more obvious than necessary).

The urge to find out the "secret" about one's self and the hidden corners of life, curiosity in the widest and most dangerous sense, is the driving force behind Hesse's work. It is a ruthless curiosity, shameless and without mercy, and it will not rest until the last veil is drawn back. For this reason then, and not for the sake of psychological subtleties, Hesse has delved again and again into the minds of vagrants and adolescents, since for them everything is unknown and without name before they have "found out." They are all spies tracking themselves down, excited by the scent of the Unknown, hankering after secrets. They are all very much akin to the Kierkegaard who admitted that it would have given him great satisfaction to be a member of the Copenhagen criminal police force. They are all brethren of Gide's protagonists, the ruthless exposers and explorers, the snoopers through *Les Caves du Vatican,* living embodiments of a curiosity which never seems to exhaust itself so that the very last sentence of *The Counterfeiters* can start with the words: "Now I am curious. . . ." In one of his early writings, a collection of fairy tales, short stories, diary pages and poems entitled *Hermann Lauscher* (1901), Hesse calls Lauscher's most characteristic feature a "self-tormenting love for truth," and he could have hardly found a more appropriate self-characterization. He is consumed by an uncontrollable and at times embarrassing desire to be naked, to show himself in so merciless a light that even the "private parts" of body and soul will not be spared exposure. In his story *Klingsor's Last Summer* (1919), the painter Klingsor gathers in his final hours the strength to do his self-portrait. And this is what his friends see when, after Klingsor's death, the picture has been found: "It is Man, Ecce Homo, the tired, rapacious, wild, child-like and over-refined man of our late period, homo Europaeus, dying and desiring to die: purified by every longing, sick with every vice, enthusiastically elated by the knowledge of his destruction, ready for every progress, ripe for each regression, all glow and all fatigue, devoted to fate and pain as the morphinist is to his drug, lonesome, hollowed out, old as the ages, at the same time Faust and Karamasov, animal and sage, all bare, without any ambitions, all naked, full of a child's fear of death and full of the weary readiness to die his death." It is Klingsor's portrait, but not Klingsor's alone. It might be Nietzsche's portrait of Man on the Eve of the Superman—if it were not Hesse's portrait of Hesse. To find the same merciless exposure in the "first person," one has only to leaf through the *Guest at the Spa,* the abysmal record of a sick man who, with masochistic satisfaction, watches the deformations, pains and ridiculous motions of his sciatica-ridden body.

But this violent urge for confession is mixed with a stubborn secretiveness, a bashful hiding behind the "fig-leaf," an obstructive silence opposed to the asking and demanding voice: "Adam, where art Thou?" Guilt cries out for confession, but guilt breeds a dark recalcitrance as well. In the first story of the Lauscher collection, written as early as 1896, we meet for the first time this bliss of confession mixed with the stubborn refusal to admit one's wrong which will shake the Steppenwolf no less than Emil Sinclair, hero of *Demian*. The conflict of remorseful desire to do penance and of rebellious self-assertion in the face of the power which demands submission is being incessantly fought on the battlefield of the soul, and vests Hesse's works with an urgency and tension truly religious. In the very signature which Hesse puts under his writings we can trace this bewildering spectacle of confession and hiding. Is it not revealing that one of his very first works presented itself to the audience as *The Posthumous Writings and Poems of Hermann Lauscher, edited by Hermann Hesse;* that his latest one is entitled *The Glass Bead Game, A Tentative Sketch of the Life of Magister Ludi Joseph Knecht, edited by Hermann Hesse;* that his *Demian* appeared anonymously with the subtitle *The Story of Emil Sinclair's Youth;* that *Steppenwolf* (1927) pretends to be the autobiography of a certain Harry Haller, found in his room after he has mysteriously left the town where he lived for a few months? There is a permanent hiding behind pseudonyms, behind a mere editorship—in short: a recalcitrance to "admit" which is ironically counteracted by the urge to expose himself, to "confess." Lauscher's first name is not Hermann by chance; the initials of the Steppenwolf are not incidentally H. H. (which, by the way, are the initials of the hero of *Journey to the East* [1932] as well), and for good reasons the first Magister Ludi, the inventor of the *Glass Bead Game,* is called Calwer, the man from Calw, the little town in Swabia where Hesse was born in 1877, and which with its old houses, narrow streets and murmuring brooks appears in so many of Hesse's stories. These are more than playful attempts to mystify the reader. They are true symptoms of this bliss of confession mixed with the stubborn refusal to admit one's wrong. And it seems quite characteristic that Hesse has never called any of his books a "novel" but has rather chosen the non-committal term a "narrative," which leaves the question between "confessional" authenticity and "impersonal" fiction in an ambiguous balance.

## II. Father and Mother Image

A balance? Rather an indication of the basic polarity which runs through all of Hesse's works. Except for the two "narratives" which present Harmony Regained, *Siddhartha* (1922) and the *Glass Bead Game*, it will be obvious even to the casual reader that each of Hesse's major books has a double focus, has two heroes which are "two" in the sense in which a schizophrenic is "two": in *Beneath the Wheel* Hans Giebenrath and Hermann Heilner; Narcissus and Goldmund in the novel of that title (1930); Demian as the companion of Emil Sinclair, the narrator; and finally the Steppenwolf, who is equally two, if not many more, in one. This cleavage of personality symbolizes the two elements which constitute man and his world: the father-element and the mother-element. It is only during the war years that the metaphysical polarity of these two worlds finds its full and unambiguous expression in Hesse's work. While the mother, embodiment of all sensuous, vital and elemental principles, remained inconspicuous and pale in *Peter Camenzind*, she was totally absent in *Beneath the Wheel*. In *Rosshalde* (1914), the story of an artist's unhappy marriage, man and woman are pitted against each other, but they are seen from the "wrong angle," as husband and wife rather than as father and mother. The war is still waged on the physical and psychological front; it is only after the "awakening" that it will be shifted to the mythical level, that father and mother will emerge as archetypes, as the embodiments of the spiritual and vital energies fighting in and for man.

In *A Child's Soul* the two worlds are seen as opposite polarities. "Downstairs in our house mother and child were at home, a harmless air pervaded the place; but upstairs power and spirit were dwelling, here was tribunal and temple and the realm of the father." This Upstairs (we cannot help associating the structure of the Christian cosmos) "smelled of sternness, of law, of responsibility, of father and God." The rule and suppression which the father-God imposes upon Hesse's heroes are responsible for the wild outbursts of rebellion with which his books, written in the late teens and early twenties, are swarming. No psychoanalyst is needed to diagnose the neuroses and violent traumas of the patients. Oedipus is at work in Emil Sinclair's frightful dream in which he sees himself hiding behind the trees, armed with a glittering knife which the seducer has put into his hands, ready to jump upon the tall figure walking down the alley: his father. Oedipus is at work in the blasphemous and delirious ravings of the youngster in *A Child's Soul,* after the sin has been committed: "I have killed, I have burned down houses, because I had fun doing it and because I wanted to mock at you and rile you. See, I hate you, I spit at your feet, you God. You have tortured and flayed me, you have given laws which nobody can obey."

Even though these and similar quotations point strongly in the psychoanalytic direction, it would be wrong to tag Hesse too ostentatiously with the ever-handy Freudian label. Hesse's concern is a truly religious one, the groping and hoping for personal salvation, and Freud's secularization of God as a pure magnification of the individual father, his interpretation of the religious emotion as a disease-symptom, would seem to Hesse no less unacceptable than they were to Kafka. It is characteristic enough that in the earlier works, in which the father-son conflict is at its highest pitch, the mother is totally or almost totally absent. It is only in *Demian* that "the mother" plays a decisive role in the development of the hero. Yet, her very name, Mrs. Eve, identifies her as the mythical All-Mother, the great womb in which life rests,—and not as the individual Freudian libido-object. Those who have tried to fit Hesse to the Procrustean bed of Freudianism overlook the fact that Mrs. Eve is not "mother" but "mother-image," not a psycho-physical reality but a myth, clearly evidenced by the fact that she is not Sinclair's mother (who does not appear in the book at all), but the mother of Sinclair's "double," Demian. To be sure, she is sex-object, too (the gossip about the incestuous relations between her and her son Demian is revealing). But the emphasis lies on her relationship to and meaning for Sinclair, and in this relationship the Oedipus-Jocasta motif is entirely lacking. Sinclair's long and painful pilgrimage to the "mother" does not describe the process of emerging from a dark individual neurosis to the unmysterious and rational daylight, but rather a descent into the dark mysteries of the "essence," into the procreativeness of motherly life. A Freudian interpretation would achieve here what it always achieves: the reduction of a symbolic image to its purely psycho-physical elements, and, by the very rationalistic process of this reduction, the destruction of the ontological authenticity of the symbol. (It is not surprising that for many years Hesse was under treatment by a disciple of C. G. Jung, whose objection to Freud is mainly based on Freud's rationalistic destruction of the super-individual myth, and that *Demian* was written as part of his phycho-therapeutic cure.)

It is in *Steppenwolf* that the two elements clash most violently: man, the detached and cool evaluator of values, the rational and demanding law-giver and judge locked in deadly battle with the animal, whose ambition it is to break all "civilized" fetters by the assault of his vital instincts, sneering triumphantly at the hopeless attempt to keep the mother-world, the drives and desires of the amoral natural forces of life, in chains. This schizophrenic duel finds its most nightmarish expression in the double taming scene which Harry Haller witnesses in the "magic theatre," the place where his inner turmoil is externalized on an imaginary stage in a series of wild spectacles. In a merciless mirror, Harry Haller sees himself cracking the whip over the well-trained, emasculated wolf, until the wolf takes over and now, whip in his paws, forces Harry to walk on all fours, to debase himself to the lowest animal level.

These shrill and cacophonous tones, which remain unresolved in *Steppenwolf,* find their harmonious resolution in *Narcissus and Goldmund.* Clearer than ever before, father and mother principle, Spirit and Life, are confronted: Narcissus, abbot of the monastery, the thinker who lives in the self-sufficient loneliness of the intellect, and Goldmund, the young novice whose very name (Golden Mouth) indicates his hunger for life, the joyful exuberance of pouring himself into the stream of being. It is Goldmund's story which is being told, his tours and detours in search of the Great Mother. "Strange haunting dreams of delight and triumph, visions of her in whom all his senses had his share, and then, with its scents and longings, the mother world would be about him: its life calling enigmatically; his mother's eyes were deeper than the sea, eternal as the gardens of paradise. Life would taste sweet and salt upon her lips; his mother's silky hair would fall around him, tenderly brushing his mouth. And not only was this mother all purity, not only the skyey gentleness of love: in her, somewhere hidden between enticements, lay all the storms and darkness of the world, all greed, fear, sin and elemental grief, all birth, all human mortality." With these visions before his eyes, Goldmund breaks out of the cloister and starts upon his enraptured dance of love. An endless chain of sensuous and sexual experiences: the gypsy girl, the peasant's wife, the two high-born sisters, the servant maid, the Jewess Rebecca, the count's mistress. If Hesse avoids monotony in this merry-go-round of the senses, it is due to the fact that with each new beloved Goldmund becomes a new lover. He is a true vagabond, a true explorer of the delights and ills of the mother world, an artist not only when he tries to carve in wood the faces and bodies he has loved, but also when he becomes one with them in flesh. His vagrancy is in truth an earnest and pious quest, his hunger for life does not taste of the nihilistic attempt to plunge headlong into life out of fear of death. In Klingsor's hectic vitality the panic of the "last summer" still reared its ugly grimace. His craving for burning and intoxicating colors was nothing but a running away from death already waiting at the gates. There is no panic in Goldmund's rovings. The Black Death, which hits the country while Goldmund's roaming is in its height, and which throws the world around him into a delirious frenzy of lust and greed, only helps Goldmund to strengthen his equilibrium and to withdraw into an idyll, one of the very few that the vagabond finds in his restless wanderings. Goldmund's pilgrimage is an act of self-realization, not of self-defense. His in-dulgence is not born out of the dogmatic, purposeful opposition of an anti-intellectual intellectual, as is the case in so many of D. H. Lawrence's writings with which *Narcissus and Goldmund* has been quite unjustifiably linked. *Lady Chatterley's Lover* is repellent for the very reason that it represents a "gospel" (though it is the resent-ful gospel of an Anti-Christ) which by its very opposition to the values it wishes devaluated, destroys the innocence of the flesh it strives to celebrate. Goldmund's exuberance is free of the corrosive gnawing of an anti-intellectual revelation; his devotion to the All-Mother is borne up by the all-embracing pantheism of a St. Francis of Assisi. (It is not without interest that very early in his career [1904] Hesse published a short monograph of the child-like saint whose exalted love for all beings flowed into the dithyrambic Song to the Sun.)

The violent tension of *Steppenwolf* is overcome. Father and mother worlds have ceased to be irreconcilable enemies. In *Narcissus and Goldmund* the two worlds are conceived from the outset as op-posite yet complementary poles between which man's existence is suspended. No longer is the father the exacting and punishing authority set over life as a stern and hostile ruler. As a monk, and later abbot of the cloister, Narcissus is at the same time "father" and "brother" to the mother-child. From his face all the threatening and antagonistic features have vanished. Brooding in monastic loneliness over the timeless rules and patterns, he is the embodiment of the pure Spirit, remote from ever-changing life with its organic rhythm of birth, growth and decay. He is the *logos* which was "in the beginning" (it is not by chance that he is presented as a distinguished logician and mathematician), in him rests the dead eternity of the Spirit. But this father, "Father" Narcissus is no longer hostile to life, to the world of fleeting phenomena. It is Narcissus who opens for Goldmund the door into life; it is he who takes him back to his heart after the lost son has spent strength and life in his search for the Mother. Goldmund was in his mind during all the years of separation, but he was no less in Goldmund's life during all the stages of the wild pilgrimage. For to Goldmund, the artist, who, in his creations, immortalizes the mortal moment, snatches lasting images from the ever-changing stream of life, the world of the father is always present. And it is highly fitting that, when Goldmund carves his first sculpture, the figure of St. John the Baptist, it is Narcissus' face which takes shape under his hands. In art the two poles, the world of the father and the world of the mother, seem to merge into a synthesis. And yet, a full and permanent union is impossible. The Matrix which is the chaos will always elude the grip of the *logos*. The supreme image, the statue of Eve, the All-Mother, which Goldmund has carried in his heart all his life, he will never be able to finish. Death, the world of the father, in which there is no growth, no form, no dream, where there is only the imageless stillness of the thought, will overcome Goldmund before the supreme achievement is even begun. But where, Narcissus, is your victory? The last words of Goldmund, ringing forever in the Father's ears long after the beloved vagabond has died in his arms, are a last and paradoxical defiance of the mother world: "But how will you ever die, Narcissus? You know no mother. How can we love without a mother? Without a mother, we cannot die." In this last scene in which Narcissus sees life slowly fade out of the eyes of his beloved one, there is a gleam of the Beatific Vision in which the word has become flesh and the flesh has become word.

## III. The Great Exorcism

There is only a gleam of the Beatific Vision, and to achieve even that much, one has to "travel through the hell in myself," a phrase by which Hesse has summarized the substance of his *Demian*. And this phrase is the theme of all of Hesse's works, at least up to *Narcissus and Goldmund*. What is this hell in myself? It is the religious term for the conflicts arising from man's divided nature, for the chaos of chthonic, inchoate forces in us which, as long as they are not integrated in a controlled and controllable order, exert a subterranean but no less tormenting tyranny over us. In the exposition of this chaos and of the anxiety which it breeds in us, Hesse has been untiring. *In Sight of Chaos* he called a series of essays on Dostoevsy (1919), whom he has rightly considered his closest fellow-traveller into the abyss of the human soul, and "in sight of chaos" might well be the general title of all his works from *Rosshalde* to *Steppenwolf*. No Freud was needed to open his eyes to the "dark aspects of the soul"; he had learned from the "original" masters, the German Romanticists, Dostoevsky, Nietzsche. At the age of 23 he wrote in his diary (later included in his *Hermann Lauscher*): "At that point I began to feel that the hour of a long-postponed battle had inexorably come, that everything suppressed, chained, half-tamed in me was tearing at the fetters, exasperatedly and threateningly. All the important moments of my life in which I had deprived the feeling of the Eternal, the naïve instincts, the innate unconscious life of some of their territory, gathered before my memory like an enormous, hostile host. Before their onslaught all thrones and columns trembled. And now I knew suddenly that nothing could be rescued. Unloosened, the lower world in me was reeling forth, it broke and sneered at the white temples and favorite images. And still I felt these desperate rebels and iconoclasts related to me, they wore the features of my dearest memories and childhood days."

It is this division in us that is the source of all our anxieties. "And why are they frightened?" asks Demian. "One is frightened when one is not in self-agreement. They have fear because they have never said 'yes' to themselves. A community of human beings who are afraid of the Unknown in them." To cure this disease no short-cut is available. The first therapeutic step is to decompose by relentless probings the easy securities which tend to divert our attention from the schism which rages in us. The first duty is the confession of the disease, the almost proud admission that we are psychopathics. Such was the courage of Dostoevsky: he was a prophet, a messenger of a higher and truer life because he was a hysteric and epileptic (*The Brothers Karamasov or the Decline of Europe*); such was the courage of Nietzsche, who had dared to ask the "terrible and harassing question whether under certain historic and cultural conditions it was not worthier, nobler and more proper to become psychopathic than to adjust oneself to these conditions by sacrificing one's ideals" (*Guest at the Spa*). This, so Hesse continues at this point, "has been the topic of almost all of my writings." It has indeed. And it was this very courage to "become psychopathic" which, in the eyes of post-war German youth, raised his *Demian* to the level of a revelation. Here was a man who, after all the false securities had broken down, did not offer them a new program by which to adjust themselves, by which to join quickly the broken pieces into a new but certainly not firmer structure. Here was a man who showed them that there was only one thing left: to be glad that all the deceptive supports and props had gone, that the road was clear now for the investigation of the disease and for its possible cure. The message that resounded from *Demian* echoed forth even more strongly from Hesse's philosophical essay, *Zarathustra's Return* (1920). It was Nietzsche's message, but already the literary presentation—the sage walking with his disciples at the outskirts of the town, provoking questions and answering them—made it clear that it was another philosopher's message as well, Socrates' message: Know Thyself.

To know oneself, to explore the hidden corners in one's soul, not to flinch even if one finds these corners populated with beasts and demons, this is the purpose of Emil Sinclair's, Steppenwolf's, Goldmund's travels. These descents into the subconscious, into the lower world, may, at times, read like samples from a psychoanalyst's handbook; but again, the direction of Hesse's genius was established long before he was ever exposed to Freud. It is the following program which, in 1900, Hesse outlines in "Lauscher's" diary: "To lift everything to the surface, to treat oneself to everything Unspoken and Unspeakable as to an unveiled mystery!" And not knowing Freud yet, he continues characteristically enough: "I know very well, this is Romanticism." If *Demian* and *Steppenwolf* are applied Freudianism (we have made our qualifications above), they are at least as closely related to the great "midwifery" of Socratic dialogues; they are records of a merciless exorcism and conquest of the dark powers which we have "to lift to the surface" in order to know ourselves. It is Narziss who quite consciously formulates the principle of midwifery: "Some demon must be at work in Goldmund, a hidden fiend to whom it was permitted to divide this noble being against itself. . . . Good then, this demon must be named, exorcised and made visible to all and, when this was done, he could be conquered."

As every patient has his analyst, so every one of Hesse's travellers on the *Road into the Interior* (under this title Hesse collected a number of his shorter stories) has his midwife Socrates: Hans Giebenrath his Hermann Heilner, Emil Sinclair his Demian, Goldmund his Narcissus, the Steppenwolf a whole group of them: the mysterious author of the inserted "Treatise Concerning the Steppenwolf," the girl Hermine who is only a female materialization of his schoolmate Hermann, and the strange musician who is Pablo and Mozart in one. They are all externalizations of the inner teacher who leads the hero on his way; and that the name "Demian" resembles in sound so closely to "daimon," the voice which, according to Socrates, guides and awakens the soul of the disciple, is certainly not accidental. (It may be mentioned in parenthesis that the name of the hero of *Demian*, Emil Sinclair, equally evokes in the German reader the association with Greece. Sinclair was the closest friend of Germany's most exalted and tragic spiritual traveller to Greece, Friedrich Hölderlin, whose main work, *Hyperion*, represents the most magnificent transplantation of the Greek "paideia" onto German soil.) What these "midwives" impart to their disciples is the "viper bite of philosophy" of which Alcibiades speaks in his eulogy to Socrates, this festering sting driving to self-realization. It is the supreme and most subtle form of seduction because it does not quench the thirst but heightens it, the thirst and longing to know onself. And when Sinclair calls his friend Demian a "seducer," he is as clairvoyant as were the archons of the city of Athens who condemned Socrates to death for seduction of the youth. For he who has learned to know himself will no longer bow to the lures and threats of authority. He has become free.

On this road to freedom travels Emil Sinclair, driven on by

Demian's voice, the permanent and catalytic mobilizer of "anamnesis," although here we are not faced with the remembering of innate "ideas" but with the rediscovery of all the emotional and vital urges which are lurking underneath the surface and have not yet become "members" in the chain of Sinclair's being. "You know that 'your permitted world' was only half of the world, and you have tried to suppress the other half as the priests and teachers are doing"—this is Demian's "viper bite of philosophy," and it tears open the wound through which Sinclair's lower world will tumble into the light of day: a series of dreams, drawings and paintings welling up from the unconscious, haunting reminiscences of images which he has seen in his childhood. And there will always be Demian or one of his mysterious messengers who will interpret these symbols for him, will throw open the door to a world which "the priests and teachers" laboriously try to camouflage, until Sinclair finally reaches Mrs. Eve, the source of all life, until he finds and learns to know—himself.

It is in much wilder and dissolute stages that the Steppenwolf is exorcised. Already the composition of the book makes it plain that we are again on the "road into the interior." The first observation point is still far outside; the anonymous young man in whose house the Steppenwolf used to live and with whom he had an occasional talk. The second step brings us closer: the Steppenwolf's diary, by which Harry Haller introduces himself, has been found. The third step takes us inside: it is the inserted "Treatise Concerning the Steppenwolf" ("For Madmen Only"), a mercilessly rational exposition of the "case" drawn up by a mysterious, completely detached observer. The fourth step: Harry Haller's life as the concrete presentation of the problems which the Treatise has analyzed theoretically, and finally, the fifth step, the initiation into the "magic theatre" where the pandemonium of his soul materializes itself before his eyes in a series of punch-and-judy shows. It is a boring beneath the surface until at the end the hidden demons appear in a frightening and unbridled mummery. So complete and ruthless is the unmasking of the subconscious powers and drives that a realistic frame, which still existed in *Demian,* can no longer accommodate them. Only a "magic theatre," working with all the ghoulish tricks of a Grand Guignol, can furnish the proper stage for this supreme exorcism.

However, the heightened frenzy of this raising of the demons does not only indicate that the schism between the two worlds has become deeper and more dangerous; it points toward a much more serious affliction: the raging against the principle of "personality," of individuation as such. Emil Sinclair was groping for the road to himself, for self-encounter which would lead to self-realization and freedom for himself. What Harry Haller is after is freedom from himself, the complete destruction of the bond which holds the particles of the Ego together and establishes the unity of the person. It is an "analysis" whose aim is no longer integration but utter dissolution of the Ego. Harry Haller does not suffer from a "split" personality, but from the individuation of man in personality as such. The "Treatise Concerning the Steppenwolf" describes the situation aptly: "The body is always one, but of the souls that live in it, there are not two or five, but innumerable ones. Man is an onion consisting of hundreds of layers. . . . The old Asiatics realized and knew it very well, and in the Buddhist yoga they invented an exact technique for unmasking the delusion of personality." Harry Haller is afraid of self-encounter (again and again suicide seems to him the only possibility of deliverance); his descent into the hell is not guided by the demand for re-membering, but by the desire for complete dis-membering. His watchword is no longer "find yourself," but "dissolve yourself into nothingness": his exorcism is yoga. It is only at the end of the self-annihilating magic-theatrical performance, which Haller watches with masochistic desire to punish himself for his individuation, that he is called to order by Mozart: "Of course, you'd fall for every stupid and humorless arrangement, generous gentleman that you are, for anything full of bathos and devoid of wit. Well, I shan't fall for it, I won't give you a nickel for your whole romantic penitence. You want to be beheaded, you want to have your head chopped off, you madman. For this idiotic ideal you might commit another ten murders. You want to die, coward that you are, but not live. But in the devil's name: live—that's just what you are to do." The road into the interior, which threatened to become a road into nothingness and dissolution, has led once more to the self. The mirrors of the magic theatre, which might have refracted the rays of the personality into infinity, have merged into a lense where the beams are gathered again in a cone. Analysis has resulted in *Gestalt,* the unleashing of the demons in a conquest over them. At the end of the exorcism the door of the magic theatre leads into the open and Harry Haller knows: "Mozart is waiting for me."

## IV. Individuation, Time and Irony

It is in *Steppenwolf,* which again and again has been proclaimed as plainly "psychoanalytic," that the decisive difference between Hesse and Freud becomes apparent. What Freud tries to repair is the disturbance of man's functional existence in the world; the malady which Hesse exposes time and again is the disturbance of man's authenticity, his *Eigentlichkeit,* as Heidegger puts it. Freud is a reformer who points at curable diseases; Hesse is an existentialist who points at the malaise inherent in the *condition humaine.*

Before Harry Haller enters the magic theatre, his psychogogue Pablo (who will later appear as Mozart) opens his eyes to the real root of his sufferings: "Undoubtedly you have guessed long ago that the conquest over time, the deliverance from reality is nothing else but the desire to get rid of your so-called personality. This is the jail in which you are sitting." The true (and incurable) plight of man began with his individuation, with his separation from the All-ness, with the beginning of time. Time is the horrible proof that paradise is lost, that man is no longer living in his *Eigentlichkeit,* but in the all-powerful and tormenting sequence of moments (this is what Heidegger calls *die Geworfenheit*), the permanent transiency of all things and of his own existence. It is man's curse that he can no longer live in the simultaneousness of his experiences, that he is suspended between eternity which knows only past and future, and time which knows only the transitory moment. Now it becomes evident that the great exorcism which we tried to analyze above means more than the schism in the individual soul: it is the paradoxical attempt to mobilize all the powers, actions and reactions of the soul into an ever-present simultaneity (Heidigger calls it *Zuhandenheit*) which will be capable of outwitting the deadening course of time. Klingsor's desperate cry "Why does time exist? Why always only this idiotic one-after-the-other and never an effervescent, satiating at-the-same-time?" rings through all of Hesse's writings up to *Magister Ludi.* If one could keep the moment alive, if one could rescue all one's yesterdays, then the suffering would be gone. And in this attempt to conquer time, Hesse's heroes are the true companions of Proust's, Joyce's, Thomas Mann's protagonists. They are all *à la recherche du temps perdu* (although their tensions and their revolts against the "idiotic" one-after-the-other are much more violent than Proust's, and much more akin to James Joyce's); they are all in the process of a re-membrance of things past (which, however, is a suitable title for Proust's *oeuvre* only when the word "remembrance" is taken in the special sense suggested here).

But how is the eternalization of the moment possible? Hesse does not attempt to give an answer to the unanswerable question. In none of his "solutions" is finality. But in every single one of his books there is the attempt to face the insoluble bravely and honestly. There are the attempts of the "artists," of Klingsor and Goldmund, who give themselves to the moment so unreservedly in the hope that the very intensity of living will save it from destruction. But in the case of Klingsor the insatiability is nothing but an outgrowth of the horror vacui, and Goldmund must realize that his life is spent before the ultimate task, the sculpture of Lady Eve, can take shape. Still, art seems to hold a promise: it might become the powerful weapon which can defeat the dance of death. And Goldmund ponders: "When as craftsmen we carve images or see laws to formulate our thoughts we do it all to save what little we may from the linked, never ending dance of death." In music, above all, the solution seems to be reached. In *Steppenwolf,* and particularly in *Magister Ludi,* music appears as deliverance from the curse of the one-after-the-other. On one of the mysterious streamers over the different show-cases in the magic theatre, Harry Haller reads the inscription: "The Essence of Art. The Transformation of Time into Space through Music." And even before he entered the magic theatre, he had come to the realization: "Yes, that was it, this music was something like time frozen to space and above it hovered a superhuman serenity, an eternal, divine laughter." To "live in music"—that might be the answer, to develop in time but not to be subject to the law of succession and transiency, to transcend each moment by fitting it into a timeless harmony, in short, to live in humor. "To live in the world as if it were not the world, to respect the law and yet to stand above it, to possess as if one did not possess, to renounce as if it were no renunciation: all this only humor is capable of achieving" (*Steppenwolf*). It means what one might call to live symbolically, to be in the things but to be beyond them at the same time, to analyze while experiencing and to experience while analyzing. It is exactly what Thomas Mann has defined again and again **as** the attitude of irony. It is, in terms of Heidegger's Existentialism, the permanent blending of *Geworfenheit* with *Vorlaufen zum Tode*. In his *Guest at the Spa*, Hesse has given, with the help of a clinical case, an example of how the ironic solution can lift us beyond the tormenting pressure of the "moment," of the cage in which we sit. By living in irony, by living as if he were playing a rôle which he can watch and analyze as an outsider, the sciatica-ridden guest of the health resort has cured himself, perhaps not from the disease of his swollen and creaking joints, but from the much deeper disease which made the physical illness unbearable. One day, after having dragged for many weeks his painful limp through the deadly monotony and the dead-earnest healing routine of the sanatorium, he lifts himself above his miserable existence and looks at himself from the outside. And seeing a ridiculous hypochondriac, worried about every motion that might cause him pain, shuffling down the staircase, putting the chair at the right angle so that sitting down will become easier, he bursts out into laughter which opens the road to recovery. It is the salvation through irony, the annihilation of the moment by transcending its laws and conditions, it is the being oneself and not being oneself at the same time which, on the intellectual level, is expressed in the patient's ironic statement: "I have the misfortune that I always contradict myself."

It is the very attitude which Kierkegaard scorned in his *Either-Or* as the "aesthetic" one because it lacks the absoluteness, the firm conviction that time and eternity are irreconcilable antipodes, that we cannot save ourselves under any circumstances. It is man's sinful attempt to play God, to bridge the unbridgeable gap between here and there, to "communicate" without undergoing and reliving the stages of Christ's Passion. And Kierkegaard would have been seized with rage, had he been able to read in *Demian*: "Instead of crucifying oneself or somebody else, one can with solemn thoughts drink wine from a chalice and while doing it think the mystery of sacrifice." For Kierkegaard this substitution would have been stark paganism, as would be the Franciscan mysticism which we so frequently encounter in Hesse's works, the attempt to break the cage of individuation by expanding the soul so that it will become the lost All-ness again. It is quite characteristic that the Christian Hesse again and again substitutes for Christ's words "Love Thy neighbor as Thyself" the Buddhist's *"tat twam asi,* Love your neighbor for he is yourself."

His yearning for deliverance from the Ego, from the tyrannical dictate of temporality, has frequently led Hesse onto the road to India. The atmosphere of the Orient was familiar to him from his earliest childhood (both his father and his maternal grandfather were leading figures in the German-Swiss Indian Missionary Association; his mother, in fact, was born in Malabar), and this made access to the wisdom of the Orient particularly easy. But even without this stimulating heritage, Hesse would have found the way to Buddhism. For Buddhism offers the most radical possibility of undoing the curse of individuation, of annihilating the "idiotic one-after-the-other" by the postulation of the eternal simultaneity of Nirvana. What the East means to him, Hesse has expressed in his *Journey to the East*: "not only a country and something geographical, but the home and the youth of the soul, the everywhere and nowhere, the oneness of all times." However, it should be made quite plain that Buddhism (at least the Mahayana Buddhism with its extreme vision of the Universal Void) remains for Hesse a radical possibility, but by no means the solution to the problem. The extinction of the Ego, of the will to be, the kingdom of a lifeless and motionless eternity, in short: the realm of the Father, is only one station of the road to redemption, only one pole in the basic polarity of man's existence. Mozart's angry exhortation in *Steppenwolf*: "in the devil's name: live—that's just what you are to do" has rung down the curtain over the Nirvana, over Harry Haller's suicidal attempts to break out of the cage of individuation. But even in his Indian legend *Siddhartha* (Siddhartha, of course, is the historical name of the Gautama Buddha), which to many seemed a complete affirmation of the Buddhist faith, the dividing line is quite sharply drawn. It is again a quest for self-realization and salvation, and Siddhartha's travels lead through all the stages of self-fulfillment: life among the ascetic brethren who kill the desires of the flesh by flagellation in order to approach the "atman," life among the courtesans and nabobs of the big cities who, by draining the cup of pleasure to the last, hope to enter into the essence. But early in his travels Siddhartha has grasped the "ironical" solution: "Both, the mind and the senses, were pretty things behind which the last meaning was hidden, both had to be listened to, with both one had to play, neither of them was to be despised nor overrated." And when Siddhartha finally meets the great teacher Buddha, it dawns upon him that he cannot become his disciple either. For Buddha's division of the world into Samsara and Nirvana, deception and truth, phenomena and essence, time and eternity, is in Siddhartha's eyes no more than a pedagogical device. The true wisdom Siddhartha finds as a ferryman, as the link between the shores while watching the water and realizing "that the river is the same at all places, at its origin and its mouth, at the waterfalls, at the ferry point, at the rapids, in the ocean, in the mountains, everywhere, always simultaneous, and that for it there exists only presence, not the shadow of the past, nor the shadow of the future." This, then is the solution: the stream itself is the coeval unity, the rhythm of fleeting moments is the everlasting presence.

This paradoxical oneness of the opposites, of time and eternity, individuation and Universal Self, life and death, mother and father, the apparent two which are essentially one, will show us again how wrong it is to interpret the polarity of Hesse's heroes in terms of narrow Freudianism. (It would be about as fitting to discover in the Indian gods Shiva and Vishnu "neurotic cases of split personalities.") That the tension between the poles is insoluble, that a definite fixation of the *condition humaine* is impossible, that the problem of man is beyond solution, can be learned from the very rhythm of Hesse's works. His books bear the relationship of complementary colors to each other. A great many of his readers found it baffling (and many even shocking) that *Siddhartha,* the serene Oriental legend in which all doubts seemed to be stilled, was followed by the weird Grand Guignol of the *Steppenwolf.* But the extreme amplitude of the pendulum's swing is just Hesse's unmistakable rhythm. "I have the misfortune that I always contradict myself"—*Demian,* the travel through "the hell in myself," is followed by *Siddhartha.* The companion piece to Siddhartha's saintly pursuit is the Witches' Sabbath of *Steppenwolf.* From Harry Haller's shrill dissonance, the pendulum swings to the tense but harmonious duo of Narcissus and Goldmund. But "since the paradox has to be risked again and again, the essentially impossible undertaken always anew," Goldmund's story, the love song to the fully experienced moment, to the intoxicated dance of life, required as a complementary color the lofty kingdom of Nirvana, the dead Void of eternity. It presented itself as the life story of Josephus Knecht in *Magister Ludi.*

This, Hesse's last work is—not only in volume—his most ambitious achievement. That it does not quite succeed has nothing to do with his artistic skill. The kingdom of eternity, "the extinction of the individual," cannot manifest itself in the framework of a realistic prose narrative however esoteric and legendary it may be. Without the help of a "magic theatre," the attempt to render visible the place which is beyond space and time must end in failure, although, in Hesse's case, it is a most magnificent and noble failure. The story of Joseph Knecht takes place at a nowhere, in a completely secluded statehood of lay-brethren whose only pursuit is learning and research. It takes place at no-time, at a period hundreds of years after the "age of wars" in which European civilization went to pieces. And the highest symbol of this citadel of the Spirit is the glass bead game, "the sum total of everything spiritual and artistic, a sublime cult, an Unio Mystica of all the shattered branches of the Universitas Litterarum," a strange device by which, according to the highest rules of mathematics and musical harmony, one can "play" and vary all the distraught contents and values of mankind's spiritual manifestations into an all-embracing syncretism. If it can be fathomed at all (and it is Hesse's great achievement that it can—almost—be fathomed) it might be the invention of Chinese sages helped along by the great German mystic Jakob Boehme. In the glass bead game the Spirit has—to use a Hegelian term—come to itself; it no longer creates but hovers in the immobility of self-meditation, introspection and auto-association. And its purest vessel is the Magister Ludi Josephus Knecht whose very name (Knecht-bondman) indicates that he is a function and not an individuality. (There has probably never before been written a "biography" which is so drained of *bios* and any individual psychology.) Here is the austere world of the father —until shortly before the end not a single woman appears on the pages of this book—and it is quite fitting for "life" in the Nirvana that Knecht refers to his own development as a succession of "awakenings" and "transcendencies." But this fortress of eternity, in which Knecht rises to the highest office, is only part of his "home." Against the advice of his superiors and colleagues he indulges in the study of history, the concern with the living moment, and at the height of his career he renounces his lofty office and leaves the world of the pure Spirit in order to dedicate himself to the modest service of an educator of a young man of the world. As Goldmund returns to the Father Narcissus after he has plumbed the depth of the mother-world, so Knecht, who is Narcissus reborn, finally finds his way into life after he has plumbed the depth of the father-world. The "ironic solution" is found again. And highly ironic is the end of the book. The very day Knecht enters into the service of life, he dies by drowning in a mountain lake. He, the unrivaled and idolized master of the great game, dies in the services of an immature youth who seems hardly worthy of this extreme sacrifice. But there is no futility in this irony. When the boy sees the master perish in the waters, the moment of his awakening has come: he knows that from now on he will have to live a life which will not only be his but that of the Magister Ludi as well. The transiency of man's existence, the fleeting instability of the moment, does not mark the victory of death but the triumph of eternal rebirth. Time, the one-after-the-other, is in the ironic vision eternity, the everlasting at the-same-time. The "idiotic" rhythm of birth, unfolding and decay is the very heartbeat of the eternal, the great law of Hegel's dialectics: *Aufgehobensein* with the threefold meaning which the word *aufgehoben* carries in the German language: annulled, preserved, and raised to a higher level.

In the summer of 1947 Hermann Hesse reached the biblical age. His latest work, magnificent in spite of its failures, seems to indicate that the storm has subsided. But we should not be unduly surprised if, provided that his almost complete blindness should ever allow him to return to writing, he were to continue to "contradict himself." He who has glanced so deeply into the chaos, who has felt so closely the grip of the "daimon," is not likely to catch more than a glimpse of the great calm in which the antinomies are resolved and reconciled. The balance is too precarious to be upheld, and even in the serene and austere pages of *Magister Ludi* we find confessions like the following: "There is no noble and lofty life without the knowledge of the devils and demons and without a perpetual battle against them." He is of the family of Dostoevsky, of those who tear out their hearts so that grace may be bestowed upon them. Peace in God, that is the goal, but the price they have to pay is tremendous. "Serenity"—this word sounds like an echo from the celestial city through Hesse's later books, and in his last work he has tried to catch its sublime reflection: "This serenity is neither frivolousness nor self-complacency; it is the highest wisdom and love, the affirmation of all reality, the wide-awakeness at the brink of all depths and abysses, the virtue of the saints and the knights." But only the one who is willing to recognize and confess his sinfulness has a slight chance to become a saint. Exactly that Hesse has done all through his life: he has beaten his breast praying for grace. "There are two roads to salvation, the road of justice for the just ones, and the road of grace for the sinners. I who am a sinner have again committed the mistake of seeking the road of justice" (*A Guest at the Spa*). Only by an act of grace can serenity be envisaged; man cannot deserve it, he can only hope for it. The ironic attitude itself is not man's achievement, but the highest blessing that sainthood can bestow.

Again and again, Hermann Hesse has been compared and linked to Thomas Mann. To be sure, they are contemporaries. But the human attitude and the emotional climate of the two are vastly different. Hesse himself felt it very clearly when he drew in *Magister Ludi* the loving and astute portrait of Thomas von der Trave. (The Trave is the river on whose banks Lübeck, Thomas Mann's birthplace, is situated.) A sketchy comparison must of needs work injustice upon both of them. Thomas Mann—at least the mature Thomas Mann—is the apex of civilization; the demons, who are by no means alien to him, are subdued and neutralized. In this he is a true heir of Goethe. Hesse is the heir of Dostoevsky, whose concern is not man's autonomous dignity but man's saintliness, not justice but grace. The demons are on the loose in Dostoevsky as well as in Hesse. Thomas Mann is, if these geospiritual generalizations be taken with a grain of salt, a Westerner, Hesse an Easterner. For Thomas Mann, the East is the danger zone which has to be warded off if man wants to live (Tadziu in *Death in Venice,* Mme. Chauchat and Naphta in *The Magic Mountain*), while Hesse has again and again seen the light arising from the East. Hesse has loudly proclaimed his love for Dostoevsky; Thomas Mann has published a beautiful essay on the great Russian with the characteristic title: "Dostoevsky—but in Moderate Doses." And the heroes of Thomas Mann's greatest *oeuvre* are Abram, Jacob and Joseph, proud men who have concluded a covenant with God, a Magna Charta of almost equal partners; the hero of Hesse's greatest *oeuvre* is Josephus Knecht, the humble servant. If the serenity for which Hesse so fervently strives is the "virtue of the saints and knights," Thomas Mann's serenity is knightly, Hermann Hesse's saintly.

There is nothing in Hesse's work to remind the reader of Thomas Mann's superior and, at times, olympic equanimity, the smoothness and ease of his transitions from one phase to the next, even in political matters. And if Thomas Mann's supreme vision is the Third Humanism, Hermann Hesse's is the eschatological Third Kingdom. Thomas Mann's work is undoubtedly wider in scope, richer with meaning and purer in outline; yet his heart never pulsates so visibly, audibly and close beneath the surface as does Hesse's. It is a tormented and struggling heart, beset by the tragic upheavals of our times, but much more thoroughly beset by the unalterable and timeless tragedy of man's existence. With the single exception of Franz Kafka, there is in contemporary German literature hardly anyone who has so valiantly and incessantly struggled with the angel as Hermann Hesse. Out of these struggles cries arose, but some of the purest and most beautiful poetry as well, some prose reminiscent of Mozart in its graceful serenity, short stories like *Knulp, In the Old Sun, How Beautiful Is Youth,* where tensions and conflicts only grumble on in the bass accompaniment while the leading melody rises to lofty mirthfulness. These are the short moments of paradisiac bliss which grace bestows upon the sinner. But the battlefield remains always close, the demons are lurking, smashing the peace so hardly won. And it is as deeply moving as it is revealing to read in one of Hermann Hesse's late poems:

> Heaps of shards and shambles far and wide:
> Thus ends the world, thus ends this life of mine.
> And I wished but to cry and to resign—
> If there were not this stubbornness inside,
>
> This stubbornness to ward off and to fight,
> Defiance deep deep in my heart below,
> And then my faith: that what torments me so
> Must, must one day turn into light.

# Hermann Hesse and the "Age of the Feuilleton"

## by Hans Mayer

Hermann Hesse's late masterpiece, *The Glass Bead Game* (1943), is dedicated to "the Journeyers to the East." But any reader, confronted unwittingly with Hesse's irony, who expected a work of fictional exotica, would be quite disappointed. After finishing the book he would look back at the dedication with consternation, for there is nothing Oriental far and wide, no landscape of the East either Near or Far. On the rare occasions when Castalia, the home of the Glass Bead Game players, is topographically fixed, when recognizable landscape images actually occur in the biography of the *magister ludi* Joseph Knecht, they are Alemannic rather than Oriental: Aargau and the Bernese Highlands provide a highly satisfactory background for the "pedagogical province." But there is no trace of the legendary lands of the East.

The dedication amounts to a self-quotation by the author, reminding the reader of Hesse's tale *The Journey to the East,* which appeared in 1932. Simply by means of the dedication the author establishes a link with the past: the reader is expected to assimilate the world of *The Journey to the East* into the substance of the story of the Glass Bead Game and its master-players. But as it turns out, *The Journey to the East* itself has a deceptive title, for it has nothing to do with the Orient, with travel accounts, or with the external agitation of adventure. The Eastern Wayfarers of 1932 share a conception of their destination that is anything but commonplace. Hesse explicitly and scornfully denies that the "traveling philoso-

"Hermann Hesse and the 'Age of the Feuilleton,'" by Hans Mayer. From Hans Mayer, *Studien zur deutschen Literaturgeschichte* (Berlin: Rütten & Loening, 1954), pp. 225–40. (Originally in *Aufbau*, 8 [1952], 613–28.) Copyright 1952 by Hans Mayer. Reprinted by permission of the author. Translated by Theodore Ziolkowski.

pher" Count Keyserling or the travel journalist Ossendowski could be designated as "Journeyers to the East" in his sense. The narrative leads us no further east than South Germany, Switzerland, and northern Italy: and even these landscapes bear a closer resemblance to the Italy of Eichendorff's tale *The Ne'er-do-well* than to any real geography. Suddenly in the course of the report we come upon the bewildering sentence: "We were encamped, after boldly crossing half of Europe and part of the Middle Ages, in a deep rocky gorge, a wild mountain ravine on the Italian border." Part of the Middle Ages? So we are dealing with a journey that leads simultaneously through space and through time! The participants in this Journey to the East also constitute a strange assemblage: they are actual people from the present as well as great masters from the past. Not only "the musician H. H." (who bears the author's initials) is a member of the Eastern Wayfarers, but also the Romantic poet Clemens Brentano and the composer Hugo Wolf. Even the painter Paul Klee has come along. And joining them, in fraternal community, the figures of writers. E. T. A. Hoffmann takes part in the expedition, but also Archivist Lindhorst, whom we recognize as a figure out of Hoffmann's tale *The Golden Pot*. Stifter's Witiko travels beside Sterne's eccentric hero, Tristram Shandy. In addition we find many figures from Hesse's own works: Pablo from *Steppenwolf*, the painter Klingsor from the novella *Klingsor's Last Summer*, Siddhartha from the "Indic poem" of that title, and Goldmund, the friend and complementary counterpart of Narcissus, who here rides along with Stifter's Witiko through half of Europe and part of the Middle Ages into the Orient. There are reports concerning the "Guardians of the Crown," whom we know from Achim von Arnim's famous novel. And when we learn the motto of the remarkable Journey to the East, it turns out to be the familiar sentence from Novalis: "Where are we going?" "Ever homeward."

All of this seems to have little to do with reality, although the external framework of the narrative appears to refer to our present era and to the living conditions of the twentieth century. A joint journey of artists both living and dead? A community of writers and their own characters? This is bound to produce unendurable tensions, and there is no lack of tensions among these Eastern Wayfarers. Occasionally the voyagers get sick of "the confusion of life and poetry." Throwing down their league rings, they take their leave and return to their homes and their useful jobs "by means of the reliable railways." Even the violinist H. H. (that is, Hesse himself) seems to break away from this community of journeyers. Suddenly finding himself back once more in the humdrum of bourgeois reality, he has a hard time reestablishing contact with the community with which he had set forth. In any case, he never arrives at his destination, the "Orient."

This tale from the year 1932 surely belongs among Hesse's most revealing poetic documents. By dedicating *The Glass Bead Game* to the "Journeyers to the East" he underlined once again the key position of the earlier story. The writer seems to regard the motifs, figures, and conflicts of *The Journey to the East* as representative and as forces that continue to be functional in his works. So it ought to be fruitful to examine a few motifs of Hesse's poetry and thought in this context.

Most accounts of the development of Hesse's life and works refer to a sharp break produced by World War I. A "new" Hesse is said to have appeared on the literary scene around 1919, and it is assumed that very little connects this artist and his themes with the author of the early poems or of the novels *Peter Camenzind, Beneath the Wheel,* and *Rosshalde.* The literary historian Hanns W. Eppelsheimer, whose *Handbook of World Literature* attests his skill in the art of brief characterization, puts it as follows: "Hesse began as an heir of Swabian Romanticism and as an admirer of Gottfried Keller, then (at age forty) broke out of the lyrics and epics of a sheltered idyll into uncertain spiritual horizons—borne along by his own destiny into the eddy of a culture grown problematic, which he sought to shape from a relentlessly penetrating observation of his own ego." For all the correct statements here, the seemingly irreconcilable opposition between the "early" and the "later" Hesse is highly debatable. To be sure, Eppelsheimer and others who offer similar analyses can appeal to Hesse himself. It is well known that the writer published his novel *Demian* in 1919 under the name of its leading character, Emil Sinclair (a name borrowed from the circle of friends surrounding Hölderlin) and that he did not acknowledge his authorship until the ninth printing of the sensationally successful book (1920). Hesse was not simply curious to find out whether this book by the unknown writer "Sinclair" could make its way on its own without the benefit of the famous name of Hermann Hesse, although this consideration naturally played a role in his decision. But at the same time Hesse wanted to suggest something like a new start, a new stage in his career, an artistic and intellectual rebirth. The implications are similar in his "Life Story Briefly Told" (1925), where Hesse seems to distance himself disapprovingly from the works of his youth, from such novels of love and marriage as *Gertrude* or *Rosshalde*, from Peter Camenzind's expedition into the world and his return to his village, from the schoolboy Hans Giebenrath, who gets mangled "beneath the wheel." To be sure, the years immediately preceding World War I and his experiences during the war affected Hesse deeply, producing a crisis in his marriage as well as illnesses and dislocations of his spiritual equilibrium. Above all, the experience of the war seems to have rendered questionable everything that he had valued. Hesse was not one of the bards of unleashed chauvinism and composed no war songs. On the contrary, during those years he discovered a friend and companion whose name and efforts in those days were virtually synonymous with cosmopolitanism and pacifism: Romain Rolland. Hesse's writings and proclamations in the years 1914 to 1918, with their dignity and decency, are the documents of a genuine humanist, whose goal is to save the great heritage of human culture from the fray, to maintain a distinction between politics and culture. (Here we note many points in common with Thomas Mann's *Reflections of a Non-Political Man* of 1918.) Hesse wanted to urge the artists, the creators of culture, not to take sides with either of the battling fronts; but he was not heard: the separation of politics and culture could not be accomplished. But it should not be forgotten that Hesse proclaimed his message during an imperialistic war in which imperialistic interests were opposed on every side. And the great bourgeois humanists that Hesse represents could not possibly identify themselves with any of these embattled interest groups.

His subsequent work was to prove that Hesse did not intend to stand still at this point. In the long run the pose *hors de combat* satisfied him as little as it had satisfied Romain Rolland, who was the first to coin the formula *au-dessus de la mêlée*. Hesse's new departure in 1919, the path of the "new" Hesse, was therefore explicitly meant to lead ever closer to a relationship between culture and society. Perhaps it seemed to Hesse at that time as though his early writing—narratives as well as poems—had devoted too little attention to these burning issues, to these relationships that were illuminated so harshly by the conflagration of the war. Yet it can be shown that while Hesse's war experiences summoned up a pro-

nounced new goal and sense of responsibility for his art, the most
important themes of his later work—clearly evident in retrospect—
are already preformed, often in an amazingly profound and clairvoyant manner, in his early creations.

What becomes of art when certain events take place, like those
that occurred in the imperialistic war of the years 1914 to 1918?
This is what the writer asked again and again in his "Reflections on
War and Politics." He had chosen as the title for an essay of September, 1914, the words from Beethoven's Ninth Symphony: "O
Friends, Not These Tones!" The same disturbing and probing question—"What is going to become of art in today's world?"—occupied
the artist, now somewhat older, who was working on *The Glass Bead
Game* during World War II. In fact, that question constitutes the
real central theme of this late work, which has been so radically
misunderstood—not without some fault on the part of the author.
The theme of the hostility toward art in the late-bourgeois world
resounds repeatedly in Hesse's works. A turning point in his development is evident in the increased urgency with which these matters
are treated from 1919 on. But they are already present in Hesse's
first books, and even *Peter Camenzind* is basically concerned with
nothing else.

To be sure, it is no simple matter to trace this continuity in Hesse's
work and in his questioning. It is present there, but often concealed
in true Romantic fashion beneath a confusion of textures, tendrils,
arabesques, and secondary lines. This explains why Hesse has so
often been designated as the ostensible promulgator of an apolitical
"subjectivism"—especially when readers take individual books out
of context and read only those. Yet these very works display an obsession with the same question: the artist's progress from isolation
toward a new and valid humanistic community. It was because of
misunderstandings of this sort that Hesse, during the regime of German fascism, received letters from readers who professed their simultaneous faith in him and in the dogmas of Hitlerism! The selection
of letters that Hesse published in 1951 reveals the contempt with
which he rejected any such associations, emphasizing the fact that
no coexistence was possible between humanism and antihumanism.
But he had not made it easy for the reader to recognize the great
cultural-philosophical critique and exhortations of his books as
clearly as he himself had understood and intended them.

For Hesse's art in all its manifestations is humanistic, even when its paths run in circles and lead back to the starting point. Let us identify a few of the more frequent misunderstandings immediately. Hesse's writing is not "buddhistic": in its essence it has nothing to do with nirvana, with renunciation of the world, with Schopenhauer's pessimism. Of course, Hesse is an extraordinary connoisseur of Eastern philosophy and poetry: Indian and especially Chinese culture, as one can best ascertain from *The Glass Bead Game*. But even his first early experience with the real India, his journal notes *Out of India* (1913), constitute a diary of disappointment. And as far as its decisive message and statement are concerned, the "Indic poem" of 1922, *Siddhartha*, stands in direct contrast to flight from the world or any Schopenhauerian negation of the will to life. This is what Siddhartha tells his friend Govinda: "It doesn't matter whether the things of reality are an illusion or not. If they are, then I too am an illusion, and so they are always of the same nature as myself. It is that that makes them so lovable and venerable to me. That is why I can love them. And this is a teaching at which you will laugh: it seems to me, o Govinda, that love is the most important thing of all. It may be important to great thinkers to comprehend the world, to explain it, to despise it. But it is my sole concern to be able to love the world, not to despise it, not to hate it and myself, but to be able to contemplate the world and myself and all beings with love and admiration and veneration." These are the words of a European humanist, not an advocate of escapism and contempt of mankind. Here again we note the propinquity to Thomas Mann, whom in philistine circles it is fashionable to play off against Hesse (and vice-versa). Yet what was Hans Castorp's famous insight, which Thomas Mann, similarly matured by the experiences of World War I, placed in the center of *The Magic Mountain* just around the time when Hesse's *Siddhartha* was published? "Man shall, for the sake of goodness and love, concede to death no power over his thoughts."

Not flight from the world, then, but the search for a new human community and a new possibility for art. But this puts Hesse's central figures into a different light: they should not be interpreted as psychological exceptions, but as representative types who embody differing responses to society. It has often been remarked that the same pairs of contrasting figures move repeatedly through Hesse's narrative oeuvre. This also helps to explain the fact that in *The*

*Journey to the East,* the author seems to control and watch over all of them at the same time—those that have already been artistically shaped and those that are not yet born. These opposites are frequently presented to us as a pair of friends, as comradely constellations of contrary human types: Giebenrath and Hermann Heilner (once again a playful allusion to Hesse's own name) in the novel *Beneath the Wheel;* Demian and Emil Sinclair; Siddhartha and Govinda; "the Steppenwolf" Harry Haller (Hesse's initials) and Pablo; and finally, in the purest incarnation, Narcissus and Goldmund. Common to them all is a deep bond linking the opposing figures, a fundamental congruity that is more than friendship. All of these friends and rivals seem, like Leverkühn and Zeitblom in Thomas Mann's *Doctor Faustus,* to be concealing something: "the secret of their essential identity" (to use Mann's words). Thus Giebenrath and Heilner, Demian and Sinclair, Narcissus and Goldmund appear to represent two aspects of their author's own nature. He seems to be active in both of them—like Goethe in Tasso and Antonio, or in Faust and Mephisto. Hesse has implied this relationship plainly and with a good deal of self-irony. *The Guest at the Spa* (1924), Hesse's account of his experiences during a cure, reports that any physician should be able to recognize in him, simultaneously the victim and narrator of this treatment, "a moderately gifted lone-wolf belonging to the family of schizophrenics but not requiring commitment." Schizophrenia, which means a split in the personality, is the expression of a spiritual illness; but at the same time it is an essential formal component of Romantic art. It is a motif that we know from such pairs of friends and rivals as Schubert's Florestan and Eusebius, Walt and Vult in Jean Paul's *Years of Indiscretion;* almost all Romantic literature teams with these "doubles." Naturally this Romantic theme plays a decisive role for Hesse, the admirer and heir of German Romantic poetry and music. But it is not simply Romantic playfulness or literary imitation that has shaped these friends, opposites, and doubles, who so typically people Hesse's works. Nor does a psychological interpretation really help us along. The author's characterization of himself as a moderately gifted schizophrenic can be taken as a kind of irony that is pedagogical and by no means simply Romantic: it is intended as a defense against the philistine's claim that he knows all the answers. Basically these figures in opposition always represent the two possible attitudes of the artist to reality: a turning away from the world, or the attempt to function within the human community. Of the friends Narcissus and Goldmund, the thinker and philosopher Narcissus remains in the monastery while the sensuous Goldmund, thirsting for experience and the artistic shaping of these experiences, rushes out into the world. Here again the basic question is posed: Is art possible only in the rejection of present-day society, or can it be combined with some sort of activity within this society? Neither Narcissus nor Goldmund, each of whom chooses one of the two ways, manages to become completely happy. In *The Glass Bead Game* Joseph Knecht, attempting as a single individual to follow the two paths successively, fails twice. And *The Journey to the East* deals with essentially the same theme, for the "hero" (who shares his author's initials) founders both during the journey out of reality into old Romantic lands and, again, on the occasion of his return into the reality of everyday bourgeois life.

So neither a buddhistic proclamation of worldly vanity can be acknowledged as Hesse's principal theme nor is the resolution of figures and conflicts into psychological (even psychoanalytical) spiritual problems. Here, instead, a great friend of mankind and of human cultural achievements unwearyingly asks how we can improve the lot of man and preserve the balance of our cultural heritage from destruction. But if Hesse incessantly circles around this central theme concerning the possibility of art in our reality, then despite all their Romantic arabesques we may properly call these formulations of a great humanist genuinely realistic.

But while Hesse is inquiring into the possibility of genuine art in the society that surrounds him, he also poses several preliminary questions that he seeks to answer. First, how does this reality look? Do the people who live in it still have any true relationship to art and to works of art? Second, is a creative continuation of classical art still possible, or has art reached a terminal point at which it is irrevocably doomed to decline? Further, what can the individual artist do to halt this decline? Should he struggle within society to preserve the cultural heritage, or should he, acting in the role of executor of the cultural estate, take his heritage and withdraw from the scene of social struggle? Precisely the purest and most genuine artists of German literature in the Age of Imperialism have suffered from the modern bourgeois hostility to art, which they have portrayed in their works. Depending upon the breadth and depth of their social understanding, the artists have reacted with grief or indictment, with the arguments of the satirist or the ironist against an order whose social laws deny true art ever more strongly. Imperialism's hostility to art— this theme permeates the work of Thomas Mann's youth with its opposition of bourgeois and artist, which recurs almost as a leitmotif; it underlies the depiction of those *artistes* in the fifth of Rilke's *Duino Elegies,* who lack foundation and hope; it sustains the cultural criticism of Karl Kraus and affords the point of departure in Romain Rolland's *Jean Christophe;* the famous Lohengrin scene in Heinrich Mann's *Man of Straw (Der Untertan)* is based on this motif; and even in the feeble neo-Romanticism of Hauptmann's *Sunken Bell* the bell-founder Heinrich stands for the function of the true modern artist over against a social environment that is hostile and unreceptive to any true art.

Hermann Hesse, too, was forced to accommodate, in his first poems and stories, the realization that his conception of art was radically opposed to the official currents of the times, as manifested in the literary trade and the publishing business, in the cultural pretensions of the philistine world. Peter Camenzind, who sets out into the world to become an artist and the creator of a poetic reality, is swept up into the hustle and bustle of the literary marketplace. At the end he returns to his village in the Alps: repairing the roof of his parental farmhouse becomes more meaningful to him than the rat race for an artistic success whose stipulations he had come all too clearly to recognize. So already *Peter Camenzind* stands in the tradition of those novels of disillusionment, all those portrayals of the conflict between true artistic existence and the merchandise character of art in a capitalist society, a series that Balzac had initiated with his *Illusions perdues. Peter Camenzind* is also a book about lost illusions, about art as commodity, and about the isolation of the artist who refuses to be content with producing and selling his work and his characters as though they were nothing but goods. But this necessarily creates a conflict between the artist and a cultural-literary business that is dominated by the fetish of commodities. In this conflict Hesse believes that he can choose the way of rejection and isolation. Peter Camenzind retreats, as it were, into a "precapitalistic" sphere. The "Steppenwolf," Harry Haller, remains in this world as a being with a real existence, but he is an eccentric, a loner, a peripheral creature wrathfully prowling around the tame realm of domesticated animals. The Steppenwolf's clash with the literary salons and business interests also ends in hostility, reciprocal rejection, and a new alienation of Haller from "business as usual." We are not dealing here merely with the commercial exploitation and prostitution of artistic achievement. To make a "thing," a fetish, out of art represents a great danger to the very process of artistic creation. For the capitalistic art consumer demands from the artist the production of "pleasing" subjects and entertainments: splendor and glitter to conceal real horrors, pseudo-problems to distract us from fundamental social questions. But such ready-made artistic products are undermined by the model of the great masters of the past. For the great literature of the past is always a poetry of authenticity and humanitarianism, while the artistic hostility of bourgeois society in its late stages demands a false artistic virtuosity and —the further the process of decay progresses—an appeal to anti-humanity, that is, if artists expect their works of art to be acknowledged. At such times the pseudo-greats of the present are praised as the true new masters by a corruptible guild of scribblers offering itself to the highest bidder. The real masters of the past are silent— and they are left in silence.

Hesse, however, gratefully pledges his allegiance to the great tradition of German poetry. He wants to be bound by that tradition and to continue to act in its spirit. This intention leads to a collision between the literary market and the poet who regards himself as the pupil and successor of the German classics. In his autobiographical narrative *The Guest at the Spa* Hesse declared his contempt for this pseudo-world by means of an ironic comparison of stars and rockets. "It is the same with my judgment of the great German poets whom I do not honor, love, and make use of any the less because the great majority of living Germans do the opposite and prefer rockets to the stars. Rockets are beautiful, rockets are enchanting, long life to rockets! But the stars! An eye and a mind filled with their quiet lights, filled with the vast resonance of their universal music—oh friends, that after all is something quite different!"

Hesse's disagreement with the modern bourgeois era and its hostility to art reached its sharpest critical formulation in the famous and incisive depiction of the "Age of the Feuilleton" in *The Glass Bead Game*. Even at the time of its appearance the book aroused considerable consternation and disapproval among the *feuilletonistes,* the opinion-makers of the bourgeois press and critical establishment. And with good reason. For Hesse's analysis amounted to a veritable negation of the so-called cultural production in a commodity society. To be sure, Hesse's depiction does not go into the reasons underlying this prostitution and leveling-down of the mind: the poet simply surveys the effects of capitalism in the realm of art, but not the connections between the social basis and its literary-artistic superstructure. But the condition of the cultural realm is rendered with a precision that is matched only by its virulence. The author of *The Glass Bead Game* is looking back at our epoch, the "Age of the Feuilleton," from a viewpoint in an imaginary future, so he is able to show neither the causal relationships nor a means of overcoming this spiritual decay (unless one chooses to regard the world of Castalia as a way out—a matter that must still be discussed). This "feuilletonistic" age gets its name from its "feuilletons," which have taken the place of all serious concern with spiritual and artistic values. What matters nowadays is simply to entertain the public— an ignorant and unprepared public that responds rapidly and forgets just as quickly—with little anecdotes that provide a few minutes of distraction. Artistic experience, the discovery of truth, teaching, strong emotions no longer matter—just intoxication, distraction, amusement. The lives and struggles of the great masters are transformed into a continuing series spiced with piquant anecdotes and psychological trivialities. The Age of the Feuilleton, as depicted in *The Glass Bead Game,* was "an era emphatically 'bourgeois' and given to an almost untrammeled individualism." The artists and intellectuals in that late stage of bourgeois and individualistic culture were obsessed "with the rapid and easy acquisition of money, with public fame and honors, with the praise of the newspapers, with marriages to the daughters of bankers and industrialists, with indulgences and luxury in the material life." But Hesse, going even further, also betrays the function that this prostitution of art and scholarship filled for the people living in the feuilletonistic age with its hostility to art. "They assiduously learned to drive automobiles, to play difficult card games, and lose themselves in crossword puzzles —for they faced death, fear, pain, and hunger almost without defenses, could no longer accept the consolations of the churches, and could obtain no useful advice from Reason. These people who read so many articles and listened to so many lectures did not take the time and trouble to strengthen themselves against fear, to combat the dread of death within themselves; they moved spasmodically on through life and had no belief in a tomorrow."

Unmistakably, the writer has here attained a profound critical insight into the symptoms manifested by the decay of the bourgeois world. But if the environment in which Hesse's life and creativity take place is hostile and averse to genuine artistic creation, if it is always concerned with violating, corrupting, or—if necessary—destroying the artist and his art, then the question remains whether at that juncture the terminal point of any true artistic creation has been reached. Hesse seems inclined to draw this conclusion, and it is here that our principal objection must be raised against him. He sees the symptoms of the bourgeois era, but not its causal connections, its "anatomy." He is incapable of visualizing the reality of a different society, one that is no longer bourgeois, no longer individualistic. To be sure, *The Glass Bead Game* contains splendid remarks about a conception of the personality that has transcended bourgeois individualism. For instance, the narrator observes that we should "not even speak of major personalities until we encounter men who have gone beyond all original and idiosyncratic qualities to achieve the greatest possible integration into the generality, the greatest possible service to the suprapersonal." But Hesse does not show us the way to that goal. For him the terminal stage of bourgeois society implies the end of all art as it has been known and practiced.

But if the writer is unable to grasp and visualize a new order that is no longer bourgeois, then the end of bourgeois art must strike him as the end of art altogether. This is the social basis of Hesse's alleged "pessimism." Already in *Peter Camenzind* the writer had attempted to imagine a poetry and a poetics that strived for the most precise reproduction of reality and nature, but that excluded mankind and human society from its poetic realm. It was the notion of a poetry devoid of human beings and hence a nonhumanist poetry, conceived out of the passionate anguish of a genuine humanist who despaired of being able to make the men of his age and environment into worthy objects of a beautiful work of art. That was a false path, like Rilke's flight into the *Dinggedicht* ("thing-poem"), which was produced from a similar disenchantment with the people and circumstances of late bourgeois society. Hesse realized that this direction was not viable, and his character, Peter

Camenzind, soon rejected this plan. In Hesse's case, the alternative was an art that dedicated itself ever more consciously to the emulation of German Classicism and Romanticism—without wondering whether or not this kind of creativity would meet with the approval or the contempt of the mighty men of the present-day marketplace. The poet felt himself to be the heir and successor to a great tradition during a time when this heritage was being denied. He considered himself to be an epigone, a last offshoot, and this sense bestowed upon his work an element of grief and hopelessness. He belonged to the stars, not to the "rockets" of the capitalistic fairground. At the end of his prologue to *The Guest at the Spa* he calls himself "a belated minor poet." Out of a similar combination of modesty and pride Karl Kraus had written the verses:

> Ich bin nur einer von den Epigonen,
> Die in dem alten Haus der Sprache wohnen . . .
> Bin Epigone, Ahnenwerthes Ahner.
> Ihr aber seid die kundigen Thebaner!

[I am merely one of the epigones, who inhabit the ancient house of language . . . An epigone, guessing at things worth inheriting. But you are the learned Thebans.]

Virtually the same poem can be found among Hesse's mature verses. Already in the earliest poems of 1902, just as in *Peter Camenzind,* there resounds this lament over the terminal state of the spirit, of true poetry. Movingly, but also with accents of hopelessness, Hesse confided a similar thought, in 1937, to his poem, "The Last Glass Bead Game Player":

> Jetzt blieb er übrig, alt, verbraucht, allein,
> Es wirbt kein Jünger mehr um seinen Segen,
> Es lädt ihn kein Magister zum Disput;
> Sie sind dahin, und auch die Tempel, Bücherein,
> Schulen Kastaliens sind nicht mehr. Der Alte ruht
> Im Trümmerfeld, die Perlen in der Hand,
> Hieroglyphen, die einst viel besagten,
> Nun sind sie nichts als bunte gläserne Scherben. . . .

[Now he was left, old, exhausted, alone; no disciple any longer seeks his blessing, no master invites him to a debate; they are gone, and also the temples, libraries, schools of Castalia no longer exist. The old man rests amid the ruins, the beads in his hand, hieroglyphs that once meant much. Now they are nothing but bright bits of glass. . . .]

In *Doctor Faustus* Thomas Mann speaks of loyalty to the practice of an art in which one secretly no longer believes, adding that this produces the artistic form of parody. Hesse retains his loyalty to an art in which he himself still believes, but in which only a few loners, Steppenwolves, bead game players, and Eastern Wayfarers seem to have faith—a handful of genuinely artistic individuals who are conscious of tradition. The appropriate form for this loyalty of grief is the elegy, a mode that suggests both the greatness and the limitations of Hesse's artistic achievements.

If the artist and the writer are going to resist this decline and the continual deterioration of art into feuilletonism and commodity, they must be able to believe that resistance is possible and meaningful. Hesse seems disposed to equate the end of the bourgeois world with the end of all art, without conceding the possibility of a new society and hence a renewal of art. But the way of the Steppenwolf, the attitude of "the last glass bead game player" patiently waiting for the end, does not suffice for the humanist Hesse. That is why, in his work, the ascetic—the intellectual and artist in flight from the world—is always counterbalanced by his antipode: the man of action, of worldliness, of sensuality. Hesse's faith in the isolated effectiveness of individual humanists who might perhaps succeed in preserving the cultural heritage for the future repeatedly turns out to be questionable and even covertly nonhumanistic. For humanism presupposes the commitment to work and fight for humanity. In *Narcissus and Goldmund* the attitudes of escapism and worldiness were juxtaposed with no decision in favor of the one or the other. Then came the domination of fascism in Germany, the preparations for war, and the war itself. And in those years, when Hesse was committed both publicly and privately to the antifascist cause, he also began to reexamine his previous attitudes and theses. The result of this reappraisal is displayed in *The Glass Bead Game*. It is not a result in the sense that he formulated a new maxim or thesis. It is both a humanistic exhortation and, at the same time, in some sense a "retraction" of this exhortation. The story of Joseph Knecht (who wants only to be a modest servant—*Knecht*—in the following of the great Wilhelm Meister) is located in a utopian future sometime after the twentieth century. The Age of the Feuilleton has been overcome, and a Pedagogical Province, modeled after Goethe's *Wilhelm Meister's Travels* and bearing the name Castalia, has been established. The order of Castalia exists wholly apart from the rest of society and humanity. Science and art are their only concern. And even here the most rigorous selection has been made: philology, mathematics, music—and the Glass Bead Game. Four seemingly pointless, seemingly "impractical" disciplines, for even mathematics is done here with no regard for its social applicability. Social relevance is not excluded, of course, but it is not sought after.

And what is the Glass Bead Game itself? As in all true poetic creations, a clear answer is impossible because the game is a symbol, and a lofty and pure exercise of art. Perhaps it is not presumptuous to equate the Glass Bead Game, in its decisive features, with literature, with the entire corpus of writing that can be designated as *belles lettres*. It is no accident that one of the masters of the game is named Thomas von der Trave—an allusion to that master of letters, Thomas Mann, who was born in Lübeck on the Trave.

In the destiny of the Glass Bead Game, therefore, Hesse portrays among other things the destiny of literature and poetry. It too is practiced in Castalia—with no "purpose" and remote from any social effect. But even poetry, like the other disciplines and despite its ostensible Castalian serenity, is subject to a terrible law: it has ceased to be productive or generative. The players do nothing but combine the thoughts and forms of earlier masters; new art cannot arise here, nor is it supposed to. The musicians of Castalia are travelers into the land of the musical past, from which they never return. New music is not created amid the Castalian groves. The seeming purity of science and art turns out, in Hesse's secret view, to be impotent.

Even more: it reveals itself, if we look more closely, as parasitic and socially irresponsible, for it is unable to give anything to society and to people outside Castalia. In a magnificent summing-up, Joseph Knecht, the highest *magister ludi*, exposes the problematic nature of this intellectual attitude that locates itself outside of society. Knecht writes in his indictment: "We eat our bread, use our libraries, expand our schools and archives—but if the nation no longer wants to authorize this, or if it should be struck by poverty, war, and so on, then our life and studying would be over in a minute. Some day our country might decide that its Castalia and our culture are a luxury it can no longer afford. Instead of being genially proud of us, it may come round to regarding us as noxious parasites, tricksters, and enemies. Those are the external dangers that threaten us." And Knecht goes even further when he asks: "Is the present-day Castalian aware of the foundations of his existence; does he know himself to be a leaf, a blossom, a twig, or root of a living organism? Does he have any notion of the sacrifices the nation makes for his sake, by feeding and clothing him, by underwriting his schooling and his manifold studies?" The criticism could hardly be stated more clearly. But does it not imply at the same time a disavowal of Castalia and the dream of the Journeyers to the East? Of an artistic existence that stands quietly aside in matters of war and peace, culture or barbarism? Joseph Knecht is therefore unable to remain in Castalia. He has come to regard it as more worthwhile to educate a single young man in the "real" world outside than to pass his time in the rarefied administration of an unfruitful "pure" literature and intellectuality. The fact that he goes out into the world and perishes there suggests that the return into this world from Castalia is not possible without a significant shift in attitude.

But in a remarkable conclusion, which ironically relativizes the entire novel, Hesse draws away again from Joseph Knecht's action. Knecht, symbolizing the untenability of the Castalian position, perishes. Yet Castalia survives and obviously continues to function. The book gives us a report of Knecht's life and death, and neither seems to have had the least effect on the Castalian idea. Is it conceivable, therefore, that Hesse ultimately does believe in an artistic existence that stands apart from the world?

If we attentively read this mysterious and remarkable late work, which is written in the finest German, then Hesse's final word is not exhausted in the tensions between socially responsible artistry and an artistry that flees society: the motto remains. For his motto Hesse invented, whimsically, a classic writer of the Latin Middle Ages and put into his mouth a Latin quotation that is rendered in Hesse's own German translation. There is talk of a utopia, of nonexistent things whose existence is neither demonstrable nor probable. But: "The very fact that serious and conscientious men treat them as existing things brings them a step closer to existence and to the possibility of being born." That is to say: Castalia and the Glass Bead Game are nonexistent things, just as the Journey to the East was not meant to signify a voyage in reality. But all over the world there are true humanists to whom these thoughts are precious, and by remaining true to these thoughts they perhaps contribute to the possibility that, one day, the nonexistent might come into existence.

Do they have any real and tangible effect? Castalia and the Glass Bead Game will never come into being, nor would it be desirable— not even for Hesse. This is proved by the story of Joseph Knecht. But what, Hesse seems to be asking, what if precisely from these very tensions between abstract intellectuality and a concrete, nonintellec-tual, even anti-intellectual environment a new existence could arise in which it would be worthwhile to participate? What if there were a spirituality that arose from a sense of social responsibility, conscious of tradition and yet genuinely creative; what if it were hostile to feuilletonism and acknowledged personality only to the extent that it is socially committed and useful? That is the task, even in Hesse's eyes. But he does not show us the way. Not even *The Glass Bead Game* shows the way.

In a letter of August 15, 1950, to a Swiss worker, Hesse suggested how he himself conceives of his position in the here and now. The worker, who had read *The Glass Bead Game,* challenged Hesse to emulate Joseph Knecht by finding his own way back into society. Hesse replies very earnestly that there is evidently a misunderstand-ing for which perhaps the nature of his novel was not without its share of responsibility. Unwilling to accept the reproach that he does not belong to the "working" people, he says: "I believe that if one measures the degree of work by the degree of ability, I am at least as much of a worker as you—not to mention the fact that dur-ing my early youth I also spent a year and a half in a workshop, crouching over bench-vices and milling tools." What matters to him? "I have not accomplished any more in my life than to support these few people, these few students and comrades, in their struggle for a human existence with dignity and courage." After all, Joseph Knecht went out into the world as a teacher and educator: "He does what I, too, have tried to do as long as I was able to practice my profession: he puts his gifts, his personality, his energy at the service of the individual human being." And at this point the great German writer and humanist educator, Hermann Hesse, once more approaches his colleague Thomas Mann. The official literary establishment of West Germany (a grotesque reification of Hesse's image of the feuilletonis-tic age) likes to juxtapose these two writers in order to let them cancel each other out. And it is true that they display characteristic differences in their poetic vocation. In the case of Hesse the literary impulse is primarily lyrical while in the case of Mann it is essentially epic. Hesse is clearly the heir of German folk-poetry and Romanticism while Thomas Mann is the pupil of the great Russian realists. Yet their humanism shares a deep common ground in their mutual striving to overcome the bourgeois world of which Hesse remarked in a letter of August 10, 1950: "That the social conditions at the end of the capitalistic epoch are no longer capable of life and are being swept away by the revolt of the disadvantaged is unavoidable." The significance of this writer for the literature of the German Democratic Republic can hardly be defined more beautifully and precisely than with the concluding words of an essay that Thomas Mann dedicated to Hesse on his seventieth birthday on July 2, 1947. Thomas Mann quotes from the novel *Demian,* where Demian asks his friend Emil Sinclair what he intends to do when the new era begins, bringing terror to those who cling stubbornly to the old. Thomas Mann provides an answer that he considers valid for himself and for Hesse as well. "The right answer would be: 'Assist the new without sacrificing the old.' The best servitors of the new— Hesse is an example—may be those who know and love the old and carry it over into the new."

# Music and Morality in Thomas Mann and Hermann Hesse

## by G. W. Field

No one can have even a passing acquaintance with the works of Mann and of Hesse without being aware of the very special role of music in both these writers. Much has been written on various aspects of music in Thomas Mann's work, but little attention has so far been given to this theme in Hesse. So far as possible this comparative study seeks to avoid purely technical features (although in the case of Mann some involvement in musical theory is inevitable) and it is our intention to concentrate on the meaning of music in its widest sense, the role of music in life, its significance in human culture, in other words its relation to moral actions and concepts.

The divergent tendencies of our two authors are obvious enough in this regard and this difference may be illustrated by the following statements. Young Adrian Leverkühn, the hero of Mann's *Dr. Faustus,* finds that "music is systematized equivocation" [1] and this attitude is made even more explicit in the author's essay on *Germany and the Germans*: "Music is a demonic realm." Hermann Hesse, on the other hand, wrote in a letter in 1934: "What interests me . . . [is] the real spirit of genuine music, its morality."

The concept "music" is a very wide and vague one. Even apart from the music of India, China, and Japan (in which countries its development and cultural importance is considerable), within the relatively narrow confines of the Western musical system there is scope for very diverse styles and kinds of music. We must ask ourselves: what music, what kind of music have Mann and Hesse in mind? Only then may we go on to examine its relation to life and

"Music and Morality in Thomas Mann and Hermann Hesse," by G. W. Field. From *University of Toronto Quarterly*, 24 (1955), 175–90. Reprinted by permission of the author and the University of Toronto Press.

[1] All translations from the original German are by the writer. . . .

art. From this study should emerge not merely some interesting comments on music but some deeper insight into the world of thought of each author and his attitude toward life. Their last major works, *Dr. Faustus* and *The Glass Bead Game,* offer the best points of departure for this comparison. In these works each writer has distilled the product of a life full of preoccupation with music and its role in the composite cultural history of mankind. In each work music plays an almost equally conspicuous part, so that the comparison of one work with the other is facilitated. We shall deal with Mann first, not because he is the simpler, for the paradoxical complexity of his thought structure is often baffling, but because the ethical implications of music seem in his work to be more negative than in Hesse's.

## I

In *Dr. Faustus,* music is essentially Janus-faced. Its very elements, *Geist* and *Trieb* (intellect and instinct), are equivocal expressions of the antithetical forces of the divine and the demonic in life. It is significant that Adrian Leverkühn's interest in music is awakened simultaneously with the onset of sex, puberty, and with the beginning of illness, his characteristic migraine.

Adrian's guide into the world of music, Kretzschmar,[2] is himself an enigmatic, paradoxical personality, and this is no doubt intentional. For Kretzschmar's combination of physical inadequacy with intellectual and artistic insight is subtly suggestive of the ambivalent nature of music itself. Kretzschmar's commentaries give us the framework by which Adrian's later compositions are to be judged. Speaking of the antithetical components of music, aspirations of the mind and claims of the senses, he finds two opposing tendencies: on the one hand music has a latent inclination to the ascetic, the antisensuous, *nur-Geistige,* a tendency to be no longer heard or felt, to be music for the eye and intellect alone; on the other hand it has a strong atavistic drive to return to its basic material, its primitive demonic elements. This latter drive is especially ap-

---

[2] Pennsylvania-born Wendell Kretzschmar seems to be drawn at least in part from Hermann Kretzschmar (1848–1924) who, according to *Brockhaus,* was "along with Riemann the most significant musical scholar of his time." The career in Germany of Mann's Kretzschmar closely parallels that of the real Kretzschmar, especially in the geographical centres in which he was active. There may be traits also of Edmund Kretschmer, organist and composer (1830–1908).

parent in the development of orchestral music in the nineteenth and twentieth centuries with stress on harmonic texture and mass effect. Wagner is mentioned in this connection and as prime example of the tendency Kretzschmar cites the opening A flat major triad of the *Ring des Nibelungen*. Stravinski, especially his *Sacre du Printemps,* might be added as a more recent example.[3] The piano, on the other hand, is the representative of music in its intellectuality. The human voice of course bridges these two disparate tendencies and Adrian's most characteristic compositions are songs, a puppet music-drama, an opera, and an oratorio, all of which feature the human voice and all of which are based on this underlying ambivalence. It is significant that Adrian's last opus, *Dr. Fausti Weheklag,* a "symphonic cantata," ends with the extinction of the human voice and a final orchestral movement.

It becomes Adrian's aim to escape from the dead-end of post-Romantic developments, to emancipate music from the sphere of the merely musical and elevate it to the level of the universal cultural-intellectual. But it may be observed here that the so-called "merely musical" is Hesse's "genuine" music: the music which is healthy and moral, transcendent over death, decay, and disease. Mann's music, instead of serving as guide and model for mankind and man's moral status, becomes the expression of the anarchic, dissident, and demonic elements in modern culture. It is linked with death instead of life.

Hesse's music, Mann's "mere music," is an expression of faith in the human soul. Adrian Leverkühn is not only completely cynical and without faith in man, in whom he sees only weaknesses and foibles, but he himself lacks "soul." His one-sided nature—cold intellectuality—Mann, with characteristic insight, depicts as most dangerously threatened by exposure to naked impulse, *das Tierische.* We are told that "warmth and coldness prevailed concurrently in his work . . . a glowing edifice that brought home the concept of the demonic like nothing else on earth."

Adrian despairs of the possibility of genuine art in the traditional sense and in the traditional forms. The "work" of art as such, as "a

---

[3] "With *Le Sacre du Printemps,*" reads the article in Hughes' *Music Encyclopedia,* "the strident and bizarre effects that made *Petrouchka* a masterpiece of bitter irony were augmented with an unprecedented complexity of rhythm and harsh, grinding dissonances which literally portrayed the earth-beating dances of a prehistoric race in a spring festival."

structure self-sufficient and rounded out harmonically within itself," appears inadmissible, intellectually impossible in any legitimate relation to the "absolute uncertainty, ambiguity and lack of harmony that characterize the state of our society today." At this stage the only recourse for the artist appears to lie in parody and this is the direction taken by the works of Leverkühn's middle period. It involves a "mocking, ironisation of tonality, of traditional music," and to the alarmed Serenus Zeitblom it seems to involve a "mocking of humanism" itself.

Beyond the range of parody, however, there is the possibility of art breaking the bonds of art, of form, and becoming direct *Erkenntnis* (cognition). To emancipate art and make possible this immediate expression of ultimate human and cosmic fate becomes Adrian's final goal, particularly in his last work, *Dr. Fausti Weheklag.* That this is still admissible as a "work" at all is attributable to its strict external form, constructed as it is of variations on the theme "I die a good and evil Christian." In other respects it bursts the bonds of traditional art to give direct expression to the cosmic lament of doomed humanity. It is a "taking back" of Beethoven's ninth symphony and the hymn to joy. The normal or traditional relationships are present only in inversion or perversion: the theme itself is equivocal (a good and evil Christian); the admonition of Christ, "Watch with me," is inverted—"they were to betake themselves to bed and sleep peacefully"; the sacrament of the Last Supper is suggested by the *Johannstrunk*; the angel chorus of the first half is taken up in inverted form by the demonic chant of the second part. The development of *Geist,* order, form, out of the sensuous elements given by the orchestra, is reversed, so that the human voice, in this context the carrier of *Geist,* is superseded by the wail of cosmic grief in the orchestra: "I find [writes Serenus Zeitblom] that here, towards the end, the uttermost accents of anguish are attained, expression has been given to the ultimate despair. . . . Then there is nothing more—silence and night."

At this point there would seem to be the widest possible gulf between Mann's music with its dark and demonic role and Hesse's music of light and enlightenment. But Mann here introduces yet another paradox. What, he says, if the merest suggestion of hope germinated out of this deepest despair? It would be the miracle that transcends faith. We are now made aware that in the conclusion, as one choir after another falls silent in the orchestra, the last tone that remains is the high G of a solitary cello—then darkness and silence. But this last hovering note of the cello is like a light in the darkness.

This does not go far towards bridging the gulf between the attitudes of Mann and Hesse. It does introduce a parallel note of optimism. But the optimism is different in nature. Mann's optimistic note enters only after darkness and despair have engulfed the human scene. It is a transcendental, metaphysical, one might almost say theological optimism, dependent on an act of grace from above. Hesse's optimism is founded on man, on faith in the individual human being and the formative power of human reason symbolized in classical music.

## II

Turning to Hesse, we can now trace briefly in the earlier works the development of his attitude to music which comes to full fruition in *The Glass Bead Game*. Among the cultural forces which contend for the soul of the early autobiographical hero *Peter Camenzind* is Wagner. (All of Hesse's characters are in an unusually high degree autobiographical.) At first under the spell of the giant of Bayreuth, Camenzind finds his way to a rejection of this music. *Gertrude* is an artist-novel in which all the main characters and most secondary ones are musicians: Kuhn the creative artist, violinist, and composer; his friend Muoth the performing "artist," the singer whose inner emptiness and frustration are masked behind his "representation" in life and in art (a tour de force which is continuous, which demands increasing recourse to the bottle, and which finally breaks him); between them is Gertrude, the understanding woman, herself an accomplished pianist. But from this novel music emerges with a message. It teaches Kuhn to embrace and accept life despite his physical inadequacies (he is crippled in a toboggan accident in early manhood) and despite the frustration of his love for Gertrude (who marries Muoth and after the latter's death lives in semi-seclusion in Kuhn's vicinity). In *Demian*, the work in which Hesse first propounds his highly personal philosophy of life, the result of years of self-examination and questioning under the impact of the First World War, music is one of the important cultural influences by means of which an individual soul can find itself and develop into a personality. *Steppenwolf* carries his personal philosophy a stage further and develops a devastating critique of the age. Music is here one of the important symptoms in the *Kulturkritik* and at the same time is one of the chief routes of escape from the dilemma in which the contemporary individual finds himself in a disintegrating civilization. Jazz is symptomatic of this disintegration. It is "Musik des Untergangs" and it is the focus of much of the criticism levelled at society. On the other hand Mozart (along with Goethe) is one of the immortals who is ever available and ever present to the individual who will search for him. Even disfigured in such a hellish contraption as the modern phonograph or radio (the date was 1926), the mind— *Geist*—in Mozart cannot be completely extinguished. Moreover Pablo, the saxophone player, in the metamorphosis of the "Magic Theatre," to Harry Haller's astonishment, is also Mozart. Clearly this metamorphosis symbolizes Hesse's optimism on an individual plane even in the face of his pessimism where the social fabric and the historical process as a whole are concerned.[4] Every jazz fiend, he implies, has within him the potentialities which the spirit of a Mozart is capable of animating and the continued existence of such individual immortals as Goethe and Mozart is the portent of the undying potentialities inherent in the individual human soul.

It is significant that Mozart and not Beethoven is the figure chosen by Hesse to convey this message. In fact Hesse sees the symptoms of decadence and disease already setting in with Beethoven and culminating in a virtual pestilence with Brahms and Wagner. In the "Magic Theatre" at the end of *Steppenwolf* Hesse conjures up an amusing vision of Wagner and Brahms condemned to Sisyphean labours. We are transported to a vast desert ringed in by misty mountains and sea:

> In this plain we saw a dignified old bearded gentleman who, with melancholy mien, was leading a mighty procession of some tens of thousands of men clothed in black. It looked depressing and hopeless, and Mozart said:
> "Look, that's Brahms. He's striving for redemption, but he still has a good way to go."
> I learned that the thousands of black figures were all the players of those voices and notes which, according to divine judgment, had been redundant in his scores.

---

[4] Hesse's position seems close to that of M. Albert Camus, who has declared he is "pessimiste quant à la destinée humaine . . . optimiste quant à l'homme."

"Instrumentation too turgid, too much material squandered," Mozart nodded.

And immediately afterwards we saw Richard Wagner marching at the head of an equally great host and we felt the heavily laden thousands pulling and drawing on him; we saw him too drag himself along on tired, contrite feet. . . .

Mozart laughed. ". . . Turgid instrumentation was after all neither Wagner's nor Brahm's personal shortcoming, it was an error of their time."

"What? And for that they have to do such heavy penance now?" I cried accusingly.

"Naturally. It's the normal course of justice. Only when they have expiated the guilt of their age will it be evident whether there is left a large enough personal contribution to merit a balancing of accounts."

From this passage it is evident that Hesse is highly critical of the mass effects and emotional saturation achieved with too full and too elaborate harmonic emphasis. This is the dangerous, demonic, emotional side which he sees suppressing the *Geist* (the spiritual and intellectual qualities) in music, the strictly controlled and yet magically effective pattern of counterpoint melody as exemplified by eighteenth-century and earlier masters. The passage also indicates the reciprocal relationship between the decadent music of Wagner and Brahms and the decadent culture in which they lived. They could not escape their own time. Thirdly, we see that the individual, although powerless so far as the tendency of his time is concerned, is nevertheless involved in guilt for the faults of his generation. The wording suggests the connection with the religious doctrine of the fall of man. Finally, we see in the passage Hesse's characteristic optimism on an individual plane. Just as Brahms and Wagner can work their way out of the purgatory they have created for themselves, so can the individual work his way through the layers of impediments in the surrounding world and arrive at a genuine expression of his latent personality as he responds to the manifestations of *Geist*.

Since humility and a sense of humour may both be ranked among the moral virtues, it may perhaps be not altogether irrelevant before leaving this passage in *Steppenwolf* to refer to the following paragraphs. The vision of the predicament of Wagner and Brahms causes in Hesse, or rather in his hero Harry Haller, a nightmare spectacle in which he too is condemned to drag after him thousands upon thousands of similar black figures: all those words he had written that were superfluous, all the typesetters and their hours of futile toil, the labours of proofreaders, the wasted time of readers.[5]

It is characteristic of Hesse that he rejects all music after Beethoven, while Thomas Mann is fascinated by the musical trend which begins with Beethoven and culminates in Wagner and ultimately in Schönberg and the fictitious Adrian Leverkühn. Yet it is Hesse who is often curtly dismissed as an unhealthy, introspective, Romantic poet, while the world weighs gravely (not without reason) every pronouncement of Thomas Mann. We are all familiar with the latter's fascination with the spell of Romanticism, death and decay in communion with love and beauty. Even in his last cosmic encounter with this theme in *Dr. Faustus,* aware though he is of the inherent pitfalls, dangers, and disasters, Mann nevertheless leaves us with the implicit assumption that great art is possible only under these conditions and that perhaps the ineffable beauty of such creative work may be worth the grim details on the other side of the coin, the side of life. In comparison with Mann at any rate, Hesse sometimes assumes the aspect of a pure classicist and he has in fact recently been described as a true spirit of the eighteenth century, the last exponent of a cosmopolitan, classical humanism.[6] Certainly Hesse is essentially a moralist, interested primarily in the ethical implications of music, its meaning and value for the individual human soul, and it follows that Hesse's music must have a firm rational structure. Borrowing psychological terms, one might say it is under strict control of the super-ego, whereas Mann's music tends to inhabit the realm of the id, the amoral and irrational aspect of life. But to learn the full import of music in man's moral life, as Hesse sees it, we must look more closely at his last great work.

## III

In the introductory chapter of *The Glass Bead Game,* Hesse paints a grim picture of our disintegrating civilization, in which

[5] This is a striking example of the autobiographical subjectivism which runs through Hesse's work. The hero, Harry Haller, who has this experience, we know to be too much of a dilettante to have written or published much if anything. But the hero is by this time so closely identified in our minds with the author that we feel no jar at this reference.

[6] R. C. Andrews, "The Poetry of Hermann Hesse," *German Life and Letters* (Jan., 1953).

again music plays a symptomatic role. He sees nothing of value achieved in music in this age of ours: even the works of the "immortals," Bach and Mozart, are disfigured in performance by the effort to gain mass emotional appeal through dynamic effects, as conductors vie with one another to give more forceful renderings of the classical masterpieces. Productivity in music as in the other arts comes to a standstill, because of the *cul-de-sac* along which music has been travelling, towards utter anarchy, the breakdown of all forms leaving only the meaningless chaos of dynamism per se. However in the midst of this complete breakdown of all cultural forms and traditions there arise hopeful lights in isolated individuals who, in reaction against the trend of the times, become skilled musicologists penetrating to the spirit of the classical composers. From these beginnings, i.e. from the spirit of classical music, arises the "Glasperlenspiel" itself.

The "glass bead game" is the magnetic pole around which revolves the life of the cultural *élite* of Castalia. It is a synthesis of all the arts and humanistic studies, and it is significant that music and mathematics were predominant in its genesis. For music, according to Schopenhauer, is the dynamic will itself and constantly strives to break the bonds of form and return to its primeval state of chaotic energy. But Hesse clamps a Kantian moral will upon the would-be formless energy of music, in the guise of mathematics, the most formal, rational, and precise aspect of human intelligence. Eventually all the other humanistic disciplines share in this cultural synthesis which is the "Glasperlenspiel." Music is subdued, the demonic force of Schopenhauer and of Thomas Mann is bridled and made the servant and subtle instrument of intellect, *Geist*.

On the other hand, Hesse's music, deprived of its demonic, dynamic, and amoral element, is perforce sterile. Whereas Adrian Leverkühn and the Germany symbolized by him stride onwards and upwards (or perhaps downwards) in the tormenting spiral of heightened creativity, Hesse's "Glasperlenspieler" in their austere intellectual atmosphere are not only devoid of original creativity but actually have a horror of any tendency in this direction. For Hesse, genuine music, *echte Musik,* is to be found only in the sixteenth, seventeenth, and eighteenth centuries, marked by emphasis on the fugue and on counterpoint. This music underwent almost miraculous development in the hands of Monteverdi, Purcell, Scarlatti, Bach, Handel, Haydn, and Mozart. In their hands it came to express the ultimate human moral values while remaining within the confines of the strictest form.

Hesse regards form in art as simply an expression of faith, not necessarily a religious faith but at least faith in humanity. He wrote in a letter in 1932: "There can be no form without faith, and there can be no faith without prior despair, without prior (and also subsequent) knowledge of chaos." The last part of this statement indicates the extent to which Hesse has penetrated the problematic aspect of natures such as Bach and Mozart (and Goethe). Personal faith, morality, genuine art are not attained lightly, and the more gifted the personality the more desperate the struggle. Nothing irritated Harry Haller, the "Steppenwolf," so much as the conventional portrait of the calm, Olympian Goethe, which suggested nothing of the preceding depths through which he had passed. But these "immortals" of the classical centuries did not surrender to the threatening chaos and human despair that beset them. They fought their way through to a recognition of the supremacy of *Geist,* order and form, reason and morality.

The problem of form in music finds Thomas Mann on similar ground. It is one of the central preoccupations of Adrian Leverkühn who shares some of Hesse's misgivings at contemporary trends in music. Leverkühn realizes too the necessity of reimposing strict form and he also realizes he must go back to the earliest period, the sixteenth century, the age of Luther, in order to rediscover the necessary formal elements. But he does this with his tongue in his cheek. The Luther-parody makes this relationship clear. Leverkühn wants the stricter form only in order to be able to give greater sway to the dark and demonic forces. He reaches out for the form without the spirit. This is suggested by his incapacity for love, his coldness, and the palpable frigidity of the devil. He combines this strict form with the most revolutionary and destructive content, and he does it all without inner faith or conviction. Therefore he can never escape the limits of parody. In Hesse's terms this music of Leverkühn would be *unecht,* ungenuine and amoral. Thus we see that, starting from the same problem of musical form, Hesse and Mann once again emerge on different territory.

One of the key terms used by Hesse to convey the essential meaning of genuine music in its moral connotations is *Heiterkeit.* Any translation must necessarily lose some of the important overtones in Hesse's context. "Serenity" suggests calm, quiescence, passivity, and has no connotations of activity, responsiveness, cheerfulness, and gaiety all of which the German term adumbrates. Another important constituent is "balance." *Heiterkeit* connotes the transcending of dissensions, such as the conflict between *Geist* and *Natur,* and it implies a state of happy equilibrium. The supreme example is the old *Musikmeister* who is literally transfigured in *Heiterkeit* before his physical demise. He exemplifies all the virtues in music and in life. From one of his favourite ancient Chinese sages, Lü Pu Wei, Hesse in a letter in 1934 quoted the following dictum which later also found its way into the first volume of *The Glass Bead Game*: "Perfect music has its cause. It is born of equilibrium. Equilibrium arises from a meaningful universe. Hence one can talk of music only with one who has perceived the meaning of the universe." Thus we see the relationship in Hesse's mind between "perfect" or "genuine" music and that balance which results from recognition of meaningfulness in the world. It is no mere coincidence that the perfect music of the eighteenth century found its fulfillment in the age of rationalism and humanism, of the moral philosophers Shaftesbury and Leibnitz, in an ordered, harmonious universe. The obverse is evident. To Hesse the world today is meaningless and has quite lost its moral virtue as a symbol and guide.

There is, furthermore, a direct connection between music and the political organization of society, for the latter of course reflects the state of morals. The Chinese sage records that the tenor of music was regarded as a direct expression of the temper of morals and politics: "In legendary China . . . a leading role was accorded music in the life of the nation and the court; the welfare of music was directly equated with that of culture and morals and the state of the realm." The degeneration of moral and political life is mirrored in the debasement of genuine music which is replaced by a false dynamic expression lacking all *Heiterkeit*:

> Lü Pu Wei is informed on Wagner too, the pied piper and favourite composer of the second German Empire and still more of the Third Reich: "The more Saturnalian the music, the more dangerous becomes the nation, the deeper sinks the ruler" etc. Or: "Intoxicating such music is, to be sure, but it has departed from the nature of true music. Therefore this music is not serene [*heiter*]. If music is not serene, the populace grumbles and a blight descends upon life" and "The music of a well-ordered age is controlled [*ruhig*] and cheerful [*heiter*] and the régime equable. The music of an un-

easy epoch is excited and excessive and its régime is awry. The music of a decaying state is sentimental and sad and its régime is imperilled.[7]

In the well-ordered world of the Castalian *élite* of *The Glass Bead Game,* the spirit of seventeenth- and eighteenth-century music reigns supreme. Hesse suggests that there is no scarcity of this musical material, for the labours of conscientious generations of musicologists have uncovered a wealth of unknown or forgotten manuscripts, and in the case of the familiar monuments of the period they have penetrated through the false encrustations of subsequent generations to the original spirit of the work in its own time. There is such a wealth of this "genuine" spiritual and intellectual music that no need is felt in the Castalian world for any additions and the ban on creative activity is in force in music as in the other arts. What this world has accomplished can be described as an extension of the influence of this highly moral and intellectual music into all the realms and activities of life. The glass bead game itself is a sort of improvisation in which "genuine" music themes are "played" in variations architectural, mathematical, poetical, etc., comprising a sort of encyclopaedic counterpoint of all the arts and studies. It has developed, we are told, "into a sublime cult, a *unio mystica* of all the discrete members of the *universitas litterarum.*" Like eighteenth-century music, it is a subtle combination of fancy and suggestion with strict formal control. But it is not merely the cultural institution of the game which is an extension of the spirit of this music. The Castalian order and its way of life represent the transference of the values of this music into daily living and social and political intercourse. The Castalian historian of *The Glass Bead Game* writes: "We believe that in what we today call classical music we have understood and taken over as model the secret, the spirit and the virtue and the devoutness of those generations." At the end of his résumé of the institution of the game, the historian states that it is basically a "playing of music" (*Musizieren*) in the sense of the words once spoken by the central figure in the work, Josef Knecht, on classical music, its meaning and its connection with life, its moral basis:

[7] *Briefe* (Frankfurt, 1951), 137–38; also repeated, in part verbatim, in *The Glass Bead Game:* "Everywhere among the older Chinese writers he came upon the praise of music as one of the original springs of all order, morals, beauty and health, and this broad and moral conception of music had long since become familiar to him through the music-master who could be considered its very embodiment."

We consider classical music the essence and epitome of our culture, because it is its most meaningful and most characteristic expression and gesture. We possess in this music the legacy of the ancient world and of Christendom, a spirit of cheerful and courageous devotion, an unexcelled code of chivalrous conduct. For in the last resort every classical gesture of a civilization signifies a moral code, a model of human conduct contracted into a gesture. Between 1500 and 1800 many kinds of music have been composed, styles and means of expression were most diverse, but the spirit, rather the morality, is everywhere the same. The human attitude expressed in classical music is always the same; it is always based on the same kind of supremacy over chance. The gesture of classical music signifies:— awareness of human tragedy, acceptance of man's fate, courage, cheerful serenity [*Heiterkeit*]. Whether it be the grace of a minuet by Handel or Couperin, or sensuality sublimated into a delicate gesture as in many Italians or in Mozart, or the calm composed readiness for death as in Bach, there is always in it a challenge, a deathless courage, a breath of chivalry and an echo of superhuman laughter, of immortal *Heiterkeit*. Thus it shall ring out in our "glass-bead games" and in our whole life, work and suffering.

Thus far the implication has been that Castalian life and classical music, its symbol and model, represent perfection in life and art. But as we read on, it becomes increasingly apparent that the world of the "Glasperlenspiel" is in fact imperfect and especially because it is deficient in vital qualities. It is important to recognize in this connection the non-Utopian, realistic aspects of Hesse's work. Hesse himself has denounced the preoccupation with its chiliastic qualities and has insisted that Castalia and the glass bead game are symbols for what is here and now, always has been, and always will be: namely the community of art and intellect and its subject-matter, human culture, the eternal *Geist*.

Josef Knecht becomes increasingly aware of the defects and the dangers threatening Castalia. They result from a spreading hybris among the human beings who comprise the Castalian world: the assumption their world is static, perfect, complete, in a state of *Sein*. But the human vessels and institutions serving *Geist* are themselves inevitably involved in the historical process, in *Werden*. This process can only be retrograde when men and institutions are morally unprepared to face the repeated challenge.

What is it that brings Knecht to this insight? It is music again. This perception arises first from that quality of music described above, its constant struggle, its awareness of the abyss and of human tragedy: "Wachsein am Rande des Abgrundes," "Wissen um das Chaos," "Trotzdem." A prime quality in music is its constant battle with the material forces of dissolution, chaos, and anarchy, the necessity of subjecting this matter to form.

There is, however, another quality of music which is even more enlightening to Knecht, for music is itself change, process, "becoming," the very opposite of *Sein*. It fills space and time to which it gives form and meaning, but without ever lingering. It must constantly surge forward bringing light to darkness, meaning to senseless matter. This musical analogy, Knecht later realizes, lay subconsciously behind his composition *Transzendieren* which he later modestly rechristened *Stufen*. In the later crises of his life Knecht recalls this poem and especially these lines:

> Wir sollen heiter Raum um Raum durchschreiten,
> An keinem wie an einer Heimat hängen,
> Der Weltgeist will nicht fesseln uns und engen,
> Er will uns Stuf' um Stufe heben, weiten.[8]

This moral lesson from music, the necessity of change and rebirth, the transience of the material things of life, of man and his institutions, is reinforced by another aspect of music: its embodiment of *Geist* which is eternal and finds its expression in all human beings and their achievements. Another of Knecht's poems closes with these lines:

> Denn auch in uns lebt Geist vom ewigen Geist,
> Der aller Zeiten Geister Brüder heisst:
> Er überlebt das Heut, nicht Du und Ich.[9]

Early in his life Knecht had been awakened to the presence of *Geist*, when as a boy he heard the old *Musikmeister* improvise a fugue for him. As he had listened to the message of *Geist*, he had resolved to

---

[8] The writer freely but imperfectly renders the German verses:
　　　Serene and full of cheer we spur the chase
　　　And ever onwards stride through time and space
　　　And nowhere cling as to a home of yesteryear.
　　　The *Weltgeist* will us not restrain and tie:
　　　His purpose is to raise and magnify
　　　Us stage by stage beyond the hemisphere.

[9] For in us too lives spirit of the eternal spirit that is kin with the spirits of all ages: It is this spirit that survives the transitory moment, not you and I.

dedicate his life to its service: ". . . it seemed to him as if he were today hearing music for the first time. Behind the musical edifice that arose before him he felt the spirit [*Geist*], the beneficent harmony of law and liberty, of serving and swaying; he surrendered and dedicated himself to this spirit and this master." Music suggests the brotherhood of man through the potential share of each human soul in universal and eternal *Geist* and it suggests that the individual's dedication to the service of *Geist* can be, and should be, also to the service of his fellow-man. When Knecht faces the final crisis of his life—the apparent conflict between his duty to the rarefied form of *Geist* cultivated by the Castalians on the one side and his duty to mankind on the other—he has a long conversation with his friend from the outside world, Designori. He tells Designori that the genuine "Glasperlenspieler" (i.e., artist or intellectual) "should above all possess the *Heiterkeit* of music, which is after all nothing else but courage, a serene, smiling striding and dancing onward right through the horrors and flames of the world, a solemn and festive offering of a sacrifice." To emphasize the moral lesson in this musical analogy, Knecht sits down and plays for his friend a movement from the Purcell sonata that had been a favourite of Pater Jacobus (in whom we recognize the Swiss philosopher and historian Jakob Burckhardt):

> Like drops of golden light the sounds descended in the stillness, so softly that between them could still be heard the song of the old spring murmuring in the court-yard. Gently and insistently, temperately and sweetly the voices of the gracious music met and entwined with one another; bravely and serenely they paced out their intimate dance through the nothingness of time and transitoriness and made the space and the nocturnal hour wide and infinite as the universe for the short spell of their duration.

Like Purcell's music, Josef Knecht strides on, brave and serene, into the world of chaos and transcience, and in thus dedicating himself to the dual service of eternal *Geist* and ever-changing man, his life is not in vain. As he succumbs in the icy water of the mountain lake, his message, the message of *Geist* itself and of service to humanity, takes hold and glows never to be extinguished in the heart and mind of his pupil Tito. Just as the notes of Purcell's music filled the stillness "like drops of golden light" and danced their way brave and serene through the emptiness of transient time, so young Tito catches the glow of *Geist* in his master Knecht and dances in the golden light of the sun rising over the mountain rim. This, we are told, was not a dance familiar to him, nor was it invented by him as a rite to celebrate the sunrise, and only later was he to realize that his dance and his trance-like enthusiasm had been occasioned not merely by the mountain air, the sun, and the early morning feeling of freedom, but even more by the transformation and impending development in his young life heralded by the impact of the friendly but venerable figure of the former Magister Ludi, Josef Knecht. Thus it is implied that the *Geist* which is manifest in music and which is epitomized in the Purcell sonata is carried over into life, into Knecht's life of serenity and service, and after him in the life of young Tito.

Music is the key to the role of Knecht and of his pupil Tito in the interpenetration of life and intellect, *Leben* and *Geist*. The normative moral character of music is brought out most clearly in the life and death of the old *Musikmeister* who is the guiding spirit in Knecht's life. While still alive the *Musikmeister* is transfigured and translated into virtual sainthood. This almost mystical symbolism denotes the ethical import of music in the life of one wholeheartedly dedicated to its service:

> It was a life of devotion and labour, but free from compulsion and free from ambition and full of music. And it seemed as if, by becoming a musician and *Musikmeister,* he had chosen music as one of the ways to the highest goal of mankind, to inner freedom, to purity, to perfection, and as if, since choosing this path, he had done nothing but let himself become more and more penetrated, transfigured and purified by music, from the clever, skilled harpsichordist's hands and teeming, titanic musician's memory into all parts of his body and soul, even to his pulse and breathing, even in his sleeping and dreaming, and that now he was a virtual symbol, or rather an embodiment, a personification of music.

Hesse's music, "genuine" music, has then a pre-eminently moral character. It has a rational basis and it is formative and ordering in life. It is both symbolic of the meaning and purpose of human life and of man's relationship to the things of the spirit and at the same time it is a concrete guide to moral action and the virtuous life. The life of the old *Musikmeister* is one of devotion and service to music and through music he serves the highest aims of mind and spirit and at the same time exemplifies the highest virtues in life.

His life under the aegis of music is a constant progression on the path to sainthood.


## IV


We have earlier glimpsed some of the similarities in the attitudes of Hesse and of Thomas Mann to music. Both, we saw, are aware of the dark, demonic forces of chaos and anarchy that underlie music and both have a somewhat similar view of the historical development of Western music. But a sharp divergence is evident in their views of Beethoven and the subsequent course followed by nineteenth-century composers. This difference rests on the fact that Mann accepts these modern developments and the greater dangers of the demonic element entailed in them, while Hesse rejects all this later music on the ground of its demonic and amoral character, its increasing surrender to the anarchic forces of chaos, and its abandonment of its high ethical mission. Mann, on the whole, is unconcerned with the moral nexus of music. He implies that the highest aesthetic attainment in music must, especially today, involve moral compromise of the most dubious sort. Hesse believes the highest art is intimately bound up with the highest virtue. On this question he is again a disciple of the eighteenth century and in virtual agreement with such philosophers as Shaftesbury and Schiller who envision moral good and aesthetic beauty as forming a sort of *unio mystica* at the core of human culture. It may be that Mann, with his exploration of the dark demonic world, is more modern, more interesting, more subtle, more bold psychologically. It is true we need to know the dark places of the subconscious in order to be in a better position to cope with them. Thomas Mann serves us well here. But if we are looking for a normative influence and a healthier one to serve us in life and in art, we would do well to pause and listen to Hermann Hesse. Despite pessimism where the immediate future developments of society are concerned, Hesse is suffused with a fundamental optimism based on the undying potentialities in every human individual. The difference between Mann and Hesse is well exemplified in the equally significant and symbolic roles of the devil in *Dr. Faustus*[10]

[10] Whether Mann's devil be accorded any degree of fictional reality or be regarded purely as a figment of Adrian's imagination, an emanation of his subconscious, matters little for the purpose of our comparison of his symbolical role with that of the saintly *Musikmeister* in Hesse's work.

and the beatified *Musikmeister* in *The Glass Bead Game*. Each has a corresponding function in the life of the hero. Adrian Leverkühn's demonic mentor leads him away from virtue and humanism towards the ultimate in modern musical creation. Josef Knecht's mentor starts him on the path that is one of service to the highest ideals in music and in life. Adrian's mentor remains in his infernal element to which he drags down his victim. Knecht's mentor reaches a virtual apotheosis of sainthood to which he is drawing his disciple. The one ends in hell while the other is headed for heaven, a goal which may be unattainable for finite mortals but which is nevertheless worth striving for.

# Hermann Hesse and the
# Over-Thirty Germanist

*by Jeffrey L. Sammons*

For the Germanist of my own age, over thirty but not yet too far over, the great enthusiasm for Hermann Hesse among younger people poses a vexing dilemma. For the fact is that many of us, with important exceptions, do not think that Hesse is a writer of the first rank, and some of us who are concerned to develop a critical perspective on literature and its relationship to life and society are not able to look upon Hesse in a very positive light. Since there is little pedagogical profit in choosing for a subject for teaching a topic about which students are enthusiastic, only to denounce it, we find it hard to tell whether and how to teach Hesse at all. Nor is this purely a generation conflict. My experience with graduate students is that they quickly become impatient with Hesse. He does not appear to hold the attention even of younger people of literary experience and with some knowledge of the German tradition and its problems.[1] The Hesse boom, as has repeatedly been observed, is primarily an American phenomenon, thriving where awareness of the German tradition remains weak. Studies of Hesse in America

"Hermann Hesse and the Over-Thirty Germanist," by Jeffrey L. Sammons. © 1973 by Jeffrey L. Sammons. Used by permission of the author. This article appears for the first time in this volume.

[1] With undergraduates I have found that the most serious and articulate of the Hesse enthusiasts are almost always disciples of Jung. For such an audience a critique of Hesse involves a larger confrontation with Jungian principles, for which I am unequipped due to my inability to concentrate on the subject. I find its irrationalism, its metaphorical and aesthetic reading of personality, its indifference to history and social context, and what appears to me a form of occultism, arbitrary and impenetrable. I have come to understand that this uncongeniality has much the same roots as my inability to appreciate Hesse. Bringing both Hesse and Jung into a criticism of Central European neo-Romanticism is, I am convinced, the only serious way to treat the controversy. The present argument hovers on the periphery of such a purpose.

over the last half-dozen years outnumber German studies by a
factor of three to two, and I see no evidence that Hesse has any
standing among West German students, although there are some
straws in the wind suggesting that this may change.

Some of the professional objection to Hesse is on artistic grounds.
Hardly anyone has tried to argue that Hesse is outstanding as a
stylist. Even Ernst Robert Curtius, who wrote an admiring essay
on Hesse in 1947, was obliged to admit that there is no spark in his
prose, and compared it to the amateurishness of his watercolors.[2]
As for Hesse's verse, Ronald Gray has shown in some detail how
trivial it normally is in rhythm and rhyme, diction and nuance.[3]
It is true that admirers of Hesse, such as Mark Boulby,[4] make
much of the interlaced structure of his themes. But it is one of the
failings of academic criticism that it does not always ask whether
the themes woven into artistic structures are themselves worthwhile.
There are some writers who write as though their intention were to
make interpretive dissertations convenient, who invite an analysis
of thematic pattern simply because their perception of the world
is conceptually thin, thus yielding material for analytic criticism
but not necessarily meeting very high standards of humane letters.

Now it is doubtless true, as Theodore Ziolkowski has said,[5] that
the present popularity of Hesse's books is not due to their aesthetic
qualities. But the question of style cannot be easily dismissed, for
Hesse's stylistic mediocrity directs attention to other problems.
First of all, his characteristic stylistic posture is certainly willed.
There is a certain amount of vivid writing in *Steppenwolf,* here
and there in *Narcissus and Goldmund,* and elsewhere, while *Siddhartha* is, of course, exceptionally mannered, as is, to a lesser extent, *The Glass Bead Game,* of which Boulby has observed: "To
say that, generally speaking, [its language] lacks the poetic nuance
might be regarded as an understatement." [6] Boulby goes on to explain how this style fits in with the strategy of the book, and the

---

[2] Ernst Robert Curtius, *Kritische Essays zur europäischen Literatur,* 2nd ed.
(Bern: Francke, 1954), p. 161. [Reprinted here, pp. 34–50—Ed.]

[3] Ronald Gray, *An Introduction to German Poetry* (Cambridge, Eng.: Cambridge University Press, 1965), pp. xx–xxvi.

[4] Mark Boulby, *Hermann Hesse: His Mind and Art* (Ithaca: Cornell University
Press, 1967).

[5] Theodore Ziolkowski, "Saint Hesse among the Hippies," *American-German
Review,* 35 (1969), p. 20.

[6] Boulby, *Hermann Hesse,* p. 299.

studied conventionality of Hesse's style elsewhere is related to his intellectual and cultural allegiances. But aspects of his style arouse mistrust in some critics sensitive to the German language and the uses to which it has been put. Jost Hermand drew some remarkable parallels between Hesse's style and that of the most trivial and self-indulgent novelists of the time, and while Hermand exempts Hesse from some of the worst sins of these writers, it is clear that the relationship is too close for comfort. For Hermand, the stylistic strategy signifies an intentional meaning:

> One can observe that every possible dilemma, every conflict situation, every fundamental decision is evaded from the outset, in order not to be diverted from the consciously harmonized feeling of life. Most of these vagabonds are strictly opposed to thoughtful reflection. They wish to know everything only from the heart, instead of concerning themselves once in a while with the intellect. "Reflection and thinking about things has no value," says Knulp, "and one does not, after all, do what one thinks, but really takes each step quite impulsively, just as the heart wills." Consequently, what they offer as maxims are usually awful platitudes. Woe to them, if one skewers their profound-sounding aphorisms and strips them of their Romantic atmosphere.[7]

Hermand is speaking here specifically about the figure of the Vagabond, represented in Hesse by Knulp and Goldmund, and the objections would not fit all of Hesse in quite this form, but, in making such observations, one sees how directly one comes from style and sense to content and intent.

Hermand, incidentally, is not wholly unsympathetic to the posture of protest found in writing of this kind. "No one," he says, "will hold it against the Romantic ne'er-do-wells or today's flower people that they continually oppose the desolating consequences of the modern economic world with the yearning for 'a more genuine humanity' that has gone into history under the heading of 'Romantic utopian anticapitalism.'"[8] Indeed it is not difficult to understand Hesse's current popularity from this point of view. Signs of a certain elective affinity began to appear some years ago.

---

[7] Jost Hermand, "Der 'neuromantische' Seelenvagabund," *Das Nachleben der Romantik in der modernen deutschen Literatur: Die Vorträge des Zweiten Kolloquiums in Amherst/Massachusetts,* ed. Wolfgang Paulsen (Heidelberg: Lother Stiehm Verlag, 1969), pp. 112–13.

[8] Ibid., p. 114.

Hesse himself tells in 1958 of a young American who wrote him after having read the seven volumes of the collected edition and concluded: "Allow me to say that you have not invented anything; rather, you play the role of a magician, you remind your readers of their own half-forgotten memories." [9] One scholar who has addressed himself to the matter, Eugene Timpe, gives as the reason for Hesse's popularity that he is an "author of mind-expanding works," and he quotes a student opinion that Hesse "writes about troubled people trying to maintain individuality in a society which forces conformity." [10] To a generation that was reading Kerouac, Ginsberg, and Corso, Hesse also seemed to give expression to the opposition to bourgeois materialism and conventional morality, to speak for "vagrancy and amorality." [11] There is a good deal of plausibility to this, although Hesse was a man of fastidious tastes and would not have cared much for some of the literary and cultural company he has been found in recently. The psychedelic Hesse is a distortive view, reflecting what Timpe called "the students' tendency to use the text as a justification for speaking about themselves." This is, he says, the "therapeutic quality" of Hesse to which he has no objection, although one might consider that a literary object that encourages apprehension in this way fits one of the fundamental definitions of *Kitsch*.[12] It is a kind of literary perception that tends to lose sight of its object and overlooks particularly the historical and ideological resonances in Hesse's analysis of and resistance to modern society.

There is one queer paradox in Hesse's life and opinions. We know that he was a difficult child. At age six he was so obstreperous that his father thought of putting him into a foster home. Hints of his rebellion against his parents are found in a muted way here and there in his novels. Like other sensitive children of his time who were to become writers, Hesse suffered grievously from school as soon as he entered puberty. His fictionalized account of his school days, *Beneath the Wheel* (1906), belongs to an important genre of

[9] *Hermann Hesse-Peter Suhrkamp Briefwechsel 1945–1959*, ed. Siegfried Unseld (Frankfurt am Main: Suhrkamp Verlag, 1969), pp. 384–85.

[10] Eugene Timpe, "Hermann Hesse in the United States," *Symposium*, 23 (1969), p. 77.

[11] Ibid.

[12] Cf. Jochen Schulte-Sasse, *Die Kritik an der Trivial literatur seit der Aufklärung: Studien zur Geschichte des modernen Kitschbegriffs* (Munich: Wilhelm Fink Verlag, 1971), esp. pp. 22–24.

school novels that includes, among others, the Hanno episode in Thomas Mann's *Buddenbrooks* (1901), Heinrich Mann's *Professor Unrat* (*The Blue Angel*, 1905) and parts of *Der Untertan* (*The Vassal*, 1918), and Robert Musil's bloodcurdling *Verwirrungen des Zöglings Törless* (*Confusions of the Schoolboy Törless*, 1906). Hesse ran away from one school and employment after another, aggressively rejected his bewildered parents, and did not begin to make some measure of peace with his environment until a year and a half of largely therapeutic activity as an apprentice clockmaker beginning at age seventeen. It certainly looks like the childhood of an incipient dropout, and that is what Hesse became, although in a sense perhaps not always well understood in this country. What is odd, first of all, is the contrast between this clearly distraught boyhood and the nostalgic view of the organic wholeness of the childhood world that supervenes in his writings or the dreams of "heroism and fame and sacred artistry," of the "timelessness of the beautiful," that he remembered from his schooldays.[13] Wherever there is a village milieu in Hesse, it is formed on the model of his childhood home, Calw on the Nagold. The ambivalence appears explicitly in *Demian:* "My goal in life was to become like my father and mother, so bright and pure, so superior and orderly, but the way there was long, in the meantime one had to sit through schools and study and pass tests and examinations, and the way led continuously beside and through the other, darker world, and it was not impossible that one should get stuck in it and sink into it."[14]

When Hesse began to come out of his deep adolescent crisis in the spring of 1895, we find him turned resolutely away from anything modern. During the chaos of puberty there were already signs that, instead of straining forward, as adolescents normally do, toward the independence of adulthood, he began to long for the state of childlike innocence. In his teens, Hesse's interest in contemporary literature was limited; he drew gloomy support for his own pessimistic state of mind from Turgenev and read the utopian socialist Edward Bellamy's *Looking Backward* (1888) mainly, it seems, to shock his parents. Like many young men, he read and

---

[13] Bernhard Zeller, *Hermann Hesse: Eine Chronik in Bildern* (Frankfurt am Main: Suhrkamp, 1960), p. 23.

[14] Hermann Hesse, *Gesammelte Werke in zwölf Bänden: Werkausgabe Edition Suhrkamp* (Frankfurt am Main: Suhrkamp, 1970), V, 11. All translations of Hesse in this essay are my own.

admired Heine, but naïvely and primarily to nourish his self-pity. But the important turn in late nineteenth-century Germany to a literature of European significance found him at first skeptical, then hostile. "Praise God," he wrote in April, 1895, "I am converted to faith in the beautiful, in Goethe, Schiller, and antiquity, I have ceased admiring Ibsen and Turgenev." [15] He complained that the theater was becoming realistic and was no more an asylum of idealism, and that Ibsen and Gerhart Hauptmann were performed instead of Lessing—a contrast, incidentally, that is not altogether just to the latter. In May he wrote a poem entitled "Consolation," inspired, as he said, "by my warm hatred of Socialism." [16] He had made "a shift to the right, which I have not yet regretted." [17] In June he wrote that "a new art is trying to come into being and the opinions are strictly divided. I stand with the old party against the new." [18]

It is a remarkable stand for an eighteen-year-old, and thus the nature of Hesse's protest against society is quite different from that which comes naturally to a contemporary American or European student. Today's restless youth are pursuing, in various ways, a progressive utopia. It takes many different forms: political and radical, individualist, antiauthoritarian, hallucinatory, and so on. Common to most of the forms is that they are not rooted to any substantial degree in the past; the Romantic enthusiasm for Oriental and Indian culture, as well as the somersault from radical individualism to radical dismantlement of the personality, although they have clear analogues in the past, are on the whole innocent of any historical sensibility. We professors sometimes deplore this and call it "presentism." However that may be, and although Hesse slides continuously in and out of various patterns that seem at first intelligible to contemporary readers, the fact is that he is neither a "presentist" nor a progressive utopian, but one who in thought and feeling is firmly oriented toward the past.

Hesse's long career passed through several stages and several modes of expression. Two themes, however, remain fairly constant and fundamental from beginning to end: the inner way and the

---

[15] Ninon Hesse, ed., *Kindheit und Jugend vor Neunzehnhundert: Hermann Hesse in Briefen und Lebenszeugnissen 1877–1895* (Frankfurt am Main: Suhrkamp, 1966), p. 450.
[16] Ibid., p. 466.
[17] Ibid.
[18] Ibid., p. 483.

search for wholeness. Both belong to contexts that, although found in all modern societies, are especially central in German intellectual history. In order to perceive their resonances, it is necessary to give some attention to the German tradition into which Hesse determinedly placed himself. He had little profit from formal schooling and was essentially a self-educated man; nevertheless, his allegiances are by no means idiosyncratic in the Germany of his time. The inner way and the search for wholeness are aspects of a criticism of modern society with sources in the resistance to the developing phenomena of the modern world in German Classicism and Romanticism around the turn of the nineteenth century. As Hesse came out of his adolescent crisis in the mid-1890s, he began a lonely and isolated time during which he read deeply in this tradition. This reading was the formative cultural experience of his life, and indeed one that was not very different from what he would have acquired had he gone through a normal course of university education, for Goethe, Schiller, and the Romantics were the axis of German *Bildung*—although, to be sure, Hesse's point was the opposite, that he could learn as much by himself as at the university.[19] For all that he protested against the vulgarization of *Bildung*, especially in *Steppenwolf*, he shared its assumptions: that in this unparalleled flowering of German culture, along with its assimilation of Classical antiquity, Renaissance art, and Indic studies, were to be found the guidelines for responding to and evaluating the experience of the present.

The transplantation of the effort of German Classical-Romanticism to find an alternative for society into the crises of the early twentieth century is the key to neo-Romanticism, of which Hesse is one of the major exemplars. It may be seen most clearly in *Steppenwolf*, for despite the change Harry Haller undergoes in his way of dealing with the strains between the ideal and the real, nothing has been altered in his secularized and aestheticized scheme of redemption. Salvation and truth lie in exactly the same place at the end as at the beginning: in the heritage of high culture, in that immortal community of Moses and Christ and Buddha and Lao-Tze; Dante, Goethe, and Novalis; Bach, Haydn, and Mozart; the metahistory of the great religious and literary creators, the great painters and composers. Except for Dostoevsky and Nietzsche, there

[19] Ibid., p. 499.

is scarcely an artist or thinker to whom Hesse alludes who lived later than the 1830s. These spirits are in a profound sense all alike, insofar as they are in touch with the one and all, that timeless realm where the poles of opposites touch and spark ethereal comets. This fraternity hovers above life and history, and it is only with infrequent intermittence in touch with the feeble and shabby emanation that is our environment. Harry Haller believes this at the beginning, and the truth of it is demonstrated to him at the end.

There is much in the neo-Romantic revival that is of immediate appeal to today's youth culture. The German intellectuals at the time of the French Revolution sensed the alienation that the disruption of traditional culture would bring and the potential in a liberal, individualistic society for putting every man at war with every other and splitting society into belligerent interest groups. The renowned German *Humanität* was a valiant effort to find a cultural and moral substance that would hold society together and prevent it from shattering into the frenetic battlefield on which we find ourselves today. The trouble was, however, that, since there was no political life or even any politics to speak of in the Germany of that time, there was no real need to take cognizance of the pressures of reality; and even reality itself, the grubby and gritty substance of the imperfect that offends us in our everyday life, became a pejorative word and something to be avoided in the purity of the realm of the spirit. Thus the German tradition became, in one of its main currents, antimodern and antidemocratic. The solutions to the dilemmas of the modern world were found in a desperate hold in the status quo or in a historical, premodern situation. Since there was no way in which these regressive utopias could be maintained in the face of history, a wedge was driven between the higher culture of the mind and the development of society. Ultimately this led to the spectacle of a bourgeoisie claiming to draw its inspiration from *Humanität* and Romantic inwardness while at the same time tolerating and from time to time encouraging the increasing barbarousness of German society and politics, with results that are only too well known. The conclusion to be drawn from this experience is that classical *Humanität*, Romantic inwardness, and allegiance to the timelessness of high culture, for all that they enrich the human experience, are inadequate guides to responsible and intelligent social and political attitudes. But Hesse drew the opposite conclusion, that the German vision was of immutable perfection, and if the world could not order itself on this vision, then so much the worse for the world.

It is against this background that the two themes of the inner way and the search for wholeness need to be seen. "The way within," a phrase that occurs many times and in many variations in Hesse, is an echo of Novalis and the famous dialogue in the second part of *Heinrich von Ofterdingen:* " 'Whither are we going?' 'Always home.' " The way home is a journey into the interior soul, just as *The Journey to the East* is a journey to an Eastern realm to be found only in the integral balance of an inner soul that is eclectically imbued with traditions of high culture. Hesse's orientation toward the quietist inwardness of Indian religion is a part of his paradoxical relationship to his childhood heritage; his grandfather was a student of Indian dialects, his father a missionary obliged for reasons of health to abandon his activity in India. Hesse's pursuit of the transcendental spiritualism of Indian and, later, Chinese wisdom undoubtedly has much to do with his popularity in the youth culture; but Americans may not notice how much this interest has been amalgamated with German Pietism, the other major cultural inheritance from his family. While Romanticism tended gradually toward a Roman Catholic universalism, Hesse's Protestant, Pietist heritage, for all his bitter denouncement of it during his rebellion against his parents, maintained his Romanticism in an individualist and escapist mode. Explaining the title of his first book of prose, *An Hour Beyond Midnight* (1899), Hesse wrote: "I wanted to suggest the realm in which I lived, the dreamland of my poetic hours and days, which lay somewhere between time and space." [20] The amalgamation of Indian and Pietist inwardness engenders a tenuous relationship to reality. It is well known that Hesse's journey to the real India in 1911 was a disappointment to him, as one easily might have predicted. Somewhat parallel was his effort to live out another neo-Romantic enthusiasm, Tolstoy's mysticism of the impoverished, soulful peasant life—an impulse that caused Hesse to relive a similarly misconceived experiment of Heinrich von Kleist in 1802. With the rueful honesty characteristic of Hesse, he was obliged to report: "The peasant life was fine, as long as it was a game; when it had grown to be habit and duty, the pleasure in it was gone." [21] The point

[20] Zeller, *Hermann Hesse*, p. 31.
[21] Hesse, *Gesammelte Werke*, X, 147.

here is that in the Romantic tradition, the effort to cultivate the inner man with delicacy and refinement spills over into a social attitude, so that society is judged from a determinedly asocial and individualistic position. Thus Hesse can write that the secret Germany that lives in Jean Paul has been overcome by a modern, soulless Germany.[22] However, in the first place this claim for an ideal, inward Germany is not only pure mysticism, but, because it ignores the social reality of which Jean Paul was a symptom, it can serve reactionary points of view; and, in the second place, the persistently blockaded modernization of Germany in the nineteenth century was primarily responsible for the soullessness Hesse lamented. It is characteristic of his sensibilities that he compared the first house he rented in Montagnola to "the country manor of an Eichendorff novella,"[23] and what the contemporary admirer of Hesse needs to do is to acquaint himself somewhat with Joseph von Eichendorff and decide for himself whether that is the sort of attitude toward society he would wish to share.

The inward way is a search for spiritual integrity, or, to put it another way, for the overcoming of neurosis. Hesse was well aware of the ambivalence of this endeavor. He wrote, shortly after his seventy-fifth birthday, to his publisher Peter Suhrkamp: "My life . . . strives thoroughly for the way within, for the center, in contrast to the centrifuge in which the world lives, and even if I find nothing in the center other than my own disquiet, nevertheless I must and will experience just this disquiet and possess it, without anesthetizing it."[24] Here, as so often when one tries to follow Hesse's thinking, he slips out of analytic focus. The inner way is supposed to be a way to a resolution of the restless dialectic of existence, but if it indeed leads only to the implacable, unresolved disquiet, what then is its advantage over the centrifuge of the world without? To argue only that the disquiet is my own individual possession is not a sufficient reason for recommending the inner way as the salvation of man and society.

For what of the centrifuge, Hesse's metaphor for the world without? It is a word that he uses several times to characterize the life of Suhrkamp, who, although physically broken during his imprisonment by the Gestapo, labored with iron self-discipline to

[22] Zeller, *Hermann Hesse*, p. 117.
[23] Hesse, *Gesammelte Werke*, X, 153.
[24] *Hesse-Suhrkamp Briefwechsel*, p. 226.

build a publishing house that would meet the highest standards of intellectual responsibility. The firm not only put Hesse back into circulation after the war, but in the course of time it earned him large sums in royalties, a matter in which Hesse was by no means disinterested and which brought out, in the early letters of the correspondence, a mean side of him rarely seen. The word "centrifuge" expresses pity for Suhrkamp's harassed way of life, but also some of the condescension of the sage at the this-worldly turmoil in which the publisher was involved. This pitiable and disreputable turmoil is the life of man in society, that part of human existence that is beneath the concern of the wise man. The inner way escapes and withdraws from it; the search for wholeness transcends it and discovers the cosmic unities that ultimately govern the world.

This search for wholeness, to which every one of Hesse's major works bears testimony, probably does not arouse active uneasiness in the ordinary American reader. It may seem natural enough in a world beset by atomization, abrasive conflict, and lovelessness in the life of both the individual and society. Neoradical theories of alienation, the emergence of communes, love-ins, and whatnot, along with some important aspects of the drug culture, attest to the felt need for a more unified perception of the world and a more harmonious interrelatedness of people and things. But to anyone sensitive to such matters in the German tradition, the theme is acutely troubling. For it is one thing to seek after unity in the world or in our perception of it; it is another to postulate ultimate unity and to regard all disharmonies as regrettable excrescences or ignorable and trivial aspects of an unimportant "reality." It is not wholly clear just where Hesse stands in this matter. When, in 1955, he won the Peace Prize of the German book industry, the citation spoke of his "deeply experienced knowledge of the unity of creation" and his effort to "uncover ever anew the harmony of the world," [25] a mystifying ideology the function of which is to veil the contradictions in society. Hesse's speech on this occasion is a little evasive, for it concentrates on peace in human relations, but there is reason to think that he shared this view of his own activity. We find a pursuit of a harmonious, Romantic nature mysticism early in his career, in *Peter Camenzind* (1904): "I wanted

[25] Ibid., p. 437.

to make you ashamed to know more of foreign wars, of fashion, of gossip, literature, and the arts than of the springtime." [26] In his essay on Dostoevsky of 1920, Hesse speaks of the new man, Russian man, who seeks the divine and sacred in all aspects of reality, accepting everything, not making distinctions between good and evil.[27] *Siddhartha* ends with "the smile of unity above the streaming configurations";[28] the Steppenwolf is obliged to dissolve into a *"unio mystica,"* [29] a phrase that appears again in the explication of the Bead Game in *The Glass Bead Game;*[30] the journey to the East "is the becoming one of all ages";[31] the Music Master in *The Glass Bead Game* explains that it is the task of the members of the Castalian Order to "see opposites as the poles of a unity," [32] and so on and on.

Now the one thing that Goethe, Schiller, and the Romantics knew about modern society was that it was coming apart. They knew well enough that this was happening because the stresses of inequality and injustice were becoming intolerable to people who had come to believe, through the agency of the Enlightenment, that the misery of human life was largely unnecessary and could be relieved. But the German thinkers did not agree that it could be relieved by direct action; they believed, and the course of the French Revolution seemed to bear them out, that the active, rational reconstruction of society would only make things worse and that the important thing was to find an ideology that would keep the existing society dynamic but intact. As Heine said of Friedrich Schlegel, they did not see in the stresses of modern times the pains of rebirth, only the agony of a dying culture.[33] Thus emerged the initially aesthetic concept of the organic metaphor, according to which society, and often the universe, is, or should be, like a biological whole, not stressful, but harmoniously organized, each part, each

[26] Hesse, *Gesammelte Werke*, I, 453.

[27] See the valuable explication of this essay in Theodore Ziolkowski, *The Novels of Hermann Hesse: A Study in Theme and Structure* (Princeton: Princeton University Press, 1965), pp. 17–24.

[28] Hesse, *Gesammelte Werke*, V, 470.

[29] Ibid., VII, 359–60.

[30] Ibid., IX, 37.

[31] Ibid., VIII, 38.

[32] Ibid., IX, 83.

[33] Heinrich Heine, *Die Romantische Schule, Sämtliche Werke*, ed. Ernst Elster (Leipzig and Vienna: Bibliographisches Institut, [1887–90]), V, 268.

human being, each social role in its place.[34] Thus Goethe's famous dictum that he would rather tolerate injustice than disorder;[35] thus the Romantic mythology of one harmonious imperium under one Church; thus the renunciation of the Enlightenment as a foreign element and the failure of democratic liberalism to strike roots in the intellectual community; thus the mystique of *Bildung* and the abdication of the bourgeois intelligentsia from the cause of progress. The men of Germany's golden age are not to be blamed for this; they were attempting to find solutions to a situation that was certainly baffling and discouraging. But the use made of the organic metaphor through the nineteenth century and up until the advent of Fascism made it a dubious legacy indeed. The chief mischief it caused was to make the Germans incapable of dealing with the class conflict and of constructing a society that would accommodate it. Class conflict was simply impermissible, for society was to be a harmonious, organic whole.[36] Although Nazism can hardly be called either harmonious or organic, many Germans thought it would be. Hesse never saw the connection between totalitarianism and the organic metaphor; he wrote to Thomas Mann in the spring of 1933: "The more *Gleichschalten* [the Nazi phrase for the complete coordination of society] becomes the slogan, the more fervently I hang on to my faith in the organic." [37]

[34] It is instructive to observe how the formation of Soviet literature and criticism for the purpose of defending a unitary ideology and a conservative view of existing society involved both the organic metaphor and an unspecific, generalizing style. Since this comes about on premises differing wholly from those of Hesse, it suggests that organicism is a valid touchstone of illiberal ideology in literature. See Robert A. Maguire, "Literary Conflicts in the 1920s," *Survey*, 18 (1972), 98–127.

[35] Goethe, *Belagerung von Mainz, Werke,* ed. Erich Trunz, et al. (Hamburg: Christian Wegener, 1959), X, 391. It is sometimes pointed out on Goethe's behalf that he made this utterance while preventing a mob from lynching some partisans of the French Revolution fleeing from reconquered Mainz. But the point can be turned around again, for clearly Goethe correlated "justice" with the stringing up of republican revolutionaries.

[36] On this point I have had some quarrels with undergraduates in regard to the figure of Kromer in *Demian*. Students will argue that Kromer cannot be taken as an independent character; he is the "Shadow" in the Jungian scheme of the book, an aspect of Sinclair's self that needs to be internalized. Whatever Hesse's intention, I am not sure that the text wholly supports this view. But, even so, the explicitness with which Hesse presents Kromer as a proletarian, whose evil and violence are accounted for as a threat of a working-class adolescent directed against a boy of the protected and prosperous bourgeoisie surely suggests something about the class base of the novel and its audience.

[37] *Hermann Hesse-Thomas Mann Briefwechsel,* ed. Anni Carlsson (Frankfurt

Peter Gay, describing the intellectual situation of the Weimar period, has called the syndrome the "hunger for wholeness." [38] For some time after the turn of the century, up to the First World War and beyond, this hunger generated among German and Austrian intellectuals a quantity of irrationalism, mystagogy, mythopoesis, assaults on science, democracy, and civilization, and sheer crackpot lunacy that strains belief, although today it seems that we are condemned to recapitulate some of it. Americans who really would like to learn something about this from literature would do well to lay Hesse aside and take up Robert Musil's novel *The Man Without Qualities,* which is three times as long and ten times as difficult as any book of Hesse's, but a great deal more profitable. Furthermore, unlike such contemporaries as Musil, Thomas Mann, or Hermann Broch, Hesse appears to have made little effort to understand the modern civilization and society he so deplored, and consequently any assent to his cultural critique will share a striking lack of precision. Hesse's characteristic stance before his environment and civilization is one of uncomprehending bafflement, which does not prevent him from firm denunciation.[39] Examples abound in *Steppenwolf.* What Harry Haller calls "jazz" is the very substance of the horrid vulgarity of the modern environment, when compared with the high idealism of classical music, but what he here

---

am Main: Suhrkamp, 1968), pp. 31–32. Radical individualism and organicism are somewhat awkward companions. In Hesse they are related in an eventually Jungian and primordially Goethean triadic hierarchy of separation, individuation, and reassimilation to the whole (cf. Ziolkowski, *The Novels of Hermann Hesse,* pp. 52–60). It is a major pattern with many important variants in modern thought. Ideologically, however, it has a self-serving potential, as, for example, the theory and practice of "free enterprise" shows; it requires, therefore, to be handled with intellectual rigor. Hesse's manipulation of this trap-ridden dialectic seems to me hazy and elusive.

[38] Peter Gay, *Weimar Culture: The Outsider as Insider* (New York and Evanston: Harper & Row, 1968), pp. 70–101.

[39] Cf. Hesse's reaction in *A Guest At the Spa* to objects displayed in a shop window, things "concerning which I do not dare say anything, since I could not fathom their nature and purpose despite long contemplation; many of them seem to serve the cultic needs of primitive tribes, though this may be an error, and altogether they make me sad, for they show me all too clearly that, despite all my willingness to gregariousness [*Sozialität*], I nevertheless live outside the bourgeois and real world, know nothing of it, and will really understand it as little as I will ever be able to make myself understood to it, despite all my long years of writing effort" (*Gesammelte Werke,* VII, 45). The passage continues in this vein for several pages. There is here a superlative complacency and hubris in this parade of willful noncomprehension.

abominates is not really jazz, but popular big-band dance music. It is true that this distinction was not very sharply made in the twenties, except by connoisseurs; nevertheless, Hesse was so appalled by modern culture that his alter ego flails away at an enemy of which he has a very superficial understanding. Haller's apparent reconciliation with Pablo and his music does not change much here, as can be seen in regard to that infamous radio that Mozart comes up with near the end of the novel, "the devilish tin horn" that "spits out that mixture of bronchial mucus and chewed rubber that the owners of gramophones and the subscribers of the radio have agreed to call music." [40] Mozart's reply is one of the key passages in the novel; reduced to its essentials, it is a recommendation of a Platonic view of the world, in the popular sense of the phrase. Imperfect and grubby as reality may be, one can discern the outlines of the ideal behind it and orient one's self through the dark and distorting glass toward the essential. The primeval spirit of things is indestructible and can be felt and sensed, even through the technological horror of the radio.

So far as the radio itself is concerned, Mozart agrees with Haller; it is true that the divine music is hidden and distorted behind, as Mozart puts it, the "hopelessly idiotic veil of this ridiculous machine." [41] Some of us may indeed feel a horror of technology that is loosely akin to Hesse's, so that we sense some gratification in the automobile hunt of the Magic Theater. But it is the perfectibility of technology, its autonomy, and the investment of a dehumanized faith in it, that gives us worry, not its imperfection, its distortion of its intention. The radio scene shows a profound failure to comprehend technology and its élan. Within less than ten years the complaint of bronchial mucus and chewed rubber would be wholly irrelevant, and in the age of high fidelity it appears ludicrously quaint. Hesse has a completely undynamic view of the radio; he sees in it only a fixed object, an evil plaything, the trash of a pseudoculture; he does not sense in it that intimation of expandable horizons that, rightly or wrongly, fascinated large numbers of people, especially young people, in the infancy of technology. Today we laugh at the boy-loves-tractor school of Soviet socialist realism, but this is only a matter of cultural lag; the love affair of older generations with the machine was a real and very human

[40] Hesse, *Gesammelte Werke,* VII, 406.
[41] Ibid., p. 407.

attitude. The vision here is not only conservative, it is blindered; it fails to focus upon the true shape of the problem. Hesse's lack of comprehension of the world whose rejection he insists upon could be demonstrated at length upon the inept account of the "feuilletonistic age" that is given at the outset of *The Glass Bead Game.*

At this point, a digression on Hesse's politics may be useful. Like so much else in him, the simplicity of his views creates complications. Hesse had, as far as I can see, one and only one political opinion: he was against war, and in this he was unusual in his time and appealing in our own. It is a sad commentary on the state of German and European society at the time of the First World War and afterwards that he had to suffer so much abuse for his pacifism. While the hunger for wholeness tends ordinarily to be associated with national chauvinism, anti-Semitism, and a thirst for war as a welcome holocaust that will cleanse society of philistinism and capitalism, in Hesse it is associated with gentle-spiritedness, a hatred of militarism, and a longing for amity among men and nations. This speaks for the refinement of his spirit, but in the circumstances it may suggest a certain lack of logic in his thinking; there is some evidence that this is so, especially during and after the Third Reich.

There is, I think, a simple key to Hesse's grim aloofness from any kind of political commitment: he tended to identify politics with militarism. He suggests this several times, most clearly in a passage near the end of the main narration of *The Glass Bead Game,* in which Knecht laments the politicization of intellectuals, which he equates with their cooptation into a militaristic cause.[42] There was some reason, in Hesse's time, to hold such an opinion, and there may be in our own, but it cannot, on the other hand, be said to be a very subtle one. Thomas Mann, who came to a relative degree of political enlightenment the hard way, tried tactfully in a letter of April, 1945, to make Hesse understand that "refusal is also politics; with it one aids the politics of the bad cause," [43] but he got nowhere. Hesse, who lamented Mann's public denunciation of Nazi Germany in 1936, refrained from making any similar statement because he was anxious not to be banned, in the conviction that his books would provide solace and a link to the higher things of the spirit amid the Nazi barbarity. He certainly believed this about his own books; in a rather rude and unfeeling letter to

[42] Ibid., IX, 394.
[43] *Hesse-Mann Briefwechsel,* p. 105.

Suhrkamp shortly after the war he criticized the publisher's postwar
plans to produce books that would throw some critical light on the
recent past, saying that what the people amid the ruins of Germany
needed was not "educational books and wise instruction, but
nourishment; apart from Mann and Hesse, reissue of Goethe,
Mörike, Eichendorff." [44] In 1948, while Mann was wearily speaking
out against the Red scare and the initial phases of what was to be
McCarthyism in the United States, Hesse reported with pleasure
that a musician had turned the letters of his name into a passacaglia
and fugue, and that a student had translated his poems into Gothic;
this is evidence, he observes, that the "fabulous, fairy-tale Germany,
whose demise has so often been asserted," was still alive "like the
root of an enchanted tree." [45] This political insensitivity is characteristic of him and appears also in his complacent resignation as
the tragic Weimar Republic was staggering to its end.[46] Hesse was
not alone among liberal-minded Germans in his exasperation with
the Weimar Republic, but in retrospect we can see that the failure
of intellectuals to stand by it, with all its dreadful shortcomings and
evil complicities, was a lethal error. The pity of it appears in a
letter of April 21, 1933, in which he says that he does not regret the
collapse of the Republic because it was not a living thing—an argument derived from the organic metaphor and often found in conservative and Fascist agitation—and he predicts fatuously that "it
will be a fruitful school for the German spirit when it again comes
into open opposition to the official Germany." [47] It is necessary to
remember that, by the time this school was closed, fifty-five million
people had been killed.

But to inquire after a writer's political opinions and actions is
not necessarily the only way to get at the question of his political
relevance. The vehicle of ideology is language: the way it is used,
its echoes and resonances in its time, the relationship between
thought and expression, between expression and human activity.
This is especially true in the neo-Romantic period, when there was
a vast cacophony of rhetoric and phrase-making, a paradoxically
shrill mysticism that sought any conceivable alternative to democracy and progress. In the recent analyses of Peter Gay, Fritz K.

[44] *Hesse-Suhrkamp Briefwechsel*, p. 11.
[45] *Hesse-Mann Briefwechsel*, pp. 151–52.
[46] See letters of February 20, and December, 1931, ibid., pp. 12, 18.
[47] Ibid., p. 27.

Ringer, and Jost Hermand,[48] we can see what a witches' sabbath of the intellect it was and how its irrationality made the advent of Fascism less surprising and less undeserved than many Germans since have wanted to believe. Hesse was, to be sure, a quieter man, and he did possess an instinctive sense for the worst excesses of pernicious nonsense. Sometimes he mounted a fairly coherent attack on the nonsense, such as in the often-quoted and somewhat unexpected passage in *Steppenwolf* in which the spirit of German music as a surrogate for reason is subjected to a sharp critique. Unfortunately, he is often a cliché-ridden writer, and it is the provenance of these clichés that is a cause for concern. Two examples are prominent enough in his writing to deserve some remarks.

One of these is the *Führer* principle. So to denominate it is perhaps to muddle it. But its permutations are widespread in neo-Romanticism, which developed to an extraordinary degree, following the tradition of historiography exemplified by Heinrich von Treitschke, the theme of the great, creative personality who stands above common morality and moves the world by the force of his elite genius. The ideological purpose of this theory is to counteract the analysis of the dynamics of class in the course of history. Hesse puts a pure example of this into the mouth of Demian: "If Bismarck had understood the Social Democrats and made an arrangement with them, he would have been a clever ruler, but not a man of destiny. So it was with Napoleon, with Caesar, with Loyola, with all of them." [49] Indeed, *Demian* ends with the word *Führer,* and the novel celebrates the amorality of the elite man with the mark of Cain for whom the rest of mankind is trash: "Surely," says Pistorius, "you will not regard all the bipeds running around on the street as human beings, just because they walk erect and carry their children for nine months." [50] The theme reappears in the Tractate of *Steppenwolf:* "We are not here talking about man as he is known by the academy, by economics, by statistics, not of man such as those running around on the streets by the millions and

[48] Gay, *Weimar Culture;* Fritz K. Ringer, *The Decline of the German Mandarins: The German Academic Community 1890–1933* (Cambridge, Mass.: Harvard University Press, 1969); Jost Hermand, *Literaturwissenschaft und Kunstwissenschaft: Methodische Wechselbeziehungen seit 1900,* Sammlung Metzler, M41 (Stuttgart: Metzler, 1965).
[49] Hesse, *Gesammelte Werke,* V, 145.
[50] Ibid., p. 106.

who are no more to be regarded than sand in the sea or the drops
of the surf; a couple of million more or less do not matter, they
are material, nothing more." [51] It is in the light of such careless use
of an inhumane cliché that Hesse's critique of the bourgeoisie must
be seen, for the Tractate continues shortly afterward: "A human
being who is capable of comprehending Buddha, a human being
who has a sense for the heavens and the depths of humanity, should
not live in a world ruled by common sense, democracy, and bourgeois culture." [52]

There is a continuous pattern in Hesse of subordination to a
superior, wiser authority. The will to rebel is, to be sure, always
present: Siddhartha and Goldmund insist on finding their own
route through the world; Sinclair is so uncertain within that he
has difficulty in following Demian; Haller resists for a long time
the primitive, elemental authority of Pablo; and Knecht, when he
breaks out of the Castalian order, is accused of wishing to choose
his own master. Hesse apparently could not see how parochial this
dilemma of individualism was. The model is the utopia of the
"Pedagogical Province" in Goethe's *Wilhelm Meister's Journeyman
Years,* which marshals ingenious repression in order to balance the
two desiderata of awe for authority and of developing the potential of the inner person. Nothing astonishes me more than the
popularity of this vision among a generation that is purportedly
agitating for freedom and emancipation, and I am troubled by the
suspicion that there may be a desire to replace a decrepit principle
of authority by a new and different one.

*The Glass Bead Game* indicates that Hesse moved more rather
than less in this direction. The hero's name is programmatic
enough; *Knecht* does not only mean "servant," but, originally,
"vassal"; it is cognate to English "knight" and the adjective
*knechtisch* means "servile." Josef Knecht goes from one *Führer* to
another, and if he does remain his own man and eventually breaks
out of the order, it seems that these decades of selfless subordination are necessary to the flowering of his own exceptional self. It
is hard to judge this because the narrative perspective of the novel
is so blurred. But, in his letter of resignation from the order,
Knecht reinforces his faith in the elite of great men: "In the history
of society it is always a matter of the effort to form a nobility, it is

[51] Ibid., VII, 248.
[52] Ibid., pp. 248–49.

society's peak and crown, and some kind of aristocracy, of a rule of the best, seems to be the actual if not always admitted goal and ideal of all attempts to form a society." [53]

The principle of service that Knecht's name underscores also evokes malaise because of the ease with which it can be made congruent with totalitarian purposes. The narrator of *The Glass Bead Game* speaks of the "blessed harmony of law and freedom, of serving and ruling," [54] a wholly totalitarian phrase, while of music he says that its function is to bring people together "in the same rhythm," [55] a role of music that is exemplified in the first of Josef Knecht's fictional autobiographies, "The Rainmaker." Critics differ as to how these autobiographies relate to the sense of the whole, but it is evident that in all of them Knecht turns to the authority of a wise man and eventually subordinates himself. How far this obsession with service and sacrifice can go appears in a letter of July, 1933, in which Hesse, to Thomas Mann's astonishment, said that he was moved by the "blue-eyed enthusiasm and readiness for sacrifice" that he had detected in the letters of young Nazi enthusiasts.[56] Mann, jolted for once out of his characteristic gentlemanly tolerance, replied, "so much stupidity is no longer permissible." [57]

The other complex I would call the apocalypse of the bourgeois society. I have said earlier that the hunger for wholeness did not generate in Hesse the thirst for holocaust, a loud insistence that only a cleansing bloodbath could clean the trash out of bourgeois society and restore heroism and purity. This tone is, however, deposited in Hesse's writings. Again *Demian* is the most offensive text:

> The soul of Europe is an animal that has been chained up for an infinitely long time. When it is freed, its first movement will not be the most amiable. But the paths and detours are of no importance, if only the true emergency of the soul comes to light, which for so long has ever again been lied and anesthetized away. Then will come our day, then we will be employed, not as *Führer* or new lawgivers —we will not live to see the new laws—but rather as volunteers who are ready to go along and stand wherever fate calls. You see, all men

[53] Ibid., IX, 382.
[54] Ibid., p. 54.
[55] Ibid., p. 29.
[56] *Hesse-Mann Briefwechsel*, p. 34.
[57] Ibid., p. 35.

are ready to do the incredible when their ideals are threatened. But
no one is around when a new ideal, a new, perhaps dangerous and
weird stirring of growth knocks at the door. We will be the few
who are around and go along. That is why we bear the mark—as
Cain was marked to arouse fear and hatred and to drive mankind of
that time out of the narrow idyll into the dangerous expanses.[58]

I confess that I have difficulty distinguishing this rhetoric from that
of the early years of the S.S. into which the spirit of apocalyptic,
elitist heroism eventually flowed. Even Mark Boulby was obliged
to say in this connection that "the attempt to equate the self-dis-
covery of the individual with the destruction of the old Europe
undeniably involves Hesse in the jargon of the neo-Nietzschean
evolutionists, Ernst Jünger, Moeller van den Bruck, and the rest,
with whose baneful preoccupations he was in reality so little in
sympathy." [59] But this to me is what is so exasperating. If a writer
is indeed obligated to the spirit, as Hesse so endlessly preached,
then his first duty should be a sensitivity to language and its
humane employment, not simply to be an indiscriminate blotter
that absorbs uncritically all the hysteria and nonsense that may be
in the air at the time.

Indeed, Hesse's susceptibility to such things may well account for
the phenomenal success of *Demian* among the bewildered young
veterans of the German defeat of 1918. The novel attempts to re-
cover and transvaluate the betrayed faith with which the men of
that generation went to war. The war, it turns out, is not what it
might have appeared by that time, a hoax perpetrated on the
nations, a bankruptcy leaving waste and void behind. It was what
the generation of 1914 thought it was: the great upheaval, the
cleansing holocaust, the revolution of the condition of man. It is
true that most of those who went to war were unable to understand
its nature, for they bore a sign unlike the mark of Cain; they were
heroic and intoxicated in love and death, but their heroism was
impelled by a communal ideal imposed on them, not derived from
within. How many of Hesse's readers grasped this fine distinction
is impossible to say. But that a certain proportion of them were
able to assent to the novel without at all sharing Hesse's pacifist
and internationalist convictions is surely probable. His fictions are

[58] Hesse, *Gesammelte Werke*, V, 144–45.
[59] Boulby, *Hermann Hesse*, p. 119.

in such a state of flux that readers at various times and places have been able to reform them for their own ends.

The sound of the apocalypse is heard in *Steppenwolf* also, although there it is all part of the experiment of the inner man, and consequently one does not know where to draw the line between the inner phantasmagoria and real existential choice. Here, as in other European writers of the time, there is the denunciation of the semilife of the bourgeois world, a longing for violence and the gratuitous antisocial act, along with a substantial urge to be destroyed: "The world must go smash and we with it." [60] *Steppenwolf* is the only book in which Hesse experiments with the ecstasy of violence and slaughter, although there are slight premonitions in a smaller compass in *Narcissus and Goldmund*. The destructiveness belongs, of course, to a psychodrama that takes place within the confines of Harry Haller's own skull, which is why *Steppenwolf* is Hesse's most comic book. But one may fairly ask if it is responsible or intelligent for an author of such profound pacifist convictions to give tongue, even as part of an aesthetic game, to bloodthirsty imaginings that were meant by others in dead earnest and were soon to be realized in a very concrete way.

Hesse is, by any severe artistic or intellectual standards, a minor writer, although a not uninteresting one if regarded with proper skepticism and a sufficient knowledge of his context. For all his high-mindedness and humaneness, his consciousness unwittingly reflects ideological positions that have had catastrophic consequences. The substance of his writing is not mainly artistic, but priestly and homiletic, and he was not intelligent enough to wrestle effectively with the issues he raised. There is always a kind of shrinkage in Hesse from the consequences of the doctrines he is experimenting with; they are blunted by crossing them with incompatible doctrines,[61] or they are made ultimately inconsequential by being placed in a play of the imagination that is intransitive because it is hermetically sealed from the detested world outside. His effect is to sugar-coat the dynamite of the German irrational tradition, and there is plenty of evidence that when that tradition is turned into pablum, those who overindulge in it are likely to wake up with a cosmic stomach ache.

[60] Hesse, *Gesammelte Werke*, VII, 376.

[61] For example, on the conflation of Nietzschean with Christian attitudes, see Ziolkowski, *The Novels of Hermann Hesse*, pp. 105–7.

# The Quest for the Grail in Hesse's *Demian*

## by *Theodore Ziolkowski*

Few twentieth-century novels have announced themselves as a search for identity more programmatically than Hermann Hesse's *Demian* (1919). "I have been and still am a seeker," the narrator states in his Prologue. And later he tells us that "an enlightened man had but one duty—to seek the way to himself, to reach inner certainty." To say, then, that the search for self is the essential theme of *Demian* is to belabor the obvious. The question for the literary critic is not *whether* the quest plays a role in Hesse's thought and works, but rather *how*. For the function of the writer is not merely to state a theme or idea, but to give it a form, an aesthetic shape. Let us begin by examining the plot of *Demian*.

In this first-person account, a young man named Emil Sinclair relates certain stages through which he passed in the years between 1905 and 1915 as he followed the "road toward himself"—a road marked by a series of detours and obstacles. The ten-year-old's first excursion into the world involves him with a blackmailer, from whom he is delivered by an older boy named Max Demian. After this shattering experience Sinclair retreats into the sanctuary of his childlike innocence for several more years and scarcely notices his liberator. When they are brought together in a confirmation class, Demian tries to startle Sinclair into consciousness by challenging him to think independently about the deeper meaning of the Bible stories discussed in class. But Sinclair's naïveté, coupled with his awe for the older boy, prevents him from entering Demian's private world, about which he has heard "too many legends and secrets." When he is sent away to school at fourteen, Sinclair, having forsaken the values of his Pietist home and found none to replace them, slumps into a life of cynical profligacy. His feelings toward

"The Quest for the Grail in Hesse's *Demian*," by Theodore Ziolkowski. From *Germanic Review*, 48 (1973). Reprinted by permission of the editors of *Germanic Review*.

Demian during this period fluctuate ambivalently between longing and hatred. He is finally rescued from this wastrel's existence
when he becomes infatuated with a girl he sees in a park. As he
tries again and again to paint her portrait, he realizes that it
increasingly resembles Demian. Around this time he meets a
lapsed theologian named Pistorius, whose knowledge of myth and
religion helps to clarify many of the mysteries to which Sinclair
was first exposed by Demian. By this point Sinclair realizes that the
meaning of his life is inextricably bound up with Demian, but all
his efforts to make contact with his former friend fail until he goes
to the university. Here for the first time he meets Demian's mother,
Frau Eva, who strikes him as the fulfillment of all his dreams. In
their home he is initiated into a circle of intimates, all of whom
are united by their faith in the religious rebirth of the individual
and the impending spiritual renewal of society. This idyll lasts for
about a year. When the war breaks out, both Demian and Sinclair
join the military. In the spring of 1915, Sinclair is wounded and
taken to a first-aid shelter, where he wakes up to find his friend
on the adjoining mattress. Demian, dying, gives Sinclair a farewell
kiss—from himself and from his mother. But by this time Sinclair
has found a source of sustaining values within himself. Now able to
survive in the world without the support of his friend, he continues
the struggle for the beliefs to which they both cling.

Hesse has repeatedly stated that the religious impulse is decisive
in his life and works. "During my entire life I have sought the religion that would be suitable for me. For although I grew up in a
home filled with genuine piety, I could not accept the God and the
faith that were offered to me there. . . . It was my way to search
first of all on a very individual level, that is, to seek my own identity
and to develop insofar as possible into a personality. Part of this
story is told in *Demian*." [1] In an essay entitled "A Bit of Theology"
(1932) Hesse outlined the quest for faith and identity according to
a more elaborate three-stage process.[2] The path of humanization, he
observed, begins with innocence. "From there it leads into guilt
and into the knowledge of good and evil, into the demands of
culture, morality, religions, human ideals." Anyone who seriously

---

[1] Letter of February 23, 1935; Hermann Hesse, *Briefe*, Erweiterte Ausgabe
(Frankfurt am Main: Suhrkamp, 1964), p. 137.
[2] "Ein Stückchen Theologie," *Gesammelte Schriften* (Frankfurt am Main:
Suhrkamp, 1957), VII, 388–402.

experiences this second level ends in despair—the realization that
virtue cannot be achieved, that justice is unattainable. "This
despair," he concludes, "leads either to destruction or to a third
Kingdom of the Spirit, to the experience of a condition beyond
morality and law . . . or in short: to faith." According to Hesse
this pattern is virtually universal: he detects it in Brahmanism, in
Buddhism, and in the teachings of Lao Tse. In every case "the way
leads from innocence into guilt, from guilt into despair, from
despair either to destruction or to salvation." Humanity has traced
this course of development hundreds of times in splendid images.
The most familiar one is, of course, the path leading from Adam in
Paradise through the Fall to the redeemed Christian.

Now it is clear that this triadic rhythm underlies Emil Sinclair's search for identity: he too lapses from the innocence of his
childhood into a despair produced by the knowledge of good and
evil; and this despair ultimately gives way to a new and higher
faith in himself. But since Hesse felt that this three-stage quest
amounts to the archetypal model for all human experience, it
provides the pattern for all his novels and is therefore in no sense
distinctive in *Demian*. If we hope to say anything useful about this
novel in particular, we must quickly pass beyond the general
archetypal situation to inquire about the myth's form in this specific
case.

The myth of the quest means many things to many men. The
theme is so pervasive, in fact, that some scholars have argued that
it determines virtually all mythic and literary patterns. According to
Joseph Campbell the "monomyth" underlying "the hero with a
thousand faces" can be reduced to a "formula represented by the
rites of passage: *separation—initiation—return*." [3] In a study of
"Mythic Patterns in the Literary Classics," Harry Slochower claims
that all myth addresses itself to one of three topics: Creation,
Destiny, and the Quest.[4] And Northrop Frye suggests that all the
principal literary genres amount to "episodes in a total quest-
myth." [5] But if we are to move from this general conception of
primal myth—which coincides fully with Hesse's notion of the

[3] *The Hero with a Thousand Faces* (New York: Bollingen, 1965), p. 30.
[4] *Mythopoesis: Mythic Patterns in the Literary Classics* (Detroit: Wayne State
University Press, 1970), p. 15.
[5] *Anatomy of Criticism* (1957; reprinted New York: Atheneum, 1966), p. 215.

three-stage process—toward its literary hypostasis in a particular work, we require a more specific pattern.

The archetypal myth of the quest has manifested itself in scores of mythological motifs ranging from the Argonauts' search for the Golden Fleece to Captain Ahab's pursuit of the Great White Whale. Howard Nemerov tries to persuade us that Faust is the most widespread Western embodiment of the myth,[6] while Alexander Gosztonyi finds in Orpheus' quest for Eurydice "the primal myth of all poetry."[7] But none of these distinctive patterns is helpful in connection with *Demian*. In any case, as John J. White has plausibly demonstrated, it is a methodological mistake to attempt to reduce any general archetype exclusively to a single mythological motif.[8]

We are aided in our own quest by the fact that Hesse is a writer in the German tradition; and the instinctive response of the German consciousness to the cue-word "quest" is almost totally predictable —it is Parzival and the Holy Grail. In his 1939 "Introduction to *The Magic Mountain*," for instance, Thomas Mann made no secret of his pleasure at learning from a young scholar-critic (Howard Nemerov) that his novel, published some fifteen years earlier, had all the hallmarks of the venerable tradition of the quester myth.[9] Aware that this myth is to be found in the writing of all peoples, Mann cites Faust as the most famous manifestation of the myth created in Germany. "But behind Faust, the eternal seeker," he continues, "stands the group of poems that bear the general designation of Sangraal or Holy Grail romances." And it is this Grail quester, specifically Parzival, the "guileless fool," who prefigures Hans Castorp, the hero of *The Magic Mountain*. A brief consideration of Goethe's *Wilhelm Meister* leads Mann to the sweeping conclusion that the entire tradition of the German *Bildungsroman* can be regarded as a "sublimation and spiritualization" of these ro-

---

[6] *The Quester Hero: Myth as Universal Symbol in the Works of Thomas Mann*, Ph.D. dissertation, Harvard University, 1940, p. 18.

[7] "Hermann Broch und der moderne Mythos," *Schweizerische Monatshefte*, 42 (1962), 211–19; esp. p. 214.

[8] *Mythology in the Modern Novel: A Study of Prefigurative Techniques* (Princeton, N. J.: Princeton University Press, 1971), pp. 45–51.

[9] "Einführung in den *Zauberberg* für Studenten der Universität Princeton," *Gesammelte Werke in zwölf Bänden* (Frankfurt am Main: Fischer Verlag, 1960), II, 602–617, esp. 615–17.

mances in which the legend of the Grail was originally embodied.

Mann is not an isolated example. In her lexicon of themes in world literature Elisabeth Frenzel observes that German writers of the past century have been fond of claiming this legend as "typically national" and of seeing in Parzival the epitome of "the German soul." [10] And Jost Hermand has shown that around the turn of the century in Germany the Grail-seeker, symbolizing the urge for spiritual renewal, emerged to take his place alongside such other representative types as the dandy of impressionism or the bohemian artist of naturalism.[11] The metaphysical reaction against nineteenth-century rationalism and positivism produced, in addition to an influential journal called *Der Gral* (from 1905) and various cultural or semireligious associations with such names as the "Gralsbund," a whole series of Grail-oriented writings: Karl Vollmöller's poetic cycle *Parcival* (1897–1900), Eduard Stucken's dramatic epic *Der Gral* (1901–24), Emanuel von Bodman's drama *Der Gral* (1915), or Will Vesper's novel *Parzival* (1911).

There is surely, among mythomaniacs and medievalists alike, no more hotly debated topic than Parzival and the Grail, and many a scholar has had his fingers seared. The story of Parzival's quest for the Grail is generally conceded to be a rather late syncretism of two separate narratives, one stemming from cultic ritual and the other from Indo-European folktales. In her book *From Ritual to Romance* (1920) Jessie L. Weston presented evidence that the legend of the Grail had its origins in a nature ritual associated with such vegetation deities as the Sumerian Tammuz, the Phrygian Attis, or the Greek Adonis. The purpose of the ritual, in each case, was to bring about and to celebrate the annual regeneration of the deity, whose death is synonymous with winter. In order to revive the

[10] *Stoffe der Weltliteratur. Ein Lexikon dichtungsgeschichtlicher Längsschnitte* (Stuttgart: Alfred Kröner, 1963) , p. 505. See also Wolfgang Golther, *Parzival und der Gral in der Dichtung des Mittelalters und der Neuzeit* (Stuttgart: Metzler, 1925); and Wolfgang Golther, *Parzival in der deutschen Literatur* (Berlin and Leipzig: DeGruyter, 1929).

[11] "Gralsmotive um die Jahrhundertwende," *Deutsche Vierteljahrsschrift für Literaturwissenschaft und Geistesgeschichte*, 36 (1962), 521–43; reprinted in Jost Hermand, *Von Mainz nach Weimar, 1793–1919* (Stuttgart: Metzler, 1969), pp. 269–97. Just to keep things in a proper perspective and to remind ourselves that the Germans have no exclusive claim to this mystical questing it might be pointed out that W. H. Auden has argued that the quest for the Grail is "the mirror image" of the modern detective story as a genre. See "The Guilty Vicarage" in *The Dyer's Hand and Other Essays* (New York: Random House, 1962), p. 151.

deity, the celebrants employed various symbolic objects with specifically sexual associations—notably a lance and a chalice. In medieval Europe this ritual was translated into Christian terms. The deity became "a King suffering from infirmity caused by wounds, sickness, or old age," and his infirmity, "for some mysterious and unexplained reason, reacts disastrously upon his kingdom, either depriving it of vegetation, or exposing it to the ravages of war." [12] The neophyte being initiated into the nature cult was christianized into the quester knight—originally Sir Gawain rather than Parzival—who revives the dead king by his ritual questions and thereby restores the land to fruitfulness. The traditional cultic objects were also given a new significance: the lance became the spear used at the crucifixion to pierce the side of Christ, and the chalice was transformed into the Holy Grail—the vessel used by Jesus and his disciples at the Last Supper. At some point in the process, presumably, the ritual origin of the legend was completely forgotten.

The wholly unrelated story of Parzival (or Perceval) is a variant of the Indo-European folktale formula of expulsion and return, known to classical antiquity from the stories of Perseus or Romulus and Remus. In the Welsh variant the hero is the son of a widow whose husband was slain in battle. The mother, anxious to preserve her son from a similar fate, flees to the woods, where she brings him up in ignorance of all knightly accomplishments and *courtoisie.* But the boy, encountering a wandering party of knights, is so fascinated by their allure that he deserts his weeping mother and sets out to become a knight. Arriving at Arthur's court, he succeeds in slaying the Red Knight and then, after a series of adventures, is admitted to the Round Table and wins back his father's heritage.

At some point, but probably no earlier than Chrétien de Troyes' late twelfth-century *Conte del Graal,* the two stories were fused together. Perceval displaced Gawain as the hero of the Grail legend, and the Grail legend, in turn, was expanded to include the Arthurian material—that is to say, Perceval's adventures in the years before and after his first visit to the Grail castle. If we accept Thomas Mann's suggestion that Parzival's quest for the Grail underlies the modern German *Bildungsroman*, then we have already moved out of the area of myth in any strict sense of the word into

[12] *From Ritual to Romance* (reprinted New York: Doubleday & Co., Anchor Books, 1957), p. 20.

the realm of literature. We are fortunate in being able to eliminate from our discussion a troublesome concept regarding which even ethnologists are unable to agree.[13] In German, notably, the term "myth" has assumed such mystical connotations that it has become virtually useless as a critical vocable of any precision.[14] Moreover, Hesse's attitude toward myth can be seen to vary considerably during his lifetime—from an early infatuation fed by Nietzsche, Jung, and the history of religions to a later skepticism informed by his study of history.[15] In short, we are well rid of myth. Instead, we are dealing with a relatively recent literary shaping of cultic and folklore motifs as defined by the medieval romances through which the story entered the mainstream of European culture—notably those of Chrétien de Troyes and Wolfram von Eschenbach.

Hesse's acquaintance with the medieval romances can be easily documented. In 1929 he stated that "the French, English, and German Christian heroic epics, notably those dealing with King Arthur and the Round Table, belong to the most beautiful works that the Middle Ages produced."[16] Hesse, whose knowledge of medieval literature and culture was quite extensive, had a number of these romances in his own library. Moreover, Grail motifs show up from time to time in his own works. An early story entitled "Chagrin d'Amour" (1908) is explicitly based on characters and situations taken from the second book of Wolfram's *Parzival*. And Parzival himself appears fleetingly as a figure in the fanciful *Journey to the East* (1932), where the Knight of the Grail is cited along with other quester figures from history and literature.

In addition, it is fairly safe to assume that Hesse was aware of the mythic implications of the Grail legend. The first quarter of the century was in general, and especially in Germany, an immensely fertile period for the scientific study of myth. No attentive reader—

[13] Cf. Mircea Eliade, *Myth and Reality*, trans. Willard Trask (1963; reprinted New York: Harper & Row, Harper Torchbooks, 1968), p. 5: "It would be hard to find a definition of myth that would be acceptable to all scholars and at the same time intelligible to nonspecialists."
[14] I have discussed this problem in my essay "Der Hunger nach dem Mythos: Zur seelischen Gastronomie der Deutschen in den Zwanziger Jahren," *Die sogenannten Zwanziger Jahre*, ed. Reinhold Grimm and Jost Hermand (Bad Homburg-Berlin-Zürich: Gehlen, 1970), pp. 169–201.
[15] I have sketched Hesse's attitude in an article, "Hesse, Myth, and Reason: Methodological Prolegomena," *Myth and Reason: A Symposium*, ed. Walter D. Wetzels (Austin: University of Texas Press, 1973), pp. 127–55.
[16] "Eine Bibliothek der Weltliteratur," *Gesammelte Schriften*, VII, 319.

particularly one with Hesse's interest in the history of religions—could fail to realize that a legend like that of the Grail quest touched mythic chords that lay well beneath the literary surface of the medieval romances. More specifically, the Grail legend was a lively topic of discussion during these very years in the circle around C. G. Jung. Jung's wife, Emma, devoted her entire lifetime to the writing of *The Grail Legend from a Psychological Standpoint*.[17] Jung himself observes in his autobiography that he became obsessed with the story of the Grail around the age of fifteen and makes it clear that he would have included a discussion of that central myth in his own writings if his wife had not already undertaken that analysis.[18] Now it is highly unlikely that Hesse, given his own interest in the Grail legend as well as contemporary studies of myth, should not have been aware of all this. Hesse underwent psychoanalysis in 1916 and 1917—just at the time he was writing *Demian*—with Josef B. Lang, a disciple of Jung. Lang, himself a remarkable student of oriental myth, was aware of the discussions in the Jung circle, and he was accustomed to share his ideas on such matters with Hesse.

Finally, Hesse's attitude toward literary and mythological motifs is characteristic of many modern writers, although he was not so playful as Joyce or Thomas Mann; yet, like them, he felt that myth and mythology constituted a common cultural possession that each generation must use according to its own needs. "The myths of the Bible, like all the myths of mankind," he once wrote, "are worthless to us as long as we do not dare to reinterpret them for ourselves and for our own times." [19] In other words, Hesse was familiar with the specific mythological motif in question, as well as its mythic implications; and it was absolutely consistent with his view of literature for him to employ it as a prefigurative device in a work of his own.

Assuming for the moment that this is indeed the case, by what criteria can we identify the specific mythologems of Parzival's quest for the Grail, as distinct from the general archetype of the quest and

---

[17] Emma Jung and Marie-Louise von Franz, *Die Graalslegende in psychologischer Sicht* (Zürich: Rascher, 1960); trans. Andrea Dykes, *The Grail Legend* (London: Hodder and Stoughton, 1971).

[18] C. G. Jung, *Memories, Dreams, Reflections*, recorded and edited by Aniela Jaffé, trans. Richard and Clara Winston (New York: Random House, Vintage Books, 1961), p. 165 and p. 215.

[19] Letter of April 13, 1930; *Briefe*, p. 30.

such other literary shapings of the quest legend as Faust or Orpheus? If we take as our basis the two finest and most familiar versions of the story—the romances of Chrétien and Wolfram—the narrative displays eight discernible and characteristic stages:

1. Parzival's secluded youth up to his encounter with the knights and his departure from his mother.
2. The arrival at Arthur's court: the slaying of the Red Knight and Parzival's instruction in courtly demeanor.
3. The first period of knight-errantry: liberation of a besieged city and wooing of the queen.
4. The first visit to the Grail castle: Parzival sees the suffering Fisher King and the bloody lance, but fails to ask the compassionate question; when he awakens the next morning the castle is deserted; Parzival is cursed by the Grail messengers.
5. The second period of knight-errantry: plagued by guilt and heedless of God, Parzival spends almost five years in search of the Grail castle in order to redeem himself.
6. The encounter with the pious hermit: Parzival confesses his sins and is absolved by the hermit, who initiates him into the mystery of the Grail.
7. The three combats.
8. The second visit to the Grail castle: after posing the question that heals the Fisher King, Parzival becomes the new king of the Grail.

Let us now take another look at *Demian* in the light of this outline. If we are willing, for the moment, to see Demian as prefigured structurally by the Fisher King, then we find five of the eight stages clearly evident in the novel. The three stages not represented belong basically to the Arthurian material: Parzival's arrival at Arthur's Court, the first period of knight-errantry, and the three final combats. Now, like the concept of archetypes in the conventional Jungian sense, mythological motifs are determined by form, not by content. But if any structural prefiguration is to be plausible, it should also have a thematic justification. We see this justification in the fact that Demian, like the Fisher King, is tormented by a vision of the desolate land. In his case, to be sure, the desolation is spiritual rather than vegetative, but it is no less dire:

We both know that the world is quite rotten but that wouldn't be any reason to predict its imminent collapse. But for several years I have had dreams from which I conclude, or which make me feel, that the collapse of the old world is indeed imminent. . . . The world wants to renew itself. There's a smell of death in the air. Nothing can be born without first dying. But it is far more terrible than I had thought.

Like the Grail king, Demian presides over a land that is spiritually desolate, and he is surrounded by a group of friends—the knights of his Grail—who long for the spiritual rebirth of society. This rebirth is to be brought about through the power of spiritual renewal represented by Demian's mother. "I had attained a goal," Sinclair realizes when he finally meets Frau Eva. If Demian is the Fisher King, his home the Grail castle, and the spirit of Frau Eva the Grail itself, then Sinclair's course in life follows the prefigurative pattern of Parzival's quest. And yet the goal is ultimately self-identity, for Sinclair comes to see that Frau Eva "existed only as a metaphor of my inner self, a metaphor whose sole purpose it was to lead me more deeply into myself."

Like Parzival, Sinclair is at the beginning a "guileless fool," who forsakes the innocence of his childhood for adventures in the seductive world of good and evil from which his mother has tried to shield him. Sinclair, to be sure, is not the traditional widow's son, but in his thinking the image of the mother primarily represents the innocence of his sheltered home. When he gets into trouble for the first time, he reflects that "hands were reaching out for me, from which not even my mother could protect me." And it is the mother who is alarmed and dismayed by her son's venture into the "dark" world of adventure. "My mother in particular treated me more like an invalid than a scoundrel."

Once Sinclair commits himself to the outside world, his life revolves essentially around his two encounters with Demian. Like Parzival, Sinclair is not sufficiently mature to be initiated into the mystery of the Grail the first time. (He never meets Frau Eva during their boyhood.) Although he senses the affliction that torments Demian, he does not avail himself of the opportunity to inquire. One day Sinclair comes upon Demian sitting in a kind of trance:

> He sat there completely motionless, not even seeming to breathe; his mouth might have been carved from wood or stone. His face was pale, uniformly pale like a stone, and his brown hair was the part of him that seemed closest to being alive. His hands lay before him on the bench, lifeless and still as objects, like stones or fruit, pale, motionless yet not limp, but like good, strong pods sheathing a hidden vigor or life.

> I trembled at the sight. Dead, I thought, almost saying it aloud. . . .
> Where was he now? What was he thinking? What did he feel?
> Was he in heaven or in hell?
> I was unable to put a question to him.

In this passage even the imagery—fruit and pods and hidden vigor
—suggests a vegetation deity waiting to be summoned back to life by
the ritual inquiry. But the quester, still a "guileless fool," fails to
pose the question. Immediately after this first failure the two boys
are parted for almost five years—a period that corresponds to the
interval between Parizval's first and second visit to the Grail castle.
Demian goes away on a trip, and Sinclair is sent off to boarding
school. During these years they see each other once, briefly; but
when Sinclair later tries to seek out his friend, he finds Demian's
house deserted, like the Grail castle following Parzival's first failure.
During his years of profligacy and despair, when he too loses sight of
God, he comes to think of himself as "a desecrator of the temple."
The person who fulfills the role of the pious hermit in Sinclair's life
is the renegade theologian, Pistorius, who is able to explain many
of the matters that Sinclair had failed to comprehend when he first
heard them from Demian. Speaking to Sinclair of their new religion,
he says: "There has to be a community, there must be a cult and
intoxicants, feasts and mysteries. . . ." As a result of these talks,
Sinclair is prepared for his second encounter with Demian.

The second visit to the Grail castle takes place when Sinclair goes
to the university and meets Demian again. This time he is introduced into his friend's home, which is described as being a special
and sanctified place:

> As soon as I opened the gate, as soon as I caught sight of the tall
> trees in the garden, I felt happy and rich. Outside was reality: streets
> and houses, people and institutions, libraries and lecture halls—but
> here inside was love; here lived the legend and the dream.

It is in this sanctuary that Sinclair finally meets Demian's mother,
who instantly strikes him as the fulfillment of all his dreams, the
goal of his quest. And here, finally, he has the second opportunity
to pose the question. One day he comes upon Demian in precisely
the same kind of deathlike trance that he had witnessed five years
earlier:

> I saw Max slumped on a stool by the curtained window, looking
> oddly changed, and it flashed through me: You've seen this before!

His arms hung limp, hands in his lap, his head bent slightly forward, and his eyes, though open, were unseeing and dead. . . . He resembled an age-old animal mask at the portal of a temple.

On this occasion, however, Sinclair does not fail to ask Demian what is bothering him, and it turns out that the trance is produced by Demian's vision of the desolate land seeking to renew itself. The asking of the question has the effect of healing Demian and the desolate land, for almost immediately thereafter the war breaks out —the war that, in the terms of the novel, has the positive function of destroying the old world with its false conventions so that a new and better world can be born. Demian, to be sure, is killed in the fighting. But through his symbolic kiss at the end of the novel he passes on to the now mature Sinclair his authority as king of the Grail and sovereign of a land that has renewed itself spiritually.

Can we venture to say, at this point, whether we are dealing with the conscious use of a familiar literary shaping of a mythic motif or with the unconscious adaptation of a more general archetype? Before we hazard an answer, we need to consider three matters that have a bearing on the question. First, and by way of comparison, we might cast a quick glance at two other well-known works that have made explicit use of the quest for the Grail as a prefigurative pattern. In his baseball novel, *The Natural* (1952), Bernard Malamud establishes the analogy very early. His hero is a true "guileless fool" —a country boy, with the prophetic name Roy, who is discovered in a remote pasture by a baseball scout. With his homemade bat, Wonderboy, and his Graillike dream of a golden baseball, this Parzival of the diamond eventually arrives in New York, where his batting prowess helps to revive a fading team called the Knights. The manager of the Knights is named Pop Fisher, and before the arrival of the quester his worries have produced a physical affliction—a case of athlete's foot on his hands—which is healed by the spectacular performance of the bat Wonderboy. It is unnecessary to cite further details, for on a surface level the parallels are both precise and overwhelming. The baseball park is transmuted into the modern equivalent of the jousting field, where legendary heroes meet in combat using their lancelike bats. But after the first few pages, though the details continue to accumulate, there is no consistent plot parallel between *The Natural* and the Grail romances. The hero asks no ritual questions; ultimately he strikes out in the World Series and the Knights fail to win the pennant. The novel turns out to be a parodistic inversion of Parzival's quest for the Grail, using easily recognizable details for largely humorous effect.[20] In fact, Malamud seems not to have constructed a modern version of the medieval romance but rather exposed the legendary dimension of the contemporary American phenomenon of baseball.[21]

T. S. Eliot's *The Waste Land* (1922) is a different case altogether. In his Notes, Eliot acknowledged that "not only the title, but the plan and a good deal of the incidental symbolism of the poem were suggested by Miss Jessie L. Weston's book on the Grail legend." But as one critic has noted, "The latent intention of *The Waste Land* might be called a reversal of Miss Weston's title—to translate romance back into its meaning as ritual." [22] For Eliot is concerned less with the familiar pattern of the quest romances than with the sexual rituals and vegetation myths that underlie them. In fact, Eliot actually breaks down the traditional story by fragmenting it into its primal components: in *The Waste Land* the figure of the Fisher King subsumes such disparate figures as Osiris, Christ, the Phoenician Sailor, and the Hanged Man of the Tarot deck.

*Demian* seems to occupy an intermediate position between these two works. The novel has almost none of the conspicuous surface parallels that we find in *The Natural*; and it displays less concern with the primal myth and vegetation ritual that obsessed Eliot. But much more than the other two authors, Hesse respects the organizing plot line of the quest romances. The three works, in short, represent three wholly different yet completely legitimate approaches to the use of prefiguration: Eliot emphasizes the underlying mythic substance and symbol; Malamud depends upon readily recognizable motifs and images; and Hesse adapts the story line and disposition of material.

This brings us to a second consideration. I have suggested else-

---

[20] See also Earl R. Wassermann, "*The Natural:* Malamud's World Ceres," *Centennial Review*, 9 (Fall 1965), 438–460. In this splendid study, Wassermann also suggests deeper allusions to myth and fertility rites.

[21] Although Malamud succeeds quite brilliantly, the basic observation is by no means original. As early as 1930 the German scholar André Jolles analyzed the adulation of sports heroes as a modern parallel to the literary genre of the legend. André Jolles, *Einfache Formen* (1930; reprinted Darmstadt: Wissenschaftliche Buchgesellschaft, 1958), pp. 60–61.

[22] George Williamson, *A Reader's Guide to T. S. Eliot,* 2nd ed. (New York: Noonday Press, 1966), p. 118.

where that the figure of Demian can most plausibly be understood as what might be called a fictional transfiguration of Jesus.[23] The external facts of plot help us very little. But if we consider his figure carefully, we note a group of characteristics that constitute a surprising yet unmistakable pattern. Demian's most salient physical feature is the "brightness" that illuminates his forehead. Through an uncanny skill in the psychological manipulation of others he accomplishes various deeds that astonish the other boys. We are told of disputations in which Demian surpasses his teachers with his questions and responses. When he talks to Sinclair, he tends to express himself in parables adapted freely from the Bible. He is driven by his faith in the coming of a new spiritual kingdom. And toward the end of the book he has assembled around his person a circle of admirers, all of whom strive for the spiritual kingdom that he proclaims. In short, Demian has what amounts to a halo and performs what are commonly regarded as miracles. He is a "healer" by the sheer force of his personality. He disputes with teachers, preaches a coming kingdom, and instructs his disciples through parables. His death, finally, is plainly an act of self-sacrifice in the service of the spiritual kingdom to come.

Now I see no contradiction between this interpretation of Demian's character and our reading of the novel as a postfiguration of Parzival's quest for the Grail. First, the figure of Jesus is seen here in a wholly mythic way. Pistorius, for instance, tells Sinclair that "Christ is not a person for me but a hero, a myth, an extraordinary shadow image in which humanity has painted itself on the wall of eternity." In addition, Hesse knew perfectly well from his study of the works of Jung and the historians of religion that the story of Jesus is related through the theme of resurrection to the various myths of Adonis, Tammuz, and Attis, from which the legend of the Grail was eventually precipitated. The legend of the Grail king, with its accoutrements of lance and chalice, is ultimately a reworking of the story of Jesus himself. In other words, there is a fundamental identity between Jesus and the Fisher King; and to the extent that Demian is the one, he is also the other.

[23] I first presented this interpretation in *The Novels of Hermann Hesse: A Study in Theme and Structure* (Princeton, N. J.: Princeton University Press, 1965); the idea is developed more systematically in my *Fictional Transfigurations of Jesus* (Princeton, N. J.: Princeton University Press, 1972).

Second, this kind of syncretism of mythic and legendary elements is not at all uncommon in modern literature. In *Ulysses,* for instance, Joyce elaborated the basic Odysseus theme with traits borrowed from the tales of Hamlet and Don Giovanni. The hero of Thomas Mann's *Doctor Faustus* owes as much to the historical Nietzsche as to the legendary Faust. And we have already noted that Eliot incorporated elements from various mythic-cultic figures in the person of the Fisher King in *The Waste Land.* Finally, to regard Demian as a fictional transfiguration of Jesus helps us to understand his function in the novel as well as many of his characteristics; and it justifies the gospellike tone of the narrative. But the New Testament parallel does not explain the role of Emil Sinclair, who has no real counterpart in the gospels, where all the figures surrounding Jesus are reduced to passive observers. But Parzival's quest for the Grail supplies the author with stages of plot that provide a fictional framework for Emil Sinclair's life. At the same time, the theme of the quest is completely consistent with Demian's role as a symbolic Jesus-Fisher King.

We now arrive at a third consideration. If, as I am arguing, it is essentially the plot, and not surface detail or ritual significance, that establishes the parallel between *Demian* and the story of Parzival's quest for the Grail, then we are now obliged to account for the three missing stages of the story. However, there is another version of the story, equally well known, in which these very elements—the arrival at Arthur's court, the first period of knight-errantry, and the three final combats—are missing. And that version corresponds almost exactly to the organization of Hesse's novel: I am referring, of course, to Richard Wagner's *Parsifal* (1882).

Wagner's opera opens with Parsifal's appearance in the forest near the Grail temple. The story of his youth is recounted in a flashback, but Act I moves rapidly to Parsifal's first visit to the Grail castle, where, after witnessing the King's suffering, he fails to ask the simple compassionate question. All of Act II is based upon an episode that has nothing to do with the original Parzival plot: Gawain's adventure in Klingsor's magic castle. In Wagner's version the sorcerer sends Kundry to seduce Parsifal away from his mission, but he casts her aside, overwhelmed by his sense of guilt at having failed to assuage the ailing Fisher King. In Act III, finally, Parsifal arrives at the abode of the pious hermit, where he is prepared to be admitted to the Grail castle for a second time. Without the retarding episodes of the three combats, Parsifal then proceeds directly to the castle, where he heals the suffering King by touching him with the sacred lance. A white dove descends to Parsifal in heavenly benediction as the opera comes to an end.

There are certain differences here, to be sure. Notably, Wagner has shifted the emphasis at the conclusion from the asking of the ritual question to the more effective stage gesture of touching the wound with the lance. At the same time, the compactness of the total work resembles Hesse's plot line much more closely than do the broader narratives of the medieval romances. In addition, Wagner's version supplies possible clues to an episode and a symbol in the novel that are not prefigured in the romances. The temptations by Klingsor and Kundry, namely, parallel the scenes in which Emil Sinclair, away at boarding school, is first led astray by an older boy and then, as a result of his encounter with the girl in the park (Kundry's garden!), once again put in mind of Demian and his own failures. And the motif of the sacred dove that descends at the end of the opera seems to foreshadow Sinclair's vision toward the end of the novel as he walks into a storm:

> Then a loose, yellow cloud swept across the sky, collided with the other gray bank of cloud. In a few seconds the wind had fashioned a shape out of this yellow and blue-gray mass, a gigantic bird that tore itself free of the steel-blue chaos and flew off into the sky with a great beating of wings.

As we already know from earlier occurrences of the bird image, this final vision anticipates the imminent spiritual rebirth of the world, which—like a bird breaking its way out of an egg—must shatter the old that the new may be born. Both thematically and structurally, therefore, this vision fulfills almost precisely the same function in the novel as does the sacred dove in Wagner's *Parsifal*.

Hesse was well acquainted with Wagner's music although, given his preference for Bach and Mozart, he was not fond of it. In the early novel *Peter Camenzind* (1904), the hero's friend plays *Die Meistersinger* on the piano, and the harmonies, he writes, "flowed around me like a warm, exciting bath." In *Steppenwolf* (1927) Mozart accuses Brahms and Wagner of unnecessarily "thick instrumentation." And other references are too frequent to enumerate. It is more germane to our purposes to note that during the *Demian* period, in 1919, Hesse wrote two major novellas that explicitly allude to Wagner's works and personality. In the story *Klein and Wagner* the hero dreams of *Lohengrin,* and when he peers into the mirror he sees the dark side of his character reflected with the facial features of Richard Wagner. Similarly, Wagner's sorcerer contributes to the characterization of the painter-hero of the novella *Klingsor's Last Summer.* In short, there is ample external evidence for Hesse's familiarity with Wagner throughout his entire lifetime and, more specifically, for his particular preoccupation with Wagner around the time of *Demian.* There are at least two reasons for this fascination with Wagner despite Hesse's antipathy toward the composer and his works. Most generally, Hesse saw in Wagner a striking embodiment of the dark and demonic aspect of the German character, whose ambivalence he was portraying in *Demian.* More specifically, he realized that the German public was familiar with the legend of Parzival and the Grail primarily through Wagner's opera, and not through the medieval romances. In his Introduction to an edition of the *Gesta Romanorum* that he published in 1915, Hesse noted that "we know Siegfried and Parzival, Tristan and Lohengrin, too exclusively from the theater." [24]

To sum up: I submit that in *Demian* Hesse consciously employed the story of Parzival's quest for the Grail as a prefigurative pattern for the plot of his novel. He found it useful, first of all, because the Grail quest corresponds closely to his own conception of the triadic rhythm of human development from innocence ("the guileless fool") through despair (at the failure to ask the question) to ultimate fulfillment (when the question is asked). Beyond this general pattern, the legend of the Fisher King implies the same vision of a desolate land in need of spiritual renewal as the one that obsessed Hesse during the years around World War I. (He rendered this vision not only in *Demian,* but also in a volume of essays entitled *Blick ins Chaos [In Sight of Chaos],* 1920.) The motif of Parzival had the immense advantage, for the novelist, of affording structure and details of plot that are not available in the more general archetype of the quest. A consideration of Hesse's other novels makes it clear that he often tended to adapt such specific motifs from existing legends or literary works in order to lend substance to the underlying pattern. In his

[24] Reprinted in Hesse, *Gesammelte Werke in zwölf Bänden* (Frankfurt am Main: Suhrkamp, 1970), XII, 86–88.

next novel, *Siddhartha* (1922), he exploited details taken from the legend of Gautama Buddha.[25]

In the second place, he expected the pattern to be sensed, if not consciously recognized, by most readers because for the German consciousness—notably since Wagner and the vogue of the Grail motif around 1900—that legend more than any other had come to embody the search for identity and meaning in a vaguely religious context. By using a familiar pattern, in other words, Hesse achieved additional dimensions of meaning, or at least of mood, that unlocked and expanded the implications of the specific story he was telling. The attentive reader could look beyond Sinclair to recognize not only Wagner's Parsifal and Wolfram's Parzival, but a whole troop of seekers from the Grail literature of the turn of the century.

The evidence suggests that in writing his novel Hesse did not use a specific literary text as a lexicon of imagery, as did Malamud; nor did he base his work essentially on a scholarly treatise dealing with the sources of the story, as did Eliot. Rather, his novel is based on a pattern assembled loosely from his recollection of the medieval romances, his familiarity with Wagner's opera, and his readings in the works of Jung and the currently fashionable historians of religion.

This entire interpretation can claim only a degree of plausibility, of course, and not any factual proof: Hesse has not done us the favor of confirming the conjecture in a letter or essay. But if it is correct, then it supports Thomas Mann's theory that the German *Bildungsroman* represents a "sublimation and spiritualization" of the medieval romances depicting Parzival's quest for the Grail. The process of converting the original nature ritual into medieval romance was essentially a process of *externalization*. The authors had to find in the reality of Christian Europe certain actions and symbols that adequately expressed the mystery of the cult from which the legend had emerged. In the works of Chrétien and Wolfram a balance is maintained between external action and inner meaning. But in the course of the later Middle Ages the movement toward externalization became dominant: meaning was gradually reduced, and the later epics degenerated more and more into adventure stories until, translated into prose, they supplied the form for the picaresque novels in which

---

[25] Hesse frequently used the same device in his shorter fiction as well. See my discussion in the Introduction to Hesse's *Stories of Five Decades* (New York: Farrar, Straus and Giroux, 1972).

the quest was maintained solely as an excuse for the increasingly fantastic adventures of the hero.

In the modern *Bildungsroman,* by way of contrast, precisely the opposite has taken place. Through a process of *internalization* the action has been removed from the external world and shifted back into the consciousness of the hero, as in *The Magic Mountain* and *Demian.* The goal of the quest is no longer a tangible Grail, but the self-awareness of the hero. Paradoxically, this shift in emphasis has put the modern novel quite near the point from which the medieval romances evolved. Miss Weston observed that the ancient ritual had "for its ultimate object the initiation into the secret of the sources of Life, physical and spiritual." [26] In its lower and more explicitly physical form the ritual still survives in numerous folk ceremonies all over the world. But "in its esoteric 'Mystery' form it was freely utilized for the imparting of high spiritual teaching concerning the relation of Man to the Divine Source of his being. . . ." This "high spiritual teaching" is precisely the goal of the modern quest that Hesse depicted in *Demian.* But here, to return to the words of the Prologue, the Grail has been so totally internalized and spiritualized that it is identical with the individual self. "I have been and still am a seeker, but I have ceased to question stars and books. I have begun to listen to the teachings my blood whispers to me."

[26] *From Ritual to Romance,* p. 203.

# Person and Persona:
# The Magic Mirrors of *Steppenwolf*

## by Ralph Freedman

*I*

Disclosure is always intriguing and literature is no exception. The masks artists have created for themselves with the energy of their talent have been persistently raised to allow the curious and the morbid a glimpse at the man underneath—his face often anguished and equally often quite bland. On the surface, this temptation to know more than meets the eye is easily explained. We all love gossip and biography is gossip sublime. Yet seven decades of psychoanalytic thinking have sharpened our perceptions. We look for truths about works of art not only in the texts themselves but in the personal dynamics of the men and women who produced them, in the hidden deformities, the suffering that lies behind any work. And often we even believe that these are superior truths that cannot be found in the texts. This psychic involvement, of course, has not gone unchallenged. Indeed, it may be fair to suggest that the very notion of the "intentional fallacy"—so crucial a doctrine in literary criticism a bare decade ago—may have been motivated, in part, by a delicate response to just this kind of probing, an attempt to cover up nakedness as Noah's sons, walking backward, covered the nakedness of their father. Today a new romanticism has once more placed a premium on nakedness, but the problems it has raised remain largely unsolved.

The relationship between life and art has posed a critical problem since criticism began. It also conditions our involvement in writers' lives. Our curiosity about them may be eventually satisfied, yet in the end we may often ask if the satisfaction was worth the candle. For clearly we would not indulge our need to know more about the person, if the writer had not written books that are in some sense important. And so the question, a critical question, must still be asked whether our knowledge about the life helps us in understanding the art. We must examine how our knowledge of the writer, our empathy, even our identification with him, can clarify his books for us: how the love and suffering in a man's work are illuminated by the love and suffering in a man's life. The problems this question raises are both obvious and manifold, and they are demonstrated with exceptional clarity in the life and work of Hermann Hesse.

As soon as we go beyond mere curiosity about the life and ask the hard questions of criticism about the work, the confusion is immediate. For example, when we look at that well-known photograph of Thomas Mann and Stefan Zweig meeting Hermann and Ninon Hesse for skiing in St. Moritz in 1936, we see them acting like very ordinary people on skiing trips posing for a camera. Presumably, the men smoke cigars and they all have good food and brandy together when they come down from the mountain. But their mountain is *not* a Magic Mountain; their theater is *not* a Magic Theater. Their small talk is *not* dialogue in fiction. Yet, we cannot say that this meeting was irrelevant to the work of the three men—probably the three most important German authors of the time. The matrix of their experience must have gone into their books. The question is: how did it enter them and to what extent is it relevant?

A good place to begin—and also to end—such a discussion is with the writer: with the way he presents himself, his *person*. This is especially true of writers like Hermann Hesse or André Gide who constantly wrote what A. J. Guerard, Jr., has called "spiritual auto-biographies." It is, of course, also true of other novelists who do not seek to render primarily themselves in their work—that is, who do not wish to convert their private lives into a universal spiritual existence—but it is less clear in these writers (I am thinking here of Dickens or Balzac or Tolstoy). We would need a more complex argument to relate their lives to their novels. But we have no such problem with writers like Hesse, Gide, Kafka, Joyce, and many others who have recreated the romantic version of the *Ich-Roman* (even where they have used the grammatical third person) as a modern way of making individual, unique, or singular experiences accessible to all.

In these writers, it is *easier* for us to view the man mirrored in his work, because their material is so obviously autobiographical. But it is also much *harder*. It is harder to view their books as an *appropriate* mirror of the man precisely because of our tendency to be so dazzled by biographical analogues that we forget the fact of their *transformation*. We are all like Goethe's faithful recorder Eckermann, who marvelled that the creator of *Faust* read his newspaper and had soft-boiled eggs for breakfast. Camus could not have written *L'Etranger* if he had never lived in Oran, but is he therefore Meursault? Is "Marcel" of *A la recherche du temps perdu* the same as Marcel Proust? One could go on indefinitely.

The distinction between a writer and his "other self" in art, even in so-called "spiritual autobiographies," is that between a *person* and his *persona*. Both are endowed with a consciousness. They both feel; they know, they sense; they articulate. The eyes and ears they both use, of course, stem from the same biological being—the artist. But the artist who seeks to observe everything, including himself, sees and hears on two different levels—that of the person and of the persona—which are not always readily explained by one another.[1] He is, like Thomas Mann's Aschenbach in *Death in Venice,* a "sublime voyeur." For Gustav von Aschenbach, the *man,* views the object of his passion (the boy Tadzio) in ever higher degrees of sexual excitement. But Gustav von Aschenbach, the *artist,* converts this viewing into art. He writes a panegyric to Beauty, inspired by his passion, and in the end dies while his seeing "eye" remains objectified as an abandoned camera on a tripod standing alone on the beach where he had sat and viewed. The person's viewing has turned into the persona's vision and has become something distinct and detached. A strong relationship between them remains, but it is not one-to-one. A transformation has occurred, and as readers or contemplators of art we are concerned with this transformation. The example is complicated by the fact that in this case both the person and the persona stem from a character of fiction, but it is pertinent because Mann has presented us with a very precise analogy to the creative process. Indeed, I think that few writers have developed the

[1] The relationship between the *person* and the objectified self, the *persona*, was my principal theme in *The Lyrical Novel* (Princeton, 1963). See my definition of this concept on pp. 2–3. Wayne Booth used the term more widely in defining the narrator: "The art of constructing reliable narrators is largely that of mastering all of oneself in order to project the persona, the second self, that really belongs in the book" *The Rhetoric of Fiction* (Chicago, 1961), p. 83.

relationship between person and persona, between eye and vision, as clearly as Mann has done in *Death in Venice*.


2


Hermann Hesse was deeply conscious of this duality in his existence, this split between the person and the persona and the problematic nature of their relationship. He created many heroes as deliberate images and equally deliberate distortions of himself. Peter Camenzind, Knulp, Sinclair, Klingsor, H. H. of *Journey to the East,* Josef Knecht of *The Glass Bead Game*—they all reflect (and often also refract) aspects of his own consciousness. Similarly, "dual heroes" —a favorite device of German romantic narrative—mirror the writer's features in intricate *compositions,* like Giebenrath and Heilner in *Beneath the Wheel* or Narcissus and Goldmund. Nor was Hesse afraid of relating the persona back to his own person. For a couple of years after writing *Klingsor's Last Summer* he often referred to himself as "Klingsor," even signing some of his letters that way. During the time the concept of "Steppenwolf" developed, and while he was writing the book (even for some time afterwards), he liked to call himself the "Protestant Steppenwolf." But he was always aware of the difference, which seemed to pose a problem for him as an artist. In fact, one of his most amusing works of the early 1920s was specifically devoted to the interplay between the self-in-life and the self-in-art, the former observing the latter and telling a story about him. This book is *A Guest at the Spa* (originally called *Psychologica Balnearia*), which was written in 1923 as a humorous description of Hesse's first visit to the spa of Baden near Zürich where he was to take regular cures for his gout and sciatica for the rest of his life. Here he appears as the observer who sees himself going through all the rituals of the typical *Kurgast*. But as the object of this observer-self's attention he is also visibly transformed into a character of fiction gradually succumbing to the sumptuous ease and hygienic rigors of the place—the "magic of Baden"—while at the same time constantly telling the reader what he is doing. For example, a funny episode at dinner—a paradoxically sumptuous affair for people with digestive ailments—is turned into a serious confrontation of the two selves:

In the high well-lighted dining-hall I sat down at my lonely little round table and at once observed how I sat down, how I adjusted my chair a little and bit my lips lightly because it hurt, how I picked up the flower vase mechanically between my fingers and placed it a bit closer, how slowly, indecisively, I pulled my napkin out of its ring (VII, 89) [2]

Hesse as sciatica patient was the object of Hesse as the "observing I." He looked at himself as "with a controlled but bored face" he poured water and broke bread without any intention of consuming either, while he as object, in turn, watched the busy headwaiter and his horde of pretty waitresses in black dresses and white aprons moving about against the backdrop of large walls adorned by landscape paintings. Throughout the scene, the two "eyes" remained juxtaposed:

> . . . [He] who observed me . . . was not the spa visitor and sciatica patient Hesse, but the old Hesse, the odd fellow, the misogynist, the old wanderer and poet, friend of butterflies and lizards, of ancient books and religions. . . . This old Hesse, my recently estranged and almost lost self, had returned and now observed us all (VII, 90).

He was his own secret audience aware of the amusing spectacle of the entire proceedings—including his pain.

And in the equally interesting *Journey to Nuremberg,* an account of a lecture tour through Southern Germany in the fall of 1925 which Hesse had also restructured as "art," he again made the point explicitly. "I know better than anyone," he wrote after describing the anguish of a public reading of the fairy tale *Pictor's Metamorphoses,* "the condition in which the eternal self observes the mortal self and judges its bouncing and grimacing, full of pity, full of mockery, full of neutrality . . ." (VII, 156–57).

The relationship between person and persona is as explicit in Hesse's first romantic and highly personal novel, *Hermann Lauscher* (1901), as it is in his later *Steppenwolf* (1927) and *The Glass Bead Game* (1943), and in each he plays very deliberately with these two figures. In fact, these three books, spanning his entire career, share a common bond. All three focus ultimately on crises of conscience that

---

[2] All references in parentheses preceded by Roman numerals are to *Gesammelte Werke* (hereafter referred to as *Werkausgabe*) (Frankfurt: Suhrkamp Verlag, 1970), 12 vols.

communicate themselves from the writer to his fictional doubles. Although we are mainly concerned with crisis in *Steppenwolf,* a glance at Hesse's earliest novel might prepare us for it. *Hermann Lauscher* (Hermann "Listener") is an edited version of himself, observed by the author Hesse, whose first name remains. He pretends (as does the landlady's nephew in *Steppenwolf*) to edit the notebooks his double had left behind. (The "chronicler" in *The Glass Bead Game* performs a more complex but analogous function.) These notes contain reminiscences of Hesse's own childhood (by no means filled only with unrelieved horror), the story of a suicide among drinking students in Tübingen, another story about a flirtation with a barmaid named Lulu, prose poems about insomnia, and some excerpts from his diary in Basel.

The biographical roots are clear and so is the "game" of their transformation. Hesse's listening (rather than viewing) double is a practicing poet. The book was written chiefly in 1899 and 1900 while Hesse was a bookseller in Basel, but it reflected for the most part his experiences during his years of apprenticeship in Tübingen where he had lived from 1895 to 1899. He had felt lonely and outcast because he had left school too early and had not entered a university (though he had taught himself in subjects that interested him as a writer with a great deal of tenacity). Yet he lived in a university town as a merchant's apprentice, while his contemporaries were students. And so young Hesse fitted out his room like a typical student's room, affected students' drinking habits and hung about with them wherever he could. *Lauscher,* then, was more than Hesse himself "listening." He had been heightened to a character of fiction *superior* to the students—a free-lancing, free-wheeling, footloose poet. "Lulu" was a real person—an actual innkeeper's daughter. In the book she became a charming sorceress in the dress of a barmaid, half realistic, half a fairy-tale Cinderella. Similarly, the "fever muse" of the insomnia prose poems transforms sexual fantasy into poetic imagery distinct from itself:

> How your hand knows how to caress. I feel in your touch the entire history of this hand, the entire culture of nobility in its form and gesture as it has been wrought by the painters of early Florence . . . (I, 314).

Biographically, this and similar passages may reflect Hesse's adoration of Elisabeth Laroche, a parson's daughter whom he loved after his move to Basel. But the sensations are transformed not just into fantasy reducible to vagaries of the unconscious. They are turned into a product of the artistic imagination. They become images in touch with history, with a sense of the history of art, with the form of aestheticist prose poetry. The psychic states are *consciously* re-worked. This is not a value judgment, for artistically this passage is very sentimental, although Hesse himself (as he told Hugo Ball in 1926) considered *Lauscher* the only valuable work among his youth-ful productions. But it is an interesting example of transformation from person to persona in Hesse's early work. In the concluding sec-tion of the book, "Basel Diary 1900," Hesse plays even more obvi-ously. "Hesse," he makes Lauscher say, "wants to get an article on Tieck out of me. . . ." Briefly, person and persona are set side by side.

The construct of the "Steppenwolf" grew out of this game between person and persona, which reached from Hesse's life into his art. As a person, he felt like a "lonely wolf of the steppes." At bay, sur-rounded by a hostile uncomprehending world of philistines, he sensed his isolation, his apartness. This image may well have been provided by the picture of a dying wolf drawn in a story written as early as 1907. But from 1924 on, when this concept matured, Hesse developed an even more abrasive sense of himself as an outsider. His second marriage to an aspiring young concert singer, Ruth Wenger, had been a disaster. After a lengthy courtship, he fled from her (and her expensive dogs) following only two months of married life early in 1924, yet he remained tied to her for years. In the summer of 1925, her interminable illness which had started that January was diagnosed as tuberculosis. At the same time, his first wife Maria, who had suffered episodes of nervous collapse for years, had a fresh break-down because one of her brothers had committed suicide and an-other brother (who had administered her estate) had to be confined to a mental hospital. All responsibilities for two faltering wives and three young sons were on Hesse's shoulders while he himself was oppressed by eye-aches, headaches, gout, and sciatica. His depression was intense. The attacks upon him by his political enemies on the patriotic Right hurt him even more than usual. Yet he had already formed a clear image of himself before these disasters had struck. When in March, 1925, his sister Adele had urged him to come to Germany to attend the silver wedding of their half-brother Karl Isenberg, he refused. And in refusing, he used the famous term and

applied it to himself. Family reunions, he told his sister, were not
for a "Steppenwolf."

The Steppenwolf concept, then, was immediately intertwined with
Hesse's own feelings about himself as a man, but basically it remained a construct for a book. It was the key by which his life gained
entry into his art. Hermann Hesse, who felt isolated and depressed,
was the *person*. His Steppenwolf-protagonist Harry Haller, who
played with these feelings in art, became the *persona*. In the curious
metamorphosis that transforms a life into a novel, the *pathology* of
the first became the *imagination* of the second. The two are not
identical. *Steppenwolf* is indeed the record of a crisis, but it is also
more than that. It is a crisis transformed.

The personal origins of the novel *Steppenwolf*—beyond the particular traumas I have described—may be found in Hesse's inability
to reestablish a coherent personal life after his break with the past
in 1919. Having left his mentally ill first wife and having overcome
a severe crisis of his own during the closing years of World War I,
he thought he could start afresh among the mountains and lakes of
Southern Switzerland. But after a brief period of intense productivity during the first summer and fall in his new home in Montagnola,
he felt barren and adrift. During these opening years of the 1920s
he allowed himself to be caught in the ill-advised new marriage that
soon forced him to escape; he moved about restlessly from Tessin
to Basel to Zürich to Bern to Baden with many lecture tours and
trips in between. It was a time of physical and psychic pain, accompanied by a sense of spiritual emptiness, a conviction (like Cole-
ridge's) that he had once again lost his creative powers.

This psychic matter, which seems to have molded him as a person,
Hesse clearly experienced in psychoanalytic terms, despite his dis-
claimer. For psychoanalysis continued to pervade his life and to
communicate itself to his work (done hastily between visits and vis-
itors). A trenchant phrase which he used to defend his involvement
in psychotherapy in a letter to Hugo and Emmy Ball (his skeptical
Catholic friends) describes his feelings during this entire period of
uncertainty and haphazard creation. "Psychoanalysis," he told his
friends, "has at bottom no other goal than to create a space in
oneself in which God's voice can be heard." It was a fire he had to
go through but which hurt very much.[3] In 1921, when Hesse sought

   [3] From an undated letter to Hugo and Emmy Ball. In another undated letter
from Zürich to the same friends, Hesse told of his analytic sessions with C. G.

C. G. Jung's help, he was struggling to finish *Siddhartha,* which had lain fallow since late in 1919, and which he was finally able to complete in the spring of 1922. But the statement to his friends can also be seen as a paradigm for his condition.

If this apt phrase describes Hesse's response to his ordeal in life, it also found its way into his art. Psychoanalysis, which seeks to remold consciousness and explores various layers and levels of the self, fashioned many of Hesse's artistic strategies in the early 1920s and most noticeably in *Steppenwolf.* Jung and others were undoubtedly right when they found the spirit of psychoanalysis pervading the basic substance of the novel. Harry Haller's world is largely *within*—the Magic Theater and its strange protagonists are part of his psyche—and the novel constantly tests the internal against an external reality. Fantasy and dream become artistic devices (though this practice was, of course, also part of the entire ambience of the *avant garde* from Dadaism to expressionism and surrealism). More specifically, the fantasy figures range from hermaphroditic Hermine (his own female version) to hermaphroditic Pablo (that jazz musician-Mozart who also includes the female) with a purely "female" intercessor, Maria, in between. The scene is clearly the psyche, an inner hell, that transforms a real city (compounded of Basel and Zürich) into a symbolic city that exposes the raw flesh of a crisis-ridden psyche. The arena of the novel, then, appears to be a mind in which space is created for God's voice (the "immortals") to be heard. And Haller's pilgrimage resembles that of psychoanalytic education. He seeks his ascent, and experiences his failure, among *mirrors* (in the Treatise that pictures him verbally and in the images of Pablo's Cabinet of Mirrors), which reflect various aspects of himself.

At the same time, the shift from one level of insight to another which psychoanalysis provides, is used in the book to shift the reader from the reality of life to the reality of art. Indeed, psychoanalysis,

---

Jung, which (according to information received from Mr. Heiner Hesse) took place in February and May, 1921: "I'm up and down. City and work are very tiring, but I live in a beautiful spot high up near the forest on the *Zürichberg* and occasionally I see dear people. But my psychoanalysis is giving me a great deal of trouble, and often Klingsor feels old and incorrigible, the summer is no longer his." And he adds: "I shall stay here still longer, the fruit I have bitten into must be eaten to the full. Dr. Jung impresses me very much." Unpublished letters, not otherwise identified, are part of the *Depositum* of the Hesse-Archives, Schiller-Museum, Marbach, Germany, and are quoted by permission of Suhrkamp Verlag, Frankfurt, and Mr. Heiner Hesse.

and the sense of personal crisis which it seeks to control, and occasionally serves to promote, became one of the most important intellectual ingredients in the book. It helped in the shift from person to persona.

## 3

*Steppenwolf,* then, is a record of a crisis, but if it were only a *record* it could not function as a work of art. It does function as art because Hesse made the unconscious stratagems of the person conscious by means of various devices which replaced the external references of society and nature, familiar from so-called "realistic" novels, with aesthetic and philosophical references. Construction was not haphazard, as in psychological association or undirected dream, but *composed,* as in music and abstract painting. Ideas are not fortuitous either but are directed by specific humanistic assumptions. Psychoanalytic education on the level of person becomes an ascent to the values of Goethe and Mozart on the level of persona—it becomes a humanistic *Bildungsroman.* In this way the relationship between the person's crisis and the persona's reconstructed symbolic world (that includes the world of humanistic education) provides the tension and the peculiar fascination of the book.

A key to an understanding of the relationship between the biographical and formal levels of existence that Hesse juxtaposes in his novel was provided in Theodore Ziolkowski's discussion of *Steppenwolf* in *The Novels of Hermann Hesse.* This is the concept of "double perception." Citing from Hesse's essay "On Reading Books" (1920), Ziolkowski shows that Hesse often viewed texts on at least two distinct levels which extend from the actual words on the page to "the stream of stimulations and ideas that come to us while we read." Consequently, a text like *Steppenwolf* may be an "inner biography" (or a "fantasy") on one level and at the same time may present a coherent, palpable world on another. In Ziolkowski's reading of the book these two levels are formed as a contrapuntal arrangement resembling that of a sonata. This assumption can be extended. "Double perception" within texts may also include the interplay of person and persona, of life and art, which we are examining.[4]

[4] *The Novels of Hermann Hesse* (Princeton, 1965), pp. 195–206. On counterpoints, see pp. 207–224.

The person in life, and his "record of crisis," and the persona in art are related to one another by the device of the mirror, which exemplifies "double perception" as a recurrent motif. *Steppenwolf* is full of mirrors.[5] The novel sets out with the reflection of city lights on wet asphalt streets and enters into more and more complicated worlds in which physical mirrors take a prominent place. His "sister" Hermine looks in a pocket mirror; Haller views himself and his double in mirrors, and the entire action culminates in Pablo's Cabinet of Mirrors. Even the characters are intricate mirrors for one another. Moreover, the language of the Treatise, which applies to Harry Haller, is a verbal translation of a mirrored reflection of himself. It presents a picture of his innermost being drawn by a mysterious higher authority in which he observes how his ideal self and his inadequate self-in-the-world are being pitilessly compared. In fact, the scene in which Haller sits down at his desk and reads about himself suggests a crucial scene in the German romantic novel *Heinrich von Ofterdingen* by Novalis in which the hero reads a "novel" in a hermit's cave, where he finds pictures from his own past and present and blurred suggestions of his future. This would seem to be one of those analogues to literary history through which Hesse transmutes life into art.

Combining the notion of double perception with the motif of the mirror, we can observe confrontations between Hermann Hesse's person in life with his artfully reconstructed persona. Indeed, mirroring pervades Hesse's life and thought especially at the time *Steppenwolf* was conceived, written, and digested. It was surely a coincidence, but striking nonetheless, that he was writing his *Steppenwolf* just when his intimate friend Hugo Ball was writing his biography. It had been commissioned by the publisher Samuel Fischer at Hesse's suggestion, and both books were slated to appear in July, 1927—the time of Hesse's fiftieth birthday. To compound the irony, Haller's symbolic disappearance was followed, within a very few months, by Ball's actual death. But one does not need to dwell on coincidences to perceive Hesse's awareness of these "mirrorings" between life and art. For example, Hesse wrote that his novel was an attempt to "overcome the great illness of [Haller's] time not through circumventions and embellishments of the truth but through the effort to make the illness itself the subject of the presentation." Turning the argument

<hr />

[5] Mirroring as a device and theme was discussed previously in *The Lyrical Novel*. See pp. 76, 87–94 and *passim*.

only slightly, he wrote about Ball's biography just as he was working on *Steppenwolf* (in October, 1926):

> Insofar as my biography makes any sense at all, it is, I suppose, that
> the personal, incurable, scantily mastered neurosis of an intellectual
> person is at the same time a symptom for the soul of his time.[6]

The mirroring, the double perception, then, took place not only
within the text itself. It communicated itself from the writer to his
work which, in turn, richly endowed the writer with the fruits of its
insight.

The situation is dramatized by Hesse's self-conscious awareness of
mirroring—before and after the fact. During the summer of 1927,
after both books had been completed, he wrote a note of appreciation to Ball after having seen the first printed copy of the book
about himself. In this letter, Hesse reported a dream:

> Last night I had a dream in connection with your book: I saw myself
> sitting not as in a mirror but as a second living figure, more alive
> than myself. But because of some inner prohibition I was not allowed
> to look at myself properly. That would have been a sin. So I just
> twinkled for a moment through the slit of my eyes and saw the
> living Hesse sitting there.[7]

We can ignore, I think, his denial that he saw himself in a mirror
(for he merely wanted to indicate that the reproduction of himself
was not two-dimensional). The resemblance of this dream after having read his own biography to some of the mirror images in Pablo's
Magic Theater is striking:

> . . . and I saw, a little dissolved and cloudy, a ghostly internally
> moving picture, heavily working and yeasting within itself: my own
> self, Harry Haller . . . and within this Harry [I saw] the Steppen-
> wolf, a shy, beautiful wolf . . . (VII, 367).

The personal duality recollected in a later dream appears in the
book as an "aesthetic" relationship between the protagonist Harry
Haller and his "wolf" double. The symbolic concept has transformed
the personal relationship.

---

[6] This letter, also on deposit in Marbach, was recently reprinted in *Materialien
zu Hermann Hesse 'Der Steppenwolf'*, ed. Volker Michels (Frankfurt, 1972), p.
97 (hereafter referred to as *Materialien*).
[7] From an undated letter to Hugo Ball, Montagnola, summer 1927.

## 4

A reading of *Steppenwolf* based on double perception and mirroring might show how the abundant personal evidence of psychological crisis has been utilized and transformed as an imaginative composition. Three motifs dominate the novel: (1) schizophrenia and potential suicide; (2) intoxication and full self-expression as a means of counteracting schizophrenia and suicide; and (3) the entire effort as a heightening of the deranged sensibility in humor and art. Within this scheme, Hesse used artistic devices (mostly borrowed from German Romanticism, its mirrors and pictures and its celebration of irony) and was able to project moments of detachment and humor which are real enough to keep us from thinking of all these strategies merely as intellectual exercises.

The personal evidence is recorded in Hesse's published and unpublished correspondence as well as in numerous poems which were originally published in periodical form in 1926 as "Steppenwolf: A Piece of Diary in Verse" (an expanded version was brought out in book form under the title *Krisis* in 1928). These poems are more biographical than the novel, because they were not equally filtered through a transforming process of the literary imagination. It is perhaps evidence of Hesse's obsession with mirroring at the time that he believed them to be (against his publisher's judgment, which prevailed in the end) a necessary complement to the "Prose Steppenwolf"—i.e., the novel. Both sets of documents—the letters and the poems—deal with the two periods in Hesse's life which set the scene for his book. The first setting was provided by his lonely life in Basel during the winters of 1923–24 and 1924–25 when he was trying to cope with his oncoming and soon almost defunct second marriage and felt like a lonely outsider roaming through alleys and sitting in wine shops. The second setting was derived from a terrible winter in 1925–26, extending into the following spring, when Hesse lived in Zürich in a set of small rooms in the apartment of two orthodox Jewish dwarfs presided over by a diminutive but relatively normal-sized aunt.[8] Here he spent most of his days drinking and insomnia-filled nights writing self-pitying poems. In these poems, and also in

[8] From a letter to Adele Gundert, Baden, December 25, 1925. Hesse delighted in the story about these lodgings and described them on several occasions.

his letters, we discern again and again Hesse's dependence on alcohol, his thoughts of suicide, his mental and physical dislocations.

A "Steppenwolf" poem describes his state of mind clearly:

> Every night the same misery.
> First one dances, laughs, guzzles
> Then one drags oneself, tired out,
> Into one's room, into the cold bed.
> Brief sleep, long wakefulness,
> Verses scrawled on paper
> Burning eyes rubbed till they're sore,
> Dear God, it's laughable!
> I lie amidst the debris of my dreams
> Longing for this torture to end,
>
> I press my hot face, moist hands
> Into my rumpled pillows
> Pour whiskey down my gullet
> And inside that lost gorge
> Laments my suffocated soul.
> From someplace in these depths of hell
> Morning comes on tired feet,
> And the day, with terrible eyes,
> Stares at my sins.
>
>                    (*Materialien,* p. 171)

In another poem, Hesse actually views his anguish as a reflection
in a mirror. It is a rather sentimental litany, called "After an Eve-
ning in the 'Hirsch'." The middle-aged poet finds himself sleeping,
somewhat drunk, leaning against the scented white neck, fur, and
black hair of a young lady in a bar where he had joined a crowd of
youthful people. Suddenly realizing he did not belong in this company, he takes his hat to go back to "Aquarius and Pisces / home to
my accustomed misery." Calling himself a clown and a fool, he trots
home toward the canal whose surface mirrors tired stars. An unknown cur at his door leaves him quickly after sniffing at him. Upstairs, where he drags himself on tired feet, he looks in the mirror:

> Into the mirror stared red eyelids
> And gray hair withered and gone to pot.

And upon seeing this apparition of himself, a reflection of his personal decay, his thoughts return to the dog that had left him:

Ach, if only that strange dog had bitten me and had eaten me up.

*(Materialien,* 167)

The "poem" is clearly more life than art, but in defining the poet's condition it already contains some of the artistic elements that have gone into the making of the novel: the mirror in which the disturbed psyche is not only reflected but revealed; the dog that runs away from the man as the man had run away from his friends. In the former case we see prefigured the mirror images of the "Prose *Steppenwolf.*" In the latter case, where the animal shuns the man as the man had shunned his friends, we find that reversal of "man and wolf," that inverse mirroring of the two figures, which Hesse used in the sequence he called "Steppenwolf-Training" in the final sections of his novel. The self-pitying stance, the sad surroundings, the glance into the mirror to disclose a rotten self-image, and the split between man and dog in the end—they all seem to be "life studies" for the fully deformed self-portrait which the Magic Theater of *Steppenwolf* was to provide.

This relationship between the anguish of life and its remolded artistic counterpart can, of course, also be discerned in many of the letters Hesse wrote to his friends and family at the time. For example, one of the anxieties suffered by Harry Haller is the approach of his fiftieth birthday with nothing to show for it. We are told that he had made a pact with himself to feel free to kill himself on that day if he wished, and we discover that the Magic Theater, its curious crew working under the watchful eyes of the immortals, enacts and resolves this choice in the realm of play. That Hesse, approaching the same age, had actually made such a pact with himself as a person may be an interesting sidelight, but the way he stated it in a painful letter from Montagnola (written in the spring of 1925) suggests something about the irony and artistry with which the novel accomplished its transformation:

> . . . The meadows are full of flowers [he wrote filled with his depression], but I see little of that. I'm mostly prone, because my legs are in bad shape. Every step is painful, and a walk to the end of the village is an effort I've tried to make only twice in two weeks. For a while I was very desperate. But then I discovered a way out. I resolved that two years from now, on my 50th birthday, I will have the right to hang myself if I still want to. And now everything that

seemed difficult has taken on another look. For at the very worst it can last only two years. . . .[9]

In the novel, these words are contained in that part of Harry Haller's mind which was reserved for the immortals. They are spoken in the impersonal language of the Treatise. Replacing the personal anguish of sciatica and gout with a general anxiety about contemporary culture, the "Chronicler" of the Treatise writes:

Finally, when he was about 47 years old, [Harry] had a happy, not entirely humorless, thought. He set the date of his fiftieth birthday as that day on which he could allow himself to commit suicide. On that day, he agreed with himself, he would be free to use or not to use that emergency exit . . . (VII, 232).

From then on, continues the Treatise, everything seemed much easier, and whatever had tortured him in the past was now no longer difficult to bear. The theoretical, psychologizing passage that precedes these statements is equally interesting. In a man disposed toward suicide, the Treatise suggests, the temptation to cast off his life can be converted into a very serviceable philosophy of life. The mere knowledge that such an "emergency exit" exists can give a man so inclined strength to bear his pain. Moreover, it enables him to be a detached *onlooker* who can observe the antics of his suffering self with grim *Schadenfreude*. "I am curious to see," the suicidal person might muse, "how much a man can actually bear! If I have reached the limits of the bearable, I need only open the door and escape" (VII, 231).

These passages from the Treatise are not only expansions of Hesse's own thoughts which he tried out in notes to several friends. They also represent an effort to render feelings as ideas within an intellectual framework. Since this odd pact with the devil of suicide is reported in the Treatise, its partly flippant, partly real resolution of crisis is no longer part of Hesse's own analysis, nor even quite that of his protagonist who might have introduced it immediately in his own Notebooks. It essentially concerns the "Steppenwolf" construct: a purely theoretical, literary being. Playing person and persona against one another, the Treatise mirrors this motif several times: it views Haller's psychological antics in its own perspective and even suggests how a humorously detached Haller may *look on*

---

[9] From a letter to Hugo and Emmy Ball, Montagnola, April 1, 1925. Partially reproduced in *Materialien*, p. 43.

as the anguished Haller goes through his paces much as the author Hesse in *A Guest at the Spa* had observed the *Kurgast* Hesse trying to eat his dinner. And if we understand all this interplay of mirrors as a reflection of the author who conceived of this pact in the first place, we understand something about the way Hesse tried to detach himself from his own psyche and to render it, artistically, as play.

We can easily see from this example that *Steppenwolf* takes a rather special place in Hesse's repertoire of books. For here the objective analogue to personal crisis is not found by transposing the psyche onto a sensibility rambling in nature, by identifying it with that of a young man growing up in the towns and villages of his home country or finding salvation in a mythical Orient. Nor did he find the compensating world in the Middle Ages of *Narcissus and Goldmund* or in the futuristic Eden of *The Glass Bead Game*. Rather, the objective context was supplied by a *theoretical framework* superimposed upon a psychological analysis of suicide and despair. It was formed by a set of devices culled from literary history which created a world for the *persona* apart from the mind and the city in which the *person* suffered: the mirror (a Romantic and symbolist motif); the Treatise (the capsuled work within the work also favored in Romantic narratives); the expressionistic (as well as Romantic) interplay of reality and illusion. These techniques wove the texture of the novel into a composition that created a world of its own, which is best summarized as the world of the Magic Theater. The content—the mental despair and the contemporary urban setting—could therefore be represented directly. As he summed it all up bitterly in one of his "Steppenwolf" poems:

> Soon I'm going home
> Soon I'll come apart
> And my bones will join
> Those of all the others.
> Famous Hesse has disappeared;
> Only his publisher still lives off his customers.
> *(Materialien*, p. 163)

Since the context, or world, is created by mirroring, parallels between events in the novel and events told in poems and letters are unusually illuminating. For example, in the sequence of episodes that introduced Harry Haller to the world of the Magic Theater, he stayed overnight in the *Black Eagle*. His "twin sister" Hermine, the feminine image of himself, had directed him to remain there after a series of partly real, partly dreamlike encounters. It was a kind of *initiation*. After waking up late in the morning following numbing sleep, his strength seemed miraculously restored and he could face his return to his landlady's bourgeois environment with equanimity. If we put on special glasses and perceive "doubly," as Theodore Ziolkowski suggests, it is fairly easy to reconstruct an image of physical dislocation. This scene seems to go back to early 1924 when Hesse was fleeing from his second wife, Ruth. He had awakened in a strange room and found he had been taken to a hospital near which, as he told his sister Adele, they had played when they were small children. Hesse alluded to this incident also in a letter to Romain Rolland: he found himself in a strange hospital bed and there was a poplar on the other side of the window. But in a letter to Hugo Ball he was more explicit. He presented himself as a sick man longing for his renewal:

> Dear Friend: I received your letter and am keeping it in mind along with my own drama. Here, I've been in bed for two weeks and last week, when I felt especially bad, I let the doctor send me to a clinic where I'll leave again in a few days. At one time I woke up in a room in a strange part of town and since then I've been lying here, very tired, and finding it hard to start life all over again.
>
> It seems I was pretty ill and it's a good thing you didn't see me lying there with a long grey stubble beard, shaking my head in response to everything. Now I'm shaved again. I can eat a little and feel a great longing for the yellow and blue flowers of Tessin. But it'll be a while before I'll be able to pack a suitcase again and tear myself away from here. . . .[10]

There is, of course, an enormous difference between the letter to Hugo Ball about waking up in the room and the tribulations and events of the novel written two years later, but a comparison between them may provide a further clue to the book. Both documents present illness and the desire to overcome it. In the novel, the lived episode becomes an intellectual clue: the hero does not long for the "blue flowers of Tessin," but, figuratively, for the Blue Flower of Novalis' novel *Heinrich von Ofterdingen*—the symbol of the in-

[10] Undated letter from Basel to Hugo Ball. Similar letters were written to Adele Gundert and Romain Rolland from Basel on March 10, 1924. Reportedly, Hesse suffered from an "intestinal infection." See *Materialien*, p. 30.

finite, of poetry, of transcendence. He no longer looks forward to
the time when he can pack his suitcase, but undergoes encounters
which are ultimately controlled by the figures of Goethe and Mozart.
The world of the personal letter is placed in the context of the
"magic" mirrors of art which Hesse, the author, has literally created.

In the first stages of the fantasy that forms the core of *Steppenwolf*, the hero seeks solace from despair. He meets those illusory
characters—Hermine, his spiritual guide, Maria, his physical mistress, and Pablo, who turns out to be the Master Magician—and
learns from them the art of shedding his inhibitions. He then meets
*himself* in the actual magic theater, in which he is to be tested, tried,
and eventually transformed. That sequence begins with the gigantic
ballroom scene and ends in various peepshows in which parts of his
personality are "acted out" in pantomimes. To a surprising degree,
these elements of the novel are reflected in the poems and letters.
Women, bars, and drinking, as our examples indicated, dominated
Hesse's life during this period and the apotheosis of the great
Masked Ball represents an actual landmark. Having loathed ballroom dancing most of his life, he answered the advertisement of a
dancing school and actually took lessons just as Haller had taken
lessons from Hermine. His actual life rose from drinking and bad
dreams to the ability to partake in the *Fastnacht* activities in early
1926, from which he derived the theme of the novel that saved him.
We can therefore trace his state of mind from the poems of longing
and despair (which, as we noted, had been intended as a sequel to
the novel) to a new experience that came to symbolize for him some
transcendent state.

In the novel *Steppenwolf*, the transformation from life to art is
performed by *magic*, a concept intricately involved in the image of
the mirror. Magic transforms the antics of the disturbed psyche into
coherent imagery. If sense pleasure was one of the initial stages on
the way to salvation, it became so through the artist-hero's heightened consciousness as he transforms the actual city of Zürich (not,
in the bright light of day, one of the sin capitals of Europe) into a
symbolic city where psychological crisis can be transformed into a
spiritual state. On the one hand, this is the only major work in
which Hesse made full use of the paraphernalia of contemporary
urban life—its bars, jazz, cafés, and its demimonde—not only because in real life he tried to immerse himself in this environment
or only because he viewed the city as the most palpable evidence of

cultural disintegration, but also because in it the psyche was most brutally exposed. On the other hand, it was his self-appointed task to apply *magic* to this environment. He sought to refract exposed psychic nerves so painstakingly in the mirrors of art that a sense of spiritual regeneration could emerge from their tortured material. To this end, despite allusions to Buddha and the East, he turned essentially to his basic Western heritage as a German writer—the tradition of Goethe, Mozart, Novalis, and Nietzsche—rather than to visions of the East which even after *Siddhartha* were still more distant and unfamiliar. The Master Magician remained the German Romantic Poet.

Borrowing many of his images from Novalis' *Heinrich von Ofterdingen*, Hesse drew the contours of a transcendental world in which time could be overcome by the magic of mystical union which he related to sexual communion as well. As we saw, the Treatise suggests the scene in which Heinrich reads from the Book of Life in the hermit's cave that turns out to be a mirror image of himself. But this scene corresponds not only to Haller's reading (and "viewing") to which we have referred but also to the entire constellation represented as the Cabinet of Mirrors. Finally, the resolution of crisis in a "mystical union" is introduced by Hesse, as it is by Novalis, by a gigantic dance in which individuals merge into a communion that ascends from sense to spirit.[11] This dance was to counteract crisis and death, to raise the protagonist above both. But this dance, too, existed in fact. Hesse gave it an intellectual twist to render it as a version of Novalis among the symbols of the modern city.

In the novel, then, the world of the psyche is mirrored and turned into play through the actions of the Master Magician (Pablo-Mozart) who acts through the mirror games of his Magic Theater. In life, all the motifs are furnished by the accidents of place and season: the ballrooms, the gaiety, the social get-togethers of the *Fastnacht* season which finally emerged as a key to a resolution of the book. Hesse's mood and expectations are described in the following passage from a letter written in February, 1926, the time of the *Fastnacht*:

> The day before yesterday I called on Hans Arp on a business matter, to wit, to order a ticket for a masked ball for which Arp is doing the decorations.

[11] See Kurt Weibel, *Hermann Hesse und die deutsche Romantik* (Winterthur, 1954).

But in the next paragraph he continues:

> For many months I have walked, every hour, along the edge of the abyss and did not believe that I would get off free. The coffin had already been ordered. And now I'm still around, am going to a masked ball and still don't know what will become of me. It isn't working without a great deal of alcohol and as a result the gout is back, but recently I have had . . . the feeling that life will be possible for me again.[12]

Alcohol was indeed the fuel that sustained him and provided the means of approaching a world in which time can be overcome. But in the following set of biographical quotations alcohol *and* the dance operate to transform physical isolation into mystical union, despair into play, the dance hall of actual Zürich into a fairyland of a symbolic city.

Hesse's friend, the sculptor Hermann Hubacher, who had taken him to one of the balls, recalled the scene in detail:

> After weeks of preparation . . . everything was ready for the festival which the artist folk were giving for themselves. I had been able to persuade Hermann Hesse to attend one of these masked balls at the Hotel Baur au Lac. I picked him up at the Schanzengraben at 9:30 and when we appeared there was a big hello at the table of our friends. . . . Hesse looked at the hubbub with a slightly sour face, more skeptical than anything else until a pretty Pierrette recognized him and sat down on his knees with elan. And see here, our friend was "parti pour la gloire. . . ." Laughter everywhere. The great dance hall was dark and in the midst of it, floating above, turned a huge illuminated globe bedecked with small mirrors, which cast its lights, like small flashes of lightning, over the dancing couples. . . . But where is Hesse? Has he run away? It's almost dawn. . . . But see here, here comes our Hesse again in the most genial mood, more sprightly than any of us, leaping on top of the table and dancing a Onestep for us so that all the glasses were clattering. Then he wrote some verses on our no longer pristine starched shirt fronts. Schoeck added a few musical notes. Never before have I borne my breast home more proudly. . . .[13]

But how does this scene appear in the novel, filtered by the spirit of Novalis and Hesse's imagination?

[12] Letter to Hugo and Emmy Ball, February 17, 1926, reprinted in *Materialien*, p. 63.

[13] "Mit Hermann Hesse am Künstlermaskenball," *Der Bildhauer Hermann Hubacher* (Zürich, 1965). Reprinted in *Materialien*, pp. 65–66.

. . . the exultation of a festive communion, the secret of a person's submergence in the mass, the *unio mystica* of pleasure. . . . I was no longer I, my personality was dissolved in the intoxication of the festival as salt is dissolved in water. . . . All [women] belonged to me and I belonged to them all. We all took part of each other. And also the men were part of it; in them, too, I existed. . . . Their smiles were mine, their wooing mine, my wooing theirs (VII, 359–60).

The dance as a union of multiple elements, divided among many people, also mirrors sexual union. In fact, Haller had learned earlier, in bed with Maria, that their union was mirrored at least threefold: Maria was his lover and Hermine's as well and both of them were lovers of the musician Pablo. "[And] I thought," he mused, "of the thousand souls of the *Steppenwolf* Treatise" (VII, 337).

If *magic* supplied transcendence of the divided psychic state in the mystical union of the dance, other forces propelled person and persona in an opposite direction. The plot develops in contradictions or counterpoints in which (appropriately enough for the occasion) the motif of the mirror is supplemented by the play of masks. The narrative, even at its seemingly happiest, always reflects a dimension of darkness, and this element is not absent in the personal testimonies as well. For example, in a thank-you note to Hubacher, Hesse jocularly complained that his friends had let him down. He had such a good time that he wondered why his friends had not acquainted him with the joys of *Fastnächte* before, and he asked for the name of the pretty girl he had met at the dance.[14] Implied in his enthusiastic response, then, is the same slightly querulous complaint which Haller had uttered just before he had submerged himself in the dance: "An experience . . . unknown to me in fifty years. . . . Every adolescent girl and every student finds it familiar" (VII, 359).

In this way, reversals multiply throughout the novel and array themselves as an arrangement of counterpoints. They portray the person's ambivalence. In Hubacher's description, Hesse's sour mien suddenly brightens; in the novel, both moods are rendered in rapid alternations. In one of Hesse's autobiographical poems, he is about to leave a bar—"disappointed, alone"—only to be dragged back

[14] To Hermann Hubacher, March 17, 1926. Reprinted in *Materialien*, p. 65. This letter, like the previous quotation, was first brought to my attention by Messrs. Heiner Hesse, Richard Herland, and Fred Haines.

to dance by two persuasive girls. He is "ready to start the night over again" (*Materialien,* 166–67). In the novel, a similar reversal occurs when Haller receives his invitation to join the Magic Theater just as he is about to leave the masked ball in disgust. But the invitation (mysteriously inscribed on his hat check) turns him around. He is released to dance that great dance with all men and women, which narrows to Maria, and ultimately to Hermine. True, in the novel reversals are produced by a kind of supernatural machinery which can only exist in dreams or in the fantasy of artists. (The mysterious invitation mirrors the earlier invitation to the Magic Theater flashed on the deserted wall.) But, though the mysteries are partly accounted for by the game of masks the occasion of the *Fastnacht* requires, they partly indicate the transformation of life into art, the manner in which personal ambivalence is turned into contrapuntal images and motifs. Hesse's sense of reaching out to an alluringly sensual world, and of feeling both wanted and rejected, becomes Haller's pilgrimage among alternating motifs: those depicting pleasure, a unified vision, humor, or transcendence contrasted with others which depict isolation, failure, betrayal, and despair.

Ambivalence transmuted into art is most dramatically shown in the teasing charade of masks that resolves Haller's relationship with Hermine—a resolution, however contradictory, about which the novelist had aroused the reader's curiosity early in the book. A gradual descent from joy begins as soon as Haller perceives Hermine (for the second time) under the mask of the Pierrette Hubacher had observed in life. Hesse's friends had still seen her most happily poised on his knees, but they were unaware of the contradictions which were to be made part of Haller's magical quest. In a poem entitled "Poor Devil on the Morning After a Masked Ball," however, Hesse revealed more of himself and expressed feelings quite clearly different from those he had conveyed to Hubacher in his joyful note:[15]

> I'm out of luck. At first everything was great.
> She sat on my knees and was all afire.

---

[15] Another poem called "Morning After the Masked Ball" develops the same theme of betrayal: "Lolo," after a night of passionate kisses, takes off in the morning with her "marital slave" in their "Fiat car," leaving him alone in the street. Hesse wishes them a quick demise, with a dog sniffing at their remains (*Materialien,* pp. 190–91).

Then she ran off with that Pierrot.
And I, enraged, began to guzzle again.
Now I have turned over a few tables
And have gotten a hole in my knee.
I'm out of money, my glasses are smashed.
Yes, infernal female, it's my defeat.

*(Materialien,* p. 193)

The playful resolution of Haller's love for Hermine echoes the same contradictions: the mystical union of the Grand Ballroom turns into defeat along the corridors of Pablo's Cabinet of Mirrors when the hero "kills" his lady and soils the "magic stage" with the "blood of reality," the mirrored knife in his hand forged of fragments of his own soul. Real emotion, real jealousy, and a real sense of betrayal, suggested in the poem, are refracted in an array of masks. Conversely, as Haller sits by the rigid body of the "dead" Hermine (herself a mask, a mirrored image), contemplating her ice-cold form, the author's description suggests a parallel scene in his life when, ten years earlier, he had sat by the rigid body of his dead father and had placed his hand on the cold forehead.[16] In the novel, all these relationships are extended further by the *literary* use of the mask—a favorite device of the 1920s with a distinguished history as well. The dance hall in the Hotel Baur au Lac with its mirrors and lights, its upper and lower regions, is masked by various allusions not only to Novalis but to Dante as well. At Haller's wake with the deadened part of himself, personal feelings and literary traditions combine. *Unio mystica* as a step beyond transcendence in the spirit of Novalis finds its counterpoint in the frigid damnation of Dante's *Inferno.*

This, then, is the game Hesse played with his person and persona, and the masked ball and the mirrors were convenient artistic props. They also connect the private psyche with that unifying tradition Hesse associated with his "immortals." Masks were especially suitable and the author, as artisan, knew it. In April, 1926, Hesse delightedly told his sister Adele of a *Fastnacht* procession he had watched with his friends, in which several masks represented characters from books by Gottfried Keller and Conrad Ferdinand Meyer.[17] In *Steppenwolf,* Hesse exploits this very function of the mask as an *aesthetic* front for life by using as his ultimate masks the

[16] "Zum Gedächtnis," *Werkausgabe,* X, 129–30.
[17] To Adele Gundert, Zürich, April 20, 1926.

features of Goethe and Mozart. It is at this juncture that the psychological pilgrimage through "the inferno of the self" turns into a humanistic *Bildungsroman*. And it is at this point as well that we observe person and persona existing on parallel levels that mirror one another—or are masks for one another—as encounters and feelings become motifs and themes.

There are, of course, further parallels between events in the novel and events in life, but they are usually not too different from those one might trace in any novel. For example, Hesse's attack on the stuffy professor who ruined the image of Goethe relates to his personal pique at the attacks made upon him by the political Right. But the events which I have selected are those which Hesse has made into the theme and tissue of his book: depression, orgiastic anaesthesia, *unio mystica,* betrayal of self. I would like to suggest that the techniques which transform the real city into a symbolic city, the real self into a symbolic self, are those which transform the dissolving psyche into an image of spiritual salvation. The mirror and the play with illusion which were actually present in the real dance hall allow the psyche to be refracted and multiplied. Similarly, too, the peepshow theater, the loges of the opera house —all gadgets of Hesse's own world—become the means of transforming life into an illusory, yet aesthetically reconstructed world. Even the "murder" with the mirrored knife—that suicide which never took place—remains a vivid parallel of a "real" murder. Hesse used these mirroring devices to render a credible image of a mind's departure from reality without being committed to it himself, to create with the help of his masks that "cheerful world of beliefs above person and time," which he viewed as an effective counterpoint to the cultural disintegration of his age.

Nevertheless, Hesse's game with contradictions does not exclude the psychic quest. For even where his novel alludes to Goethe, Mozart, or Dante, or where its resolutions are clearly constructed on the models of humanistic education, the ideal of art, and of Novalis's allegorical *Bildungsroman,* the effective connection with the hero's psychological pilgrimage is never broken off. It is merely transformed. For the course of the novel, taking Haller back to his origins by leading him through the "inferno of the self," where he is judged wanting, also describes that of the novel of psychoanalytic education. Reviewing some of the sources from which Haller's pilgrimage toward the grail of salvation developed, we continue to focus on ambivalence and despair from which, with painful efforts, Hesse extracts a symbolic ideal. The Treatise describes this search in language resonant with Jungian sound-effects:

> The way to innocence, to the uncreated, to God, does not lead back but forward, not to wolf or child, but always more and more into guilt, ever more deeply into the process of becoming Man. Nor will suicide seriously help you, poor Steppenwolf. You will have to go the longer, more arduous, harder way towards becoming Man; you will have to multiply your duality, to complicate further your complications. Instead of narrowing your world, of simplifying your soul, you will always have to become more world; finally, you will have to include the entire world in your painfully widened soul in order to reach, perhaps, the end, the state of peace. This is the way Buddha has gone, the way every great man has gone. . . . [Becoming] God means: so to have widened one's soul that it may again comprise the entire universe (VII, 247–48).

As we read these lines in the context of the novel as a whole (and in the context of Hesse's life, which has furnished the material), we realize that the psychoanalytic method itself has become yet another way to achieve transformation. The quest for the self and the ideal of the novel of education are therefore joined in a composition in which the individual can mirror an entire culture and present it as art.

Hesse's novel may not be a very successful work of art. It is shot through with tricks and literary gadgets. The sentimentality and self-pity that pervade the poems and even some of the letters survive in the book. But those who have praised the experimental deftness of its composition are not far wrong. The world of *Steppenwolf* emerges as an interior dimension which is individual and universal alike. It performs in the realm of art the function Hesse had foreseen for psychoanalysis in life: to create a space within the self in which God's voice can be heard. A response, indeed, to that desperate moment when "the coffin had already been ordered."

## V

The parallels between life and art which we have traced dramatize Hesse's peculiar manner of constructing spiritual autobiography. No doubt Harry Haller's crisis was also in large measure

Hesse's own—an impression he has not only failed to erase but has positively encouraged. But Hesse has also encouraged a reading of his book as an artful composition in which person and persona are intricately related to one another. When readers praised his *Narcissus and Goldmund* at the expense of the "degenerate" *Steppenwolf*, he was quick to reply that the latter had been at least as carefully constructed as the former.

The strange history of the novel's reputation in Germany and in the United States can be largely explained by the literalness of its interpretation that ignores vast areas of its meaning. Both the rejection of the novel by Hesse's German admirers of the 1920s and its unquestioning acceptance by their American counterparts in the 1960s rest on a confusion between psychic content and symbolic form, between the actual self and its mirrored image. If the book was disdained by many German readers in the 'twenties because it dealt with subjects "unworthy" of the author of *Siddhartha*—bars, liquor, whores, bourgeois sex—it was extolled with equal injustice in America of the 'sixties, when it was viewed as a psychedelic wish-dream in the spirit of Timothy Leary. It is clear from the book, and from Hesse's later comments, that neither view is fully justified.

For us, it should remain a paradigm of Hesse's perennial game in which person and persona are played against one another. The ironic way in which each mirrors the other and in which both function within a larger scheme suggests, as Lionel Trilling has said in a different context, that the writer transcends his illness by writing.[18] If the novel were unfettered psychosis, it would be hardly worth reading. If it were only life, it would not be a book. But an author who views himself in the mirror of art—as Hesse in that trenchant dream saw "the living Hesse sitting there"—reconstructs life on a universal scale. Whether Hesse succeeded in this or in any other novel is a different question. The point is that by his own testimony he worked at it very hard.

[18] "Art and Neurosis," *The Liberal Imagination* (New York, 1949), pp. 176–77. A slightly different but equally pertinent point was made by my colleague Clarence Brown in an as yet unpublished essay: "The artist has nothing but life to write from, but what he wishes to do with much of that life, especially the painful part of it which is most productive of art, is to get rid of it. This he does by writing. . . ."

# Chronology of Important Dates

1877     Hermann Hesse born on July 2 in Calw, Württemberg.

1881–86     Family in Basel.

1886–95     Return to Calw. Preparatory school in Calw, Göppingen (1890–91), and Maulbronn (1891–92). After running away from Maulbronn, Hesse is sent to institutions in Bad Boll, Stetten, Basel, and Bad Cannstatt (1892–93). Then various jobs, notably as mechanic's apprentice in Calw.

1895–99     Apprenticeship in bookstore in Tübingen. *Romantic Songs,* 1899. *An Hour beyond Midnight,* 1899.

1899–1903     Bookdealer in Basel. *Hermann Lauscher,* 1901. *Poems,* 1902.

1904–1912     Gaienhofen on Lake Constance. Marriage to Maria Bernoulli (1904). Contributor to numerous magazines. Coeditor of journal *März* (1907–1912). Trip to East Indies with the painter Hans Sturzenegger (1911). Lives of *Boccaccio* and *Saint Francis,* 1904. *Peter Camenzind,* 1904. *Beneath the Wheel,* 1906. *In this World* (stories), 1907. *Neighbors* (stories), 1908. *Gertrude,* 1910. *On the Road* (poems), 1911. *By-Ways* (stories), 1912.

1912–19     Bern. Relief work for German internees and prisoners of war (1914–19). Analysis with Josef B. Lang (1916–17). *Out of India,* 1913. *Rosshalde,* 1914. *Knulp,* 1915. *Demian,* 1919. *Fairy Tales,* 1919. *Zarathustra's Return,* 1919.

1919–22     Montagnola in Swiss Ticino. Begins to paint. Coeditor of journal *Vivos voco* (1919–22). Analysis with C. G. Jung (1921). *Klingsor's Last Summer* (including *Klein and Wagner* and *A Child's Soul*), 1920. *In Sight of Chaos* (esp. two essays on Dostoevsky), 1920. *Wandering* (prose, poems, and watercolor sketches), 1920. *Siddhartha,* 1922.

1923–31     Montagnola, with first of regular visits to spa at Baden near Zürich (1923). Becomes a Swiss citizen (1923). Divorce from

Maria Hesse (1923). Marriage to Ruth Wenger (1924) and subsequent divorce (1927). Lecture tour in Germany (1925). Winters in Zürich (1925–31). *A Guest at the Spa,* 1925. *Steppenwolf,* 1927. *The Journey to Nuremberg,* 1927. *Krisis* (a diary in verse), 1928. *Reflections* (essays), 1928. *Narcissus and Goldmund,* 1930.

1931–62    Montagnola. Marriage to Ninon Dolbin, née Ausländer (1931). Nobel Prize (1946). *The Journey to the East,* 1932. *Hours in the Garden* (idyllic poem), 1936. *Collected Poems,* 1942. *The Glass Bead Game (Magister Ludi),* 1943. *Krieg und Frieden* (collected essays on war and politics), 1946. *Dream Traces* (stories), 1945. *Late Prose* (stories), 1951. *Letters,* 1951. *Conjurations* (stories, diaries), 1955.

1962    Hesse's death on August 9 in Montagnola.

# Notes on the Editor and Contributors

THEODORE ZIOLKOWSKI, editor of the anthology, teaches German and European literature at Princeton. His most recent books are *Dimensions of the Modern Novel* (1969) and *Fictional Transfigurations of Jesus* (1972).

MARTIN BUBER (1878–1965), writer and religious thinker, was a professor of social philosophy at Hebrew University in Jerusalem. His "I-Thou" philosophy has had a profound impact on the modern mind.

ERNST ROBERT CURTIUS (1886–1956), professor of romance philology at the University of Bonn, was one of Germany's foremost men of letters. He is best known abroad for his epoch-making study, *European Literature and the Latin Middle Ages* (1948).

GEORGE WALLIS FIELD, professor of German at Victoria College (University of Toronto), is the author of articles on Schiller, Thomas Mann, and Hesse in addition to his book, *Hermann Hesse* (1970).

RALPH FREEDMAN, professor of comparative literature at Princeton, has written numerous articles on modern literature as well as a book, *The Lyrical Novel* (1963). He is currently completing a biography of Hesse.

ANDRÉ GIDE (1869–1951), Nobel Prize-winning French novelist and moralist, was long fascinated with German thought and literature—notably Goethe and Nietzsche.

THOMAS MANN (1875–1955), German Nobel-Prize laureate, knew Hesse for many years. Their relationship is recorded in a published correspondence (1968).

HANS MAYER, a leading Marxist critic and professor of German at the Technical University in Hannover, has published many books on literature from 1750 to the present. Eleven of his essays have been translated under the title *Steppenwolf and Everyman* (1971).

JEFFREY L. SAMMONS, professor of German at Yale, has written widely on nineteenth-century literature. Among his books is the highly acclaimed study, *Heinrich Heine: The Elusive Poet* (1969).

OSKAR SEIDLIN, the distinguished Germanist, is a professor at Indiana University. He has published several volumes of essays on topics ranging from Goethe to Thomas Mann, including most recently *Klassische und moderne Klassiker* (1972).

# Selected Bibliography

This Bibliography is limited to books, or chapters in books, that have appeared in English since Joseph Mileck's *Hermann Hesse and His Critics: The Criticism and Bibliography of Half a Century* (Chapel Hill, N. C.: University of North Carolina Press, 1958) and Helmut Waibler's *Hermann Hesse: Eine Bibliographie* (Bern and Munich: Francke, 1962). A list of recent articles in newspapers and journals may be found in Anna Otten's *Hesse Companion* (Frankfurt am Main: Suhrkamp, 1970).

Andrews, Wayne. "The Achievement of Hermann Hesse." In *Siegfried's Curse: The German Journey from Nietzsche to Hesse*. New York: Atheneum, 1972. Pp. 274–329. A sympathetic appraisal of Hesse as critic of Germany.

Barrett, William. "Journey to the East." In *Time of Need: Forms of Imagination in the Twentieth Century*. New York: Harper & Row, 1972. Pp. 187–213. A discussion of the conflict of opposites in Hesse's novels.

Baumer, Franz. *Hermann Hesse*. Translated by John Conway. New York: Ungar, 1969. A study of Hesse's existential consciousness.

Boulby, Mark. *Hermann Hesse: His Mind and His Art*. Ithaca, N. Y.: Cornell University Press, 1967. Excellent critical analysis.

Casebeer, Edwin F. *Hermann Hesse*. New York: Warner Paperback Library, 1972. A "personal" reading of *Siddhartha, Steppenwolf, Narcissus and Goldmund*, and *Magister Ludi* in a series called "Writers for the 70's."

Devert, Krystyna. "Hermann Hesse: Apostle of the Apolitical 'Revolution.'" In *Literature in Revolution*. Edited by George Abbot White and Charles Newman. New York: Holt, Rinehart and Winston, 1972. Pp. 302–317. A New Left critique of Hesse's apolitical stance.

Engel, Eva J. "Hermann Hesse." In *German Men of Letters*. Edited by Alex Natan. London: Oswald Wolff, 1963. Vol. II, pp. 249–74.

Farquharson, Robert H. *An Outline of the Works of Hermann Hesse*. Toronto: Forum House, 1973.

Field, George Wallis. *Hermann Hesse*. New York: Twayne, 1970.

Freedman, Ralph. "Romantic Imagination: Hermann Hesse as a Lyrical Novelist." In *The Lyrical Novel: Studies in Hermann Hesse, André Gide, and Virginia Woolf*. Princeton, N. J.: Princeton University Press, 1963. Pp. 42–118.

Hatfield, Henry. "Accepting the Universe: Hermann Hesse's *Steppenwolf*." In *Crisis and Continuity in Modern German Fiction*. Ithaca, N. Y.: Cornell University Press, 1969. Pp. 63–77.

Mayer, Hans. "Hermann Hesse's *Steppenwolf*." In *Steppenwolf and Everyman*. Translated by Jack D. Zipes. New York: Thomas Y. Crowell, 1971. Pp. 1–13.

Reichert, Herbert W. *The Impact of Nietzsche on Hermann Hesse*. Mt. Pleasant, Mich.: The Enigma Press, 1972.

Rose, Ernst. *Faith from the Abyss: Hermann Hesse's Way from Romanticism to Modernity*. New York: New York University Press, 1965.

Serrano, Miguel. *C. G. Jung and Hermann Hesse: A Record of Two Friendships*. Translated by Frank MacShane. New York: Schocken, 1966.

Simons, John D. *Hermann Hesse's* Steppenwolf: *A Critical Commentary*. New York: Simon & Schuster, 1972. (Monarch Notes 00917).

Zeller, Bernhard. *Portrait of Hesse: An Illustrated Biography*. Translated by Mark Hollebone. New York: Herder and Herder, 1971.

Ziolkowski, Theodore. *The Novels of Hermann Hesse: A Study in Theme and Structure*. Princeton, N. J.: Princeton University Press, 1965.

————. *Hermann Hesse*. New York: Columbia University Press, 1966. A brief general introduction.